M000291391

The Holt Reader
Adapted Version

Isabel L. Beck, Ph.D., Program Consultant

HOLT, RINEHART AND WINSTON

Printed in the United States of America

ISBN 978-0-03-099641-2
ISBN 0-03-099641-4

23456 179 11 10 09 08

Contents

To the Student

A Book for You

A book is like a garden carried in the pocket.
—Chinese Proverb

The more you put into reading, the more you get out of it. This book is designed to do just that—help you interact with the selections you read by marking them up, asking your own questions, taking notes, recording your own ideas, and responding to the questions of others.

A Book Designed for Your Success

The Holt Reader, Adapted Version goes hand in hand with *Elements of Literature*. It is designed to help you interact with the selections and master important language arts skills.

The Holt Reader, Adapted Version has three types of selections: literature, informational texts, and documents that you may encounter in your various activities. All the selections include the same basic preparation, support, and review materials. Vocabulary previews, skill descriptions, graphic organizers, review questions, and other tools help you understand and enjoy the selections. Moreover, tips and questions in the side margins ensure that you can apply and practice the skills you are learning as you read.

The selections in the book are all from your textbook, *Elements of Literature*. You will find that some of the selections are worded exactly as they were worded in *Elements of Literature*. In this book, those selections have been broken into sections. Each section is followed by a short note titled "In Other Words." That note restates the previous text in different words. Other selections have been rewritten or retold slightly to make them easier to understand; these are called adapted selections. You can tell which ones are adapted because you will see the words "based on" in the Table of Contents or on the first page of the selection.

A Book for Your Own Thoughts and Feelings

Reading is about *you*. It is about connecting your thoughts and feelings to the thoughts and feelings of the writer. Make this book your own. The more you give of yourself to your reading, the more you will get out of it. We encourage you to write in this book. Jot down how you feel about the selection. Write down questions you have about the text. Note details you think need to be cleared up or topics that you would like to investigate further.

A Walk Through the Book

The Holt Reader, Adapted Version is arranged in collections, just like *Elements of Literature*, the book on which this one is based. Each collection has a theme or basic idea. The stories, poems, articles, or documents within the collection follow that theme. Let's look at how the arrangement of *The Holt Reader, Adapted Version* helps you enjoy a collection as a whole and the individual selections within the collection.

Before Reading the Collection

Literary and Academic Vocabulary

Literary and academic vocabulary refers to the specialized language that is used to talk about books, tests, and formal writing. Each collection begins with the literary and academic terms that you need to know to master the skills for that collection.

Before Reading the Selection

Preparing to Read

From experience, you know that you understand something better if you have some idea of what's going to happen. So that you can get the most from the reading, this page previews the skills and vocabulary that you will see in the reading.

Literary Focus

For fiction selections—stories, poems, and plays—this feature introduces the literary skill that is the focus for the selection. Examples and graphic elements help explain the literary skill.

Reading Focus

Also in fiction selections, this feature highlights a reading skill you can apply to the story, poem, or play. The feature points out why this skill is important and how it can help you become a better reader.

Informational Text Focus

For informational, or nonfiction, selections, this feature introduces you to the format and characteristics of nonfiction texts. Those texts may be essays, newspaper articles, Web sites, employment regulations, application forms, or other similar documents.

Selection Vocabulary

This feature introduces you to selection vocabulary that may be unfamiliar. Each entry gives the pronunciation and definition of the word as well as a sentence in which the word is used correctly.

Into the Story

This feature provides an introduction about the selection related to the author, setting, historical events, or other topics that may be unfamiliar.

While Reading the Selection

Side-Column Notes

Each selection has notes in the side column that guide your reading. Many notes ask you to underline or circle in the text itself. Others provide lines on which you can write your responses to questions.

Read and Discuss These notes ask you to pause at certain points so that you can think about basic ideas before proceeding further. Your teacher may use these notes for class discussions.

A Walk Through the Book

Here's How This feature shows you how to apply a particular skill to what you are reading. It models how you might think through the text. Each Here's How note addresses the selection's Reading Focus, Literary Focus, Language Coach, or Vocabulary.

Your Turn In these notes, you have a chance to apply vocabulary skills and practice the same reading, literary, and language skills introduced and modeled earlier. You might be asked to underline or circle words in the text or to write responses in your own words.

After Reading the Selection

Skills Practice
For some selections, graphic organizers reinforce the skills you have practiced throughout the selection.

Applying Your Skills
This feature helps you review the selection. It provides additional practice with selection vocabulary and literary, reading, and informational text focus skills.

After Reading the Collection

Skills Review
On the first page of the Skills Review, you can practice using the collection's academic vocabulary and selection vocabulary.

Language Coach
The second Skills Review page draws on the Language Coach skills in the *Elements of Literature* Preparing to Read pages. This feature asks you to apply those skills to texts from throughout the collection.

Writing Activity
You may have found that you need more practice writing. These short writing activities challenge you to apply what you have learned to your own ideas and experiences.

Oral Language Activity
Writing Activities alternate with Oral Language Activities. These features are designed to help you express your thoughts clearly aloud. The features are particularly helpful if you are learning English or if you need practice with Standard English.

Plot and Setting

© Chad Ehlers/Stone/Getty Images

Literary and Academic Vocabulary for Collection 1

LITERARY VOCABULARY

conflict (KAWN FLIHKT) *n.:* a main problem or struggle in a story.
The main conflict in the story was Matt's fight with his father.

setting (SEH TIHNG) *n.:* the time and place of a story.
The setting of the story was New York City in the 1980s.

mood (MOOD) *n.:* how a story makes you feel.
The mood of the story became sad after the main character died.

climax (KLY MAKS) *n.:* the point when we learn the outcome of the story's main conflict.
The climax of the story came when the police finally caught the bank robbers.

ACADEMIC VOCABULARY

effective (UH FEHK TIHV) *adj.:* bringing about a wanted result.
Even though I did not see the surprise coming, I felt that it was an effective way to end the story.

outcome (OWT KUHM) *n.:* result; ending.
The story had a happy outcome, as the Prince and the Princess got married.

reveal (RIH VEEL) *v.:* make known.
The actions of the characters in a story reveal their true personalities.

structure (STRUHK CHUHR) *n.:* how something is organized.
Many stories follow the same structure and have conflicts and resolutions.

The Treasure of Lemon Brown

Based on the story by Walter Dean Myers

LITERARY FOCUS: CONFLICT

The plot of a story usually has a **conflict**, or a problem or struggle. Conflict often happens when a character wants something very badly but cannot get it. For example, one conflict in "The Treasure of Lemon Brown" is that Greg, the main character, wants to play basketball, but his dad will not let him.

There are two different types of conflict. One type of conflict comes from inside, and the other comes from outside. Conflicts from the inside are called **internal conflicts**. An example would be if a character is too shy to get what he or she wants. Conflicts from the outside are called **external conflicts**. An example would be if a character is stuck in a dangerous blizzard.

READING FOCUS: SUMMARIZING

Summarizing means retelling only the most important events in a story. The chart below shows one way to summarize. Look for the resolution to Greg's problem as you read the story.

Somebody (character)	Wanted (goal or desire)	But (conflict)	So (resolution)
Greg	wants to play basketball	but his dad won't let him	

VOCABULARY

Work with a partner to practice using these words in complete sentences.

eerie (EER EE) *adj.:* strange and frightening.

battered (BAT EHRD) *adj.:* badly dented.

INTO THE STORY

This story is set in Harlem, a neighborhood in New York City. After World War I, the neighborhood was home to the Harlem Renaissance. A renaissance is a rebirth of culture. During this time, many great African American writers, artists, and musicians lived and worked in Harlem.

Over the years, many of Harlem's buildings were not well kept and the people who once lived in them left the neighborhood. Recently, Harlem has seen a new wave of development and restoration.

SKILLS FOCUS

Literary Skills
Understand conflict.

Reading Skills
Summarize a text.

THE TREASURE OF LEMON BROWN

Based on the story by Walter Dean Myers

Music Lesson #2 (detail) (2000) by Colin Bootman. Oil on board.
©Private Collection/The Bridgeman Art Library

The dark sky was filled with angry, swirling clouds. **A** Greg
Ridley was sitting on the front steps of his apartment house.
His angry mood matched the clouds as he remembered his
father's voice reading out the letter. It was from the principal,
saying that Greg would probably fail math.

"I had to leave school when I was thirteen," his father had
said. "I wish I'd had half the chances that you have."

Greg had sat at the kitchen table, listening to his father.
He knew that now his father would not allow him to play
basketball. The Scorpions, the Community Center team, wanted
Greg on their team, although he was only fourteen. It was the
chance of a lifetime. That chance ended with the letter from the
principal. **B**

A   HERE'S HOW

Literary Focus

The author starts off talking
about the dark sky with its
"angry, swirling clouds." I
think this is an *omen*, or a
sign, that something bad
may be about to happen,
like a **conflict** of some kind.

B   READ AND DISCUSS

Comprehension

How is the story starting off?

Reading Focus

I will make sure I understand what has happened so far by **summarizing** the events. First, Greg feels angry that he is failing math and that his father won't let him play basketball. Next, he walks down the street and into an old apartment building. While he thinks about his father, Greg is surprised by someone who says he has a razor.

B (HERE'S HOW)

Literary Focus

Greg could be in trouble because he is being threatened by someone with a razor. I think this is an example of an **external conflict**.

C (YOUR TURN)

Literary Focus

In lines 29–30, Greg was worried about the **conflict** with Lemon Brown. Why is he relaxed in lines 38–39?

_____

_____

_____

_____

Greg knew he should go upstairs and study his math book. Instead, he walked down the street to the abandoned[1] tenement.[2] He noticed that the door was slightly open. He pushed it gently and let himself in.

In the front room, Greg could see an old table, what looked like a pile of rags in the corner, and a broken-down couch.

20 He went to the window and stood looking out at the rain. He thought about the Scorpions, and then his father. Greg's father was a postal worker. He was proud of his job. He often told Greg how hard he had worked to pass the test. Greg had heard the story too many times.

What was that sound? Greg held himself still and listened intently.[3] It was someone breathing!

Slowly he turned around.

"Don't try nothing. I got a razor here!" **A** **B**

Greg held his breath, peering[4] at the figure that stood

30 before him.

"Who are you?" said Greg.

"I'm Lemon Brown," came the answer. "Who are you?"

"Greg Ridley."

The figure shuffled[5] forward, and Greg saw an old man with a black, wrinkled face, crinkly white hair, and whiskers. He wore several dirty coats and baggy pants. From the knees on down, his legs were covered in rags tied with string. There was no sign of a razor.

Greg relaxed. He had seen the man before, picking through the trash. **C**

40 "You ain't one of them bad boys looking for my treasure, is you?" Lemon Brown asked.

"I'm not looking for your treasure," Greg answered, smiling. "If you have one."

"Every man got a treasure," Lemon Brown said. "You know who I am?"

---

1. **abandoned** (UH BAN DUHND): deserted; left empty and unused.
2. **tenement** (TEH NUH MEHNT): an old, run-down apartment house.
3. **intently**: with concentration.
4. **peering**: looking closely.
5. **shuffled** (SHUH FUHLD): dragged feet while walking.

D READ AND DISCUSS

Comprehension
What is all this telling us?

E HERE'S HOW

Language Coach
I know that *noise* is a noun. A person who makes a lot of *noise* may be called *noisy*. *Noise* and *noisy* are called **related words**.

"Your name is orange or lemon or something like that."

"Sweet Lemon Brown," the old man said, pulling back his shoulders as he did so. "They used to say I sung the blues[6] so sweet that if I sang at a funeral, the dead would start rocking with the beat.[7] Used to travel all over. You ain't never heard of Sweet Lemon Brown?"

"Afraid not," Greg said. **D**

Lemon Brown looked toward the window. "What's that noise?" **E**

Greg peered out and saw three men. One was carrying a length[8] of pipe.

"They's bad men," Lemon Brown whispered, leading Greg into the hallway and up the darkened stairs.

There was a banging downstairs and a light as the three men entered. "Hey! Ragman!" one called out. "We come to get your treasure."

"We won't hurt you," said another voice. "Unless we have to."

"You sure he's here?"

"I don't know," came the answer. "All I want is his treasure. He might be like the shopping-bag lady with that money in her bags."

---

6. **blues:** a slow, sad form of jazz music.
7. **beat:** rhythm.
8. **length** (LEHNGTH): a piece of something that is long, such as a board or a pipe.

A   HERE'S HOW

Vocabulary

I am not sure what the word *eerie* means. At first I thought it might mean "funny" or "strange." But then Greg tries to make Lemon Brown seem *eerier* by howling and scaring the men. If something is *eerier*, then it must be both strange *and* frightening.

B   YOUR TURN

Reading Focus

On this page, Lemon Brown and Greg face three men who demand Lemon Brown's "treasure." **Summarize** what Greg and Lemon Brown do in response to these men.

_____

_____

_____

C   READ AND DISCUSS

Comprehension

What have we learned about Lemon Brown's treasure now?

"You think he's upstairs?"

"HEY, OLD MAN, ARE YOU UP THERE?"

Silence.

"Watch my back, I'm going up."

70   Greg held his breath. He thought about the pipe, wondering what he would do when the man reached them.

Then Lemon Brown stood up at the top of the stairs, both arms raised high above his head.

"There he is!" a voice cried from below.

"Throw down your treasure, old man, so I won't have to bash your head in!"

Lemon Brown didn't move. He was an eerie sight, a bundle of rags standing at the top of the stairs. His shadow loomed[9] over him. Maybe, the thought came to Greg, I can make this scene

80   even eerier.

Greg wet his lips, put his hands to his mouth, and howled. **A** **B**

"What's that?"

As Greg howled, Lemon Brown hurled[10] himself down the stairs. There was a crashing noise, yelling, and running footsteps. The front door opened and slammed shut. Then there was only silence.

"Mr. Brown?" Greg called. "You OK?"

"Yeah. I got their flashlight," came the answer.

90   "They wanted your treasure." Greg ran down the stairs.

"You want to see it?" From his layers of ragged clothing, Lemon Brown produced a piece of folded plastic and carefully unfolded it. Inside were yellowed newspaper clippings[11] and a battered harmonica.[12]

"There be my treasure," he said. **C**

Greg began to read the clippings about Lemon Brown, a blues singer and harmonica player who played in shows more

---

9. **loomed:** appeared in a frightening form.
10. **hurled:** threw suddenly and violently.
11. **clippings:** pieces cut from a newspaper.
12. **harmonica** (HAHR MAH nih kuh): small musical instrument that is held in the hand and played by the mouth.

than fifty years ago. Greg looked at the harmonica. It was dented badly on one side.

100   "I used to travel around and make money to feed my wife and Jesse—that's my boy's name. He grew up to be a man and went off to fight in the war. I gave him these things that told him who I was and what he come from. If you know your pappy did something, you know you can do something, too. Then Jesse got killed. Broke my heart, it truly did."

    Greg didn't know what to say, so he just nodded.

    "They sent back what he had with him over there," said Lemon Brown. "This old mouth fiddle and these clippings. When I give it to him, he treated it just like a treasure. Ain't

110 that something?"

    "Yeah, I guess. . . . I mean, you're right."

    "You OK for a youngster." Lemon Brown carefully wrapped the clippings and the harmonica in the plastic. "Better than those bad men what come here looking for my treasure."

    "Is your treasure really worth fighting for against men like that? And a pipe?"

    "What else a man got excepting what he can pass on to his child?" Lemon Brown said. "You get home now."

    "You sure you'll be OK?" Greg asked.

120   "I'll be heading west in the morning," Lemon Brown said.

    "You take care of that treasure."

    "That I'll do," Lemon said.

    The rain had stopped. Greg climbed his front steps and pushed the button over the bell marked "Ridley." He thought of the lecture[13] that he knew his father would give him, and smiled. **F G**

Comprehension Wrap-Up

1. Sweet Lemon Brown says, "If you know your pappy did something, you know you can do something, too." How can that idea lead to a change in Greg?

---

13. lecture (LEHK CHUHR) a scolding; talking to.

D   **YOUR TURN**

Vocabulary

In line 92, Lemon Brown's harmonica is described as *battered.* Circle the words in lines 96-97 that help you figure out the meaning of *battered.*

E   **YOUR TURN**

Reading Focus

In your own words, **summarize** what happens in lines 110–118.

_____

_____

_____

_____

F   **READ AND DISCUSS**

Comprehension

What has happened between the boy and the old man?

G   **YOUR TURN**

Literary Focus

Do you think Greg's **conflict** with his dad will continue when he goes home? Why or why not?

_____

_____

_____

_____

The Treasure of Lemon Brown

USE A CONCEPT MAP

Greg faces many different **conflicts** in "The Treasure of Lemon Brown."
Identify the four main conflicts that Greg deals with in the story. Write one
conflict in each circle. Remember that conflicts can be arguments, fears, or
anything that causes a struggle or problem for a character.

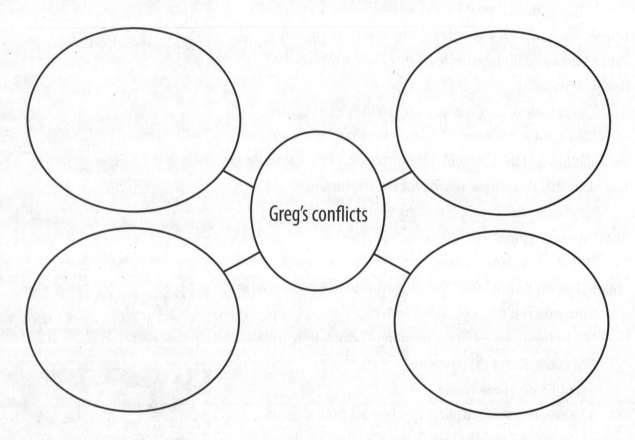

Applying Your Skills

The Treasure of Lemon Brown

LITERARY FOCUS: CONFLICT

DIRECTIONS: Write one or two sentences describing the biggest **conflict**, or problem, that Lemon Brown and Greg's dad face in this story.

1. Lemon Brown _____

_____

2. Greg's dad _____

READING FOCUS: SUMMARIZING

DIRECTIONS: Circle the letter that correctly **summarizes** each of the following parts of the story.

1. The beginning:

   a. Greg makes the basketball team; he goes out to celebrate with Lemon Brown.

   b. Greg is angry about being lectured by his dad; he goes to an abandoned apartment building; he meets Lemon Brown.

   c. Greg's dad passes his postal worker test; Greg fails math; Greg howls like a ghost.

2. The ending:

   a. Lemon Brown takes a flashlight from the bad men; he plays songs on the harmonica for Greg.

   b. Greg howls to help scare the men away; he talks about basketball; he moves out west with Lemon Brown.

   c. Lemon Brown scares the bad men away; he shows Greg his treasure; the old man and the boy part ways.

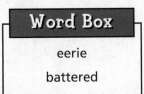

Word Box

eerie

battered

VOCABULARY REVIEW

DIRECTIONS: Fill in the blanks with the correct word from the Word Box.

1. Lemon Brown's harmonica was _____ and dented on one side.

2. The apartment looked _____ without any lights on, but Greg felt brave so he decided to investigate.

The Inn of Lost Time

By Lensey Namioka

LITERARY FOCUS: SETTING AND MOOD

When you watch a movie, do you ever feel cold during a winter scene? If so, you have felt the power of the **setting** of a story. The setting is the time and place in which a story takes place.

Setting can help create the **mood** of a story, or how it makes you feel. For example, if a story's setting is a sunny day at a park where kids are laughing, then the mood will probably be happy. Writers create certain settings and moods to help us better understand the story and the people in it.

READING FOCUS: ANALYZING DETAILS

Writers use **details** to help describe the plot and to create a setting. For example, in "The Inn of Lost Time," the author uses details to give clues to a mystery. As you read, keep a chart like the one below to record details from the "Inn of Lost Time" that help create setting and mood.

Detail: Place → **Detail: Time** → **Detail: Custom**

Japan's farmhouse → 16th Century → People drink tea by a fire and tell stories

VOCABULARY

Work with a partner to practice using these words in complete sentences.

desolate (DEHS uh liht) *adj.*: lonely; miserable.

poignant (POYN yuhnt) *adj.*: causing sadness or pain.

ruefully (ROO fuhl lee) *adv.*: with regret and embarrassment.

grueling (GROO uhl lhng) *adj.*: very tiring; demanding.

traumatic (traw MAT ihk) *adj.*: emotionally painful; causing shock.

INTO THE STORY

This story is set about 500 years ago in Japan. At that time, trained warriors called samurai protected the land. Samurai helped protect against attacks from outsiders and also kept the peace at home. They worked for rich people who owned land. They usually worked for one family their whole adult lives. Samurai who did not have a family to serve were called ronin.

Literary Skills
Understand setting and mood.

Reading Skills
Analyze story details.

THE INN OF LOST TIME

By Lensey Namioka

INTO THE STORY

"The Inn of Lost Time" was written in modern times. However, it is set in sixteenth-century Japan, when there were samurai, or special soldiers. In her storytelling, Lensey Namioka creates a story within a story. In fact, this story has two stories within it. One is an old Japanese folk tale in which a man sleeps for fifty years. The other is a story about something that happened to one of the soldiers.

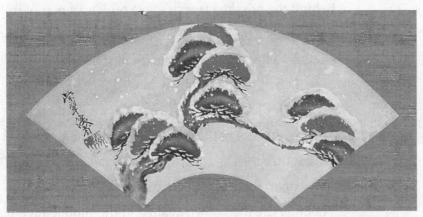

© Freer Gallery of Art, Smithsonian Institution, Washington, D.C.,
Gift of Charles Lang Freer, F1897.31a–b

A **HERE'S HOW**

Vocabulary

I do not understand what *ronin* are in line 6. I know they are "unemployed samurai," but I don't know what samurai are. I read the surrounding sentences to look for clues, but I still don't know. I looked in my dictionary, which says *samurai* are "Japanese soldiers." So *ronin* are Japanese soldiers without jobs.

B **READ AND DISCUSS**

Comprehension

What has the author set up so far? **Follow-up:** What did we learn about the ronin?

"Will you promise to sleep if I tell you a story?" said the father. He pretended to put on a stern expression.

"Yes! Yes!" the three little boys chanted in unison. It sounded like a nightly routine.

The two guests smiled as they listened to the exchange. They were wandering ronin, or unemployed samurai, and they enjoyed watching this cozy family scene. **A**

The father gave the guests a helpless look. "What can I do? I have to tell them a story, or these little rascals will give us no
10 peace." Clearing his throat, he turned to the boys. "All right. The story tonight is about Urashima Taro." **B**

YOUR TURN

Vocabulary

Defense in line 23, means "protection." Who are the samurai supposed to defend?

_____

_____

 HERE'S HOW

Vocabulary

Doubt in line 30, means "uncertainty." *No doubt* is an expression that means the writer is sure of something, even without proof. What is the writer so sure of?

_____

_____

 YOUR TURN

Vocabulary

In line 33, does *battering* mean a) covering with flour, b) hitting in baseball, or c) hitting repeatedly?

_____

Instantly the three boys became still. Sitting with their legs tucked under them, the three little boys, aged five, four, and three, looked like a descending row of stone statuettes. Matsuzo, the younger of the two ronin, was reminded of the wayside half-body statues of Jizo, the God of Travelers and Protector of Children.

IN OTHER WORDS A father tells his three sons a bedtime story about Urashima Taro. Two traveling soldiers are staying with the family. The younger soldier, Matsuzo, looks at the children and listens to the father tell the story.

Behind the boys the farmer's wife took up a pair of iron chopsticks and stirred the ashes of the fire in the charcoal brazier.[1] 20 A momentary glow brightened the room. The lean faces of the two ronin, lit by the fire, suddenly looked fierce and hungry.

The farmer knew that the two ronin were supposed to use their arms in defense of the weak. **A** But in these troubled times, with the country torn apart by civil wars, the samurai didn't always live up to their honorable code.

Then the fire died down again and the subdued red light softened the features of the two ronin. The farmer relaxed and began his story.

The tale of Urashima Taro is familiar to every Japanese. No 30 doubt the three little boys had heard their father tell it before— and more than once. **B** But they listened with rapt attention.

Urashima Taro, a fisherman, rescued a turtle from some boys who were battering it with stones. **C** The grateful turtle rewarded Taro by carrying him on his back to the bottom of the sea, where he lived happily with the Princess of the Undersea. But Taro soon became homesick for his native village and asked to go back on land. The princess gave him a box to take with him but warned him not to peek inside.

---

1. **brazier** (BRAY zhuhr): metal container that holds burning coals or charcoal, used to warm a room or cook food.

IN OTHER WORDS The farmer's wife stirs the fire as the story begins. Every Japanese person knows the story of Urashima Taro. Taro was a fisherman who saved a turtle. The turtle took him to live under the sea with a princess. But Taro missed his home and went back to land. The princess gave him a box and told him not to look in it.

When Taro went back to his village, he found the place quite changed. In his home he found his parents gone, and living there was another old couple. He was stunned to learn that the aged husband was his own son, whom he had last seen as a baby! Taro thought he had spent only a pleasant week or two undersea with the princess. On land, seventy-two years had passed! His parents and most of his old friends had long since died. **D**

Desolate, Taro decided to open the box given him by the princess. As soon as he looked inside, he changed in an instant from a young man to a decrepit old man of more than ninety. **E**

At the end of the story the boys were close to tears. Even Matsuzo found himself deeply touched. He wondered why the farmer had told his sons such a poignant bedtime story. **F** Wouldn't they worry all evening instead of going to sleep?

But the boys recovered quickly. They were soon laughing and jostling each other, and they made no objections when their mother shooed them toward bed. Standing in order of age, they bowed politely to the guests and then lay down on the mattresses spread out for them on the floor. Within minutes the sound of their regular breathing told the guests that they were asleep.

Zenta, the older of the two ronin, sighed as he glanced at the peaceful young faces. "I wish I could fall asleep so quickly. The story of Urashima Taro is one of the saddest that I know among our folk tales."

IN OTHER WORDS When Taro went home, he saw that seventy-two years had passed. He opened the box the princess gave him and turned into an old man. The story of Taro

40

50

60

D **READ AND DISCUSS**

Comprehension
The father is telling a story. What happened on land while Taro was under the sea?

_____

_____

E **HERE'S HOW**

Reading Focus
I can **analyze details** to understand what happened to Taro when he opened the box. Taro changed from a young man to an old man. I think that whatever is in the box made Taro grow older. I think this might suggest that time itself was in the box. I will read on to see if I am right.

F **HERE'S HOW**

Language Coach
I know that some words are spelled differently than they are **pronounced**. I read the word *poignant* in line 51. The *g* is silent, so I don't pronounce it.

Vocabulary

I know the word *stout* can mean "fat." However, I do not think the farmer is talking about his son's size. *Stout* must also mean "strong or brave," because the farmer says "Nothing bothers them much." I looked *stout* up in the dictionary, and it means "strong or heavy." This is close to my definition.

Vocabulary

Hastened means "did something quickly." Why is Zenta so quick to say something nice to the farmer's wife about her tea?

_____

_____

_____

Reading Focus

Zenta says he knew a man who paid gold to get years of his life back. I think this conversation has **details** that will be important to the story. I will keep reading to see if Zenta says more about this man.

Comprehension

The adults are having a serious conversation. What do we learn about Zenta from this conversation?

is a very sad one. When the father finishes telling the story, the boys go to bed.

The farmer looked proudly at his sleeping sons. "They're stout lads. Nothing bothers them much." **A**

The farmer's wife poured tea for the guests and apologized. "I'm sorry this is only poor tea made from coarse leaves."

Zenta hastened to reassure her. "It's warm and heartening on a chilly autumn evening." **B**

"You know what I think is the saddest part of the Urashima Taro story?" said Matsuzo, picking up his cup and sipping the tea. "It's that Taro lost not only his family and friends but a big piece of his life as well. He had lost the most precious thing of all: time."

The farmer nodded agreement. "I wouldn't sell even one year of my life for money. As for losing seventy-two years, no amount of gold will make up for that!"

Zenta put his cup down on the floor and looked curiously at the farmer. "It's interesting that you should say that. I had an opportunity once to observe exactly how much gold a person was willing to pay for some lost years of his life." He smiled grimly. "In this case the man went as far as one gold piece for each year he lost." **C**

"That's bizarre!" said Matsuzo. "You never told me about it."

"It happened long before I met you," said Zenta. He drank some tea and smiled ruefully. **D** "Besides, I'm not particularly proud of the part I played in that strange affair."

"Let's hear the story!" urged Matsuzo. "You've made us all curious."

IN OTHER WORDS Matsuzo thinks it is very sad that Taro lost so much time. The farmer says he would not trade his life for money. The older soldier, Zenta, says he once saw a man pay to get back years of his life that he had lost. Matsuzo wants Zenta to tell the story.

90 The farmer waited expectantly. His wife sat down quietly behind her husband and folded her hands. Her eyes looked intently at Zenta.

"Very well, then," said Zenta. "Actually, my story bears some resemblance to that of Urashima Taro. . . ."

It happened about seven years ago, when I was a green, inexperienced youngster not quite eighteen years old. **E** But I had had a good training in arms, and I was able to get a job as a bodyguard for a wealthy merchant from Sakai.

As you know, wealthy merchants are relatively new in our country. **F** Traditionally the rich have been noblemen, land-
100 owners, and warlords with thousands of followers. Merchants, regarded as parasites in our society, are a despised class. **G** But our civil wars have made people unusually mobile and stimulated trade between various parts of the country. The merchants have taken advantage of this to conduct business on a scale our fathers could not imagine. Some of them have become more wealthy than a warlord with thousands of samurai under his command.

The man I was escorting, Tokubei, was one of this new breed of wealthy merchants. He was trading not only with outly-ing provinces but even with the Portuguese[2] from across the sea.
110 On this particular journey he was not carrying much gold with him. If he had, I'm sure he would have hired an older and more experienced bodyguard. But if the need should arise, he could always write a message to his clerks at home and have money for-warded to him. It's important to remember this. **H**

IN OTHER WORDS Zenta tells the story. He was eighteen and a bodyguard for a rich trader named Tokubei. Tokubei did not travel with a lot of money, but he could always get more.

---

2. **Portuguese:** The Portuguese were the first Europeans to reach Japan, arriving in 1543. Until they were expelled, in the 1630s, they traded extensively with the Japanese.

E (HERE'S HOW)

Vocabulary

I know the word *green* is a color, but Zenta is not saying that he was actually green. I will keep reading to try to learn what he means. I know that he was young and inexperienced. Maybe this is what green means. I looked up green in my dictionary, and it means "new to some-thing," so I was right.

F (YOUR TURN)

Vocabulary

A *merchant* is someone who makes money through trade. Re-read this paragraph and circle the words that tell you about merchants and what they do.

G (YOUR TURN)

Vocabulary

Parasites are insects or ani-mals that live off of other animals. Did people in Japan see merchants as good or bad people?

H (HERE'S HOW)

Reading Focus

In line 114, the author tells me, "It's important to remember this." This tells me that what Zenta is say-ing here is very important. I should reread this section to **analyze the details** I need to remember.

Vocabulary

I do not know what the word *grueling* means. Zenta says they had to climb several steep hills. This sounds difficult, so I think *grueling* means difficult. I look it up my dictionary, and *grueling* means very tiring or demanding. This is close to my definition.

B (HERE'S HOW)

Vocabulary

How do Zenta and Tokubei feel in this paragraph? Circle the word that tells you what the word *ravenous* in line 130 means.

C (HERE'S HOW)

Literary Focus

The author does not say exactly where the men are. Based on the clues in the reading, I can try to picture the **setting**. The men are walking on a narrow, winding path off of the highway. It is probably not very well traveled because it is removed from the main road.

D (HERE'S HOW)

Vocabulary

I am not sure what the word *bamboo* means. Because of the **setting** of this scene, I know that the characters are somewhere off a main road. I read on and learn that *bamboo* can be eaten and makes a "delicious dish." This makes me think that *bamboo* may be a type of plant. I checked my dictionary, and I was right!

The second day of our journey was a particularly grueling one, with several steep hills to climb. **A** As the day was drawing to its close, we began to consider where we should spend the night. I knew that within an hour's walking was a hot-spring resort known to have several attractive inns.

120 But Tokubei, my employer, said he was already very tired and wanted to stop. He had heard of the resort and knew the inns there were expensive. Wealthy as he was, he did not want to spend more money than he had to.

While we stood talking, a smell reached our noses, a wonderful smell of freshly cooked rice. Suddenly I felt ravenous. **B** From the way Tokubei swallowed, I knew he was feeling just as hungry.

We looked around eagerly, but the area was forested and we could not see very far in any direction. The tantalizing smell

130 seemed to grow and I could feel the saliva filling my mouth.

"There's an inn around here somewhere," muttered Tokubei. "I'm sure of it."

We followed our noses. We had to leave the well-traveled highway and take a narrow, winding footpath. But the mouthwatering smell of the rice and the vision of fluffy, freshly aired cotton quilts drew us on. **C**

IN OTHER WORDS Zenta and Tokubei were very tired and hungry from traveling. They smelled rice cooking. They followed the smell, looking for an inn.

The sun was just beginning to set. We passed a bamboo grove, and in the low evening light the thin leaves turned into little golden knives. I saw a gilded[3] clump of bamboo shoots. The

140 sight made me think of the delicious dish they would make when boiled in soy sauce. **D**

We hurried forward. To our delight we soon came to a clearing with a thatched house standing in the middle. The fra-

---

3. **gilded:** here, appearing to be coated with gold.

E HERE'S HOW

Reading Focus
Zenta says there was something unusual about the girl's hand. I think Zenta includes this **detail** because it is important to the story. I underlined this detail so that I remember to look for more information about the girl's hand as I read.

grant smell of rice was now so strong that we were certain a meal was being prepared inside.

Standing in front of the house was a pretty girl beaming at us with a welcoming smile. "Please honor us with your presence," she said, beckoning.

There was something a little <u>unusual about one of her</u>
150 <u>hands</u>, but, being hungry and eager to enter the house, I did not stop to observe closely. **E**

You will say, of course, that it was my duty as a bodyguard to be suspicious and to look out for danger. Youth and inexperience should not have prevented me from wondering why an inn should be found hidden away from the highway. As it was, my stomach growled, and I didn't even hesitate but followed Tokubei to the house.

Before stepping up to enter, we were given basins of water to wash our feet. As the girl handed us towels for drying, I saw what
160 was unusual about her left hand: She had six fingers.

Tokubei had noticed it as well. When the girl turned away to empty the basins, he nudged me. "Did you see her left hand? She had—" He broke off in confusion as the girl turned around, but she didn't seem to have heard.

A **YOUR TURN**

Reading Focus

Underline **details** in lines 165–170 that the author uses to give an idea that something might be strange about this inn.

B **YOUR TURN**

Language Coach

The word *spacious* in line 171 makes an /sh/ sound in the second syllable, even though it is spelled *–cious*. What other word in this paragraph makes a similar sound in its second syllable?

C **HERE'S HOW**

Reading Focus

Zenta uses **details** to guess the innkeeper's age. He notices that the innkeeper has gray hair and a bent back, even though his face looks strong.

D **HERE'S HOW**

Literary Focus

The innkeepers are taking good care of their guests in this part. The **mood** in this part of the story is very comfortable and relaxed.

The inn was peaceful and quiet, and we soon discovered the reason why. We were the only guests. Again, I should have been suspicious. I told you that I'm not proud of the part I played.

IN OTHER WORDS The men passed bamboo plants and then saw a small inn. A girl invited them into the inn. Her hand looked strange, but Zenta was too hungry to look at her closely. Then Zenta saw that the girl had six fingers on one hand. He and Tokubei were the only guests at the inn.

Tokubei turned to me and grinned. "It seems that there are no other guests. We should be able to get extra service for the

170   same amount of money." **A**

The girl led us to a spacious room which was like the principal chamber of a private residence. Cushions were set out for us on the floor and we began to shed our traveling gear to make ourselves comfortable. **B**

The door opened and a grizzled-haired man entered. Despite his vigorous-looking face his back was a little bent, and I guessed his age to be about fifty. **C** After bowing and greeting us, he apologized in advance for the service. "We have not always been innkeepers here," he said, "and you may find the accom-

180   modations lacking. Our good intentions must make up for our inexperience. However, to compensate for our inadequacies, we will charge a lower fee than that of an inn with an established reputation."

Tokubei nodded graciously, highly pleased by the words of our host, and the evening began well. It continued well when the girl came back with some flasks of wine, cups, and dishes of salty snacks. **D**

While the girl served the wine, the host looked with interest at my swords. From the few remarks he made, I gathered that he

190   was a former samurai, forced by circumstances to turn his house into an inn.

Having become a bodyguard to a tight-fisted merchant, I was in no position to feel superior to a ronin-turned-innkeeper. Socially, therefore, we were more or less equal. **E**

IN OTHER WORDS The inn was very comfortable. Zenta and Tokubei met the man who owned the inn. He used to be a soldier, like Zenta. The girl with the strange hand brought the men wine.

We exchanged polite remarks with our host while we drank and tasted the salty snacks. I looked around at the pleasant room. It showed excellent taste, and I especially admired a vase standing in the alcove.

200 My host caught my eyes on it. "We still have a few good things that we didn't have to sell," he said. His voice held a trace of bitterness. "Please look at the panels of these doors. They were painted by a fine artist." **F**

Tokubei and I looked at the pair of sliding doors. Each panel contained a landscape painting, the right panel depicting a winter scene and the left one the same scene in late summer. Our host's words were no idle boast. The pictures were indeed beautiful.

Tokubei rose and approached the screens for a closer look. When he sat down again, his eyes were calculating. No doubt he was trying to estimate what price the paintings would fetch. **G**

210 After my third drink I began to feel very tired. Perhaps it was the result of drinking on an empty stomach. I was glad when the girl brought in two dinner trays and a lacquered container of rice. Uncovering the rice container, she began filling our bowls.

Again I noticed her strange left hand with its six fingers. Any other girl would have tried to keep that hand hidden, but this girl made no effort to do so. If anything, she seemed to use that hand more than her other one when she served us. The extra little finger always stuck out from the hand, as if inviting comment. **H**

E **YOUR TURN**

Reading Focus

What do we know so far about the hosts at the inn? What **details** does the author give to let you know this?

_____

_____

F **HERE'S HOW**

Vocabulary

I know that a panel can be a flat part of something. I am confused by the *panels* in line 201. They must be part of the door. The dictionary says *panels* can be smaller parts of a larger painting. I understand now that Tokubei is looking at two paintings on a door.

G **READ AND DISCUSS**

Comprehension

Zenta is telling a story from his past. He gives many details. What is Zenta explaining? **Follow-up:** How do the door panels connect to Tokubei?

_____

_____

H **YOUR TURN**

Reading Focus

Underline the **detail** the author wants us to remember in this paragraph.

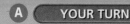

A **YOUR TURN**

Vocabulary

Blurry means "unclear." Read on and explain why things started to look *blurry* to Zenta.

_____

_____

B **READ AND DISCUSS**

Comprehension

What happened?

C **HERE'S HOW**

Vocabulary

I am not sure what the word *frantically* means. I know that Zenta is very worried because he does not know what has happened. I looked up *frantic* in the dictionary, and it means "worried or confused." I understand that Zenta is *frantic* because he does not know where he is.

D **YOUR TURN**

Reading Focus

Shakily in line 237 means "unsteadily." Circle the **details** in this paragraph that show Zenta is having difficulty standing up.

E **YOUR TURN**

Literary Focus

I know that the **setting** has changed from the inn. Zenta and Tokubei are now cold and wet, lying on the ground outside. It is now morning.

IN OTHER WORDS There were many nice things in the inn. Tokubei looked at two paintings on a door. They were expensive. The men ate dinner. Zenta was very tired. He kept looking at the girl's six fingers.

220 The hand fascinated me so much that I kept my eyes on it and soon forgot to eat. After a while the hand looked blurry. And then everything else began to look blurry. **A** The last thing I remembered was the sight of Tokubei shaking his head, as if trying to clear it.

When I opened my eyes again, I knew that time had passed, but not how much time. My next thought was that it was cold. It was not only extremely cold but damp.

I rolled over and sat up. I reached immediately for my swords and found them safe on the ground beside me. *On the*
230 *ground?* What was I doing on the ground? My last memory was of staying at an inn with a merchant called Tokubei. **B**

The thought of Tokubei put me into a panic. I was his bodyguard, and instead of watching over him, I had fallen asleep and had awakened in a strange place.

I looked around frantically **C** and saw that he was lying on the ground not far from where I was. Had he been killed?

I got up shakily, and when I stood up, my head was swimming. But my sense of urgency gave some strength to my legs. I stumbled over to my employer and to my great relief found him
240 breathing—breathing heavily, in fact. **D**

When I shook his shoulder, he grunted and finally opened his eyes. "Where am I?" he asked thickly.

It was a reasonable question. I looked around and saw that we had been lying in a bamboo grove. By the light I guessed that it was early morning, and the reason I felt cold and damp was that my clothes were wet with dew. **E**

IN OTHER WORDS After staring at the girl's hand, Zenta fell asleep. When he woke up, he and Tokubei were on the ground outside. He had no idea how he got there. Zenta was very worried. He was supposed to be looking after Tokubei. The men did not know where they were.

"It's cold!" said Tokubei, shivering and climbing unsteadily to his feet. He looked around slowly, and his eyes became wide with disbelief. "What happened? I thought we were staying at an inn!"

250

His words came as a relief. One of the possibilities I had considered was that I had gone mad and that the whole episode with the inn was something I had imagined. Now I knew that Tokubei had the same memory of the inn. I had not imagined it.

But why were we out here on the cold ground, instead of on comfortable mattresses in the inn?

"They must have drugged us and robbed us," said Tokubei. He turned and looked at me furiously. "A fine bodyguard you are!"

260

There was nothing I could say to that. But at least we were both alive and unharmed. "Did they take all your money?" I asked.

Tokubei had already taken his wallet out of his sash and was peering inside. "That's funny! My money is still here!"

This was certainly unexpected. What did the innkeeper and his strange daughter intend to do by drugging us and moving us outside?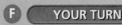

At least things were not as bad as we had feared. We had not lost anything except a comfortable night's sleep, although from the heaviness in my head I had certainly slept deeply enough—

270

and long enough too. Exactly how much time had elapsed since we drank wine with our host?

All we had to do now was find the highway again and continue our journey. Tokubei suddenly chuckled. "I didn't even have to pay for our night's lodging!"

IN OTHER WORDS Zenta and Tokubei thought the inn-keepers had given them drugs and robbed them. But Tokubei

---

F (**YOUR TURN**)

Literary Focus

Mood is the atmosphere of a story. How has the mood of the story changed in this waking up scene?

_____

_____

G (**HERE'S HOW**)

Reading Focus

Zenta does not know how long he spent sleeping. I can tell that this is an important **detail** that I will learn more about as the story continues.

had all of his money. They did not know how long they had slept. They decided to find the highway again. Tokubei was happy that he did not have to pay for the inn.

As we walked from the bamboo grove, I saw the familiar clump of bamboo shoots, and we found ourselves standing in the same clearing again. Before our eyes was the thatched house. Only it was somehow different. Perhaps things looked different
280 in the daylight than at dusk.

But the difference was more than a change of light. As we approached the house slowly, like sleepwalkers, we saw that the thatching was much darker. On the previous evening the thatching had looked fresh and new. Now it was dark with age. Daylight should make things appear brighter, not darker. The plastering of the walls also looked more dingy. **A**

Tokubei and I stopped to look at each other before we went closer. He was pale, and I knew that I looked no less frightened. Something was terribly wrong. I loosened my sword in its
290 scabbard.[4] **B**

We finally gathered the courage to go up to the house. Since Tokubei seemed unable to find his voice, I spoke out. "Is anyone there?"

After a moment we heard shuffling footsteps and the front door slid open. The face of an old woman appeared. "Yes?" she inquired. **C** Her voice was creaky with age.

What set my heart pounding with panic, however, was not her voice. It was the sight of her left hand holding on to the frame of the door. The hand was wrinkled and crooked with the
300 arthritis of old age—and it had six fingers. **D**

IN OTHER WORDS Zenta and Tokubei walked back to the inn. It looked different. Now it was very old. Something was wrong. An old woman opened the door. She had six fingers.

---

4. **scabbard:** case for the blade of a sword.

A HERE'S HOW

Reading Focus

I notice some important **details** about the inn here: it is "somehow different," the roof was now "dark with age," and the walls "looked more dingy," which means they were dirtier. By **analyzing details** about the inn, I can tell that the inn looks very different from the way it looked before.

B YOUR TURN

Literary Focus

The **mood** of the story has changed again. What is the **mood** of the story like at this point?

_____

_____

C HERE'S HOW

Vocabulary

Inquired means "asked." Circle the part of this sentence that tells you the old woman asked a question.

_____

D YOUR TURN

Reading Focus

There is a **detail** in this paragraph that surprises Zenta. What is that detail?

_____

_____

I heard a gasp beside me and knew that Tokubei had noticed the hand as well.

The door opened wider and a man appeared beside the old woman. At first I thought it was our host of the previous night. But this man was much younger, although the resemblance was strong. He carried himself straighter and his hair was black, while the innkeeper had been grizzled and slightly bent with age. **E**

"Please excuse my mother," said the man. "Her hearing is not good. Can we help you in some way?"

310 Tokubei finally found his voice. "Isn't this the inn where we stayed last night?"

The man stared. "Inn? We are not innkeepers here!"

"Yes, you are!" insisted Tokubei. "Your daughter invited us in and served us with wine. You must have put something in the wine!"

The man frowned. "You are serious? Are you sure you didn't drink too much at your inn and wander off?"

"No, I didn't drink too much!" said Tokubei, almost shouting. "I hardly drank at all! Your daughter, the one with six fingers

320 on her hand, started to pour me a second cup of wine . . ." His voice trailed off, and he stared again at the left hand of the old woman. **F**

"I don't have a daughter," said the man slowly. "My mother here is the one who has six fingers on her left hand, although I hardly think it polite of you to mention it."

"I'm getting dizzy," muttered Tokubei, and began to totter.

IN OTHER WORDS Zenta and Tokubei met a young man at the door. He said he was not an innkeeper. He did not believe that Zenta and Tokubei had stayed there. The man said he did not have a daughter. The old woman with six fingers was his mother.

"I think you'd better come in and rest a bit," the man said to him gruffly. He glanced at me. "Perhaps you wish to join your friend. You don't share his delusion about the inn, I hope?" **G**

E (HERE'S HOW)

Reading Focus

There are several **details** that tell me this man is different from the innkeeper the night before. They look alike, but this man is younger. His hair is black and he stands up tall.

F (HERE'S HOW)

Literary Focus

The **mood** of this scene is very different from the first time Tokubei arrived at the inn. Now, he is angry and confused.

G (HERE'S HOW)

Vocabulary

I do not know what a *delusion* is. I know that the man does not believe that Tokubei and Zenta were ever at his house. I look up *delusion* in my dictionary, and it is a "false belief or fantasy." This means that the man thinks Tokubei is making things up.

"I wouldn't presume to contradict my elders," I said carefully. Since both Tokubei and the owner of the house were my elders, I wasn't committing myself. In truth, I didn't know what to believe, but I did want a look at the inside of the house.

The inside was almost the same as it was before but the differences were there when I looked closely. We entered the same room with the alcove and the pair of painted doors. The vase I had admired was no longer there, but the doors showed the same landscapes painted by a master. I peered closely at the pictures and saw that the colors looked faded. What was more, the left

340 panel, the one depicting a winter scene, had a long tear in one corner. It had been painstakingly mended, but the damage was impossible to hide completely.

Tokubei saw what I was staring at and he became even paler. At this stage we had both considered the possibility that a hoax of some sort had been played on us. **B** The torn screen convinced Tokubei that our host had not played a joke: The owner of a valuable painting would never vandalize it for a trivial reason. **C**

As for me, I was far more disturbed by the sight of the sixth finger on the old woman's hand. Could the young girl have dis-

350 guised herself as an old crone? She could put rice powder in her hair to whiten it, but she could not transform her pretty straight fingers into old fingers twisted with arthritis. **D** The woman here with us now was genuinely old, at least fifty years older than the girl.

IN OTHER WORDS Zenta and Tokubei went inside. The inn looked similar, but it was now very old. The paintings were ripped. The people inside were not playing a joke on the two men. Zenta knew the old woman was really old, and not the young girl dressed up to look old.

It was this same old woman who finally gave us our greatest shock. "It's interesting that you should mention an inn, gentlemen," she croaked. "My father used to operate an inn. After he

---

A HERE'S HOW

Vocabulary

Parts of this story can be very confusing. I need to pay close attention to **details**. This way, I can tell what is different and what is the same about the inn and the people there.

B YOUR TURN

Vocabulary

Zenta thinks the innkeepers are playing a *hoax* on them. Circle the word in this paragraph that tells you what a *hoax* is.

C HERE'S HOW

Vocabulary

I know that the expensive painting has been ripped. Zenta says that someone who owns such an expensive painting would never rip it for a *trivial* reason. I do not know what trivial means, so I looked it up. My dictionary says "small or unimportant." Playing a joke would be a trivial reason to ruin a painting.

D YOUR TURN

Reading Focus

What **detail** makes Zenta decide that the little girl could not be dressed up as the old woman?

died, my husband and I turned this back into a private residence. We didn't need the income, you see."

360   "Your . . . your . . . f-father?" stammered Tokubei. **E**

    "Yes," replied the old woman. "He was a ronin, forced to go into inn keeping when he lost his position. But he never liked the work. Besides, our inn had begun to acquire an unfortunate reputation. Some of our guests disappeared, you see."

    Even before she finished speaking, a horrible suspicion had begun to dawn on me. Her *father* had been an innkeeper, she said, her father who used to be a ronin. The man who had been our host was a ronin-turned-innkeeper. Could this mean that this old woman was actually the same person as the young girl

370 we had seen? **F**

    I sat stunned while I tried to absorb the implications. What had happened to us? Was it possible that Tokubei and I had slept while this young girl grew into a mature woman, got married, and bore a son, a son who was now an adult? If that was the case, then we had slept for fifty years! **G**

    The old woman's next words confirmed my fears. "I recognize you now! You are two of the lost guests from our inn! The other lost ones I don't remember so well, but I remember *you* because your disappearance made me so sad. Such a handsome

380 youth, I thought; what a pity that he should have gone the way of the others!" **H**

IN OTHER WORDS The old woman said her father used to run an inn. Zenta and Tokubei realized that she was the young girl they had met. The two men had slept for fifty years! The old woman said their guests disappeared. She remembered Zenta and Tokubei from fifty years ago.

    A high wail came from Tokubei, who began to keen[5] and rock himself back and forth. "I've lost fifty years! Fifty years of my life went by while I slept at this accursed inn!" **I**

---

5. **keen:** cry.

E (**HERE'S HOW**)

Reading Focus

I notice the **detail** that Tokubei is repeating words and sounds as he tries to say "your father." I read this line out loud to see how it sounded. This helped me better understand that the character is surprised by the old woman's answer.

F (**YOUR TURN**)

Language Coach

Some words are spelled differently than they are pronounced. Which word in this paragraph is pronounced with a /sh/ sound, even though it is not spelled with SH?

_____

G (**READ AND DISCUSS**)

Comprehension

What do the men think has happened to them?

H (**YOUR TURN**)

Vocabulary

Re-read lines 376–381. Based on its context here, what do you think the word *confirmed* means in line 376?

_____

I (**YOUR TURN**)

Vocabulary

What smaller word do you recognize in the word *accursed*? Use this word to help you come up with a definition for accursed.

A **YOUR TURN**

Vocabulary

In line 398, does *console* mean a) to make someone feel better, b) a control panel for electronics, or c) a piece of furniture?

_____

_____

B **YOUR TURN**

Reading Focus

Remember that a *ronin* is a wandering samurai, or Japanese soldier. Why do you think Zenta was more worried about his boss than himself?

_____

_____

The inn was indeed accursed. Was the fate of the other guests similar to ours? "Did anyone else return as we did, fifty years later?" I asked.

The old woman looked uncertain and turned to her son. He frowned thoughtfully. "From time to time wild-looking people
390 have come to us with stories similar to yours. Some of them went mad with the shock."

Tokubei wailed again. "I've lost my business! I've lost my wife, my young and beautiful wife! We had been married only a couple of months!"

A gruesome chuckle came from the old woman. "You may not have lost your wife. It's just that she's become an old hag like me!"

That did not console Tokubei, whose keening became louder. **A** Although my relationship with my employer had not
400 been characterized by much respect on either side, I did begin to feel very sorry for him. He was right: He had lost his world.

IN OTHER WORDS Tokubei began to cy because he had lost fifty years of his life. The old woman said that other people had come back to the inn, telling similar stories of. Those people had also slept for many years. Zenta felt very bad for Tokubei.

As for me, the loss was less traumatic. I had left home under extremely painful circumstances and had spent the next three years wandering. I had no friends and no one I could call a relation. The only thing I had was my duty to my employer. Somehow, someway, I had to help him. **B**

"Did no one find an explanation for these disappearances?" I asked. "Perhaps if we knew the reason why, we might find some way to reverse the process."
410 The old woman began to nod eagerly. "The priestess! Tell them about the shrine priestess!"

"Well," said the man, "I'm not sure if it would work in your case. . . ."

"What? What would work?" demanded Tokubei. His eyes were feverish.

"There was a case of one returning guest who consulted the priestess at our local shrine," said the man. "She went into a trance and revealed that there was an evil spirit dwelling in the bamboo grove here. This spirit would put unwary travelers into a long, unnatural sleep. They would wake up twenty, thirty, or even fifty years later." **C**

420

"Yes, but you said something worked in his case," said Tokubei.

The man seemed reluctant to go on. **D** "I don't like to see you cheated, so I'm not sure I should be telling you this."

"Tell me! Tell me!" demanded Tokubei. The host's reluctance only made him more impatient.

IN OTHER WORDS Zenta explains that he did not have a home and a wife like Tokubei. Although he was not as upset as Tokubei, Zenta knew that he had to help Tokubei. Tokubei wanted to find a way to get back the years that he lost. A priestess said that an evil spirit in the bamboo plants made people sleep for many years.

"The priestess promised to make a spell that would undo the work of the evil spirit," said the man. "But she demanded a large sum of money, for she said that she had to burn some very rare and costly incense before she could begin the spell." **E**

430

At the mention of money Tokubei sat back. The hectic[6] flush died down on his face and his eyes narrowed. "How much money?" he asked.

The host shook his head. "In my opinion the priestess is a fraud and makes outrageous claims about her powers. We try to have as little to do with her as possible." **F**

"Yes, but did her spell work?" asked Tokubei. "If it worked, she's no fraud!"

---

6. **hectic:** feverish.

C HERE'S HOW

Reading Focus

In this paragraph, the man talks about **details** that seem to explain what happened. I learn that an evil spirit in the bamboo plants made travelers sleep for many years.

D HERE'S HOW

Vocabulary

I am not sure what the word *reluctant* in line 424 means. The man says he isn't sure whether he should be telling Tokubei about the priestess. *Reluctant* must mean not wanting to do something. The dictionary says "unwilling," so my definition is correct.

E READ AND DISCUSS

Comprehension

The man is talking about the powers of the shrine priestess. What is all this telling us?

F HERE'S HOW

Language Coach

I know that some words are spelled differently than they are pronounced. In line 436, the word *outrageous*, which means "extraordinary," is spelled with a *g*. But when I say it out loud, I pronounce the *g* like a /j/.

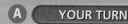

A **YOUR TURN**

Reading Focus

In this sentence, Zenta notices something. **Analyze the details** given and explain why you think this information is important.

_____

_____

B **YOUR TURN**

Vocabulary

In this context, does *remit* in line 457 mean a) to cancel, or b) to send?

_____

440 "At least the stranger disappeared again," cackled the old woman. "Maybe he went back to his own time. Maybe he walked into a river."

Tokubei's eyes narrowed further. "How much money did the priestess demand?" he asked again.

"I think it was one gold piece for every year lost," said the host. He hurriedly added, "Mind you, I still wouldn't trust the priestess."

"Then it would cost me fifty gold pieces to get back to my own time," muttered Tokubei. He looked up. "I don't carry that

450 much money with me." **A**

"No, you don't," agreed the host.

Something alerted me about the way he said that. It was as if the host knew already that Tokubei did not carry much money on him.

IN OTHER WORDS The priestess charged a lot of money to get rid of the evil spirit. The man said he did not trust her. Tokubei thought her spell might work. The host already knew that Tokubei did not have enough money with him to pay the priestess.

Meanwhile Tokubei sighed. He had come to a decision. "I do have the means to obtain more money, however. I can send a message to my chief clerk and he will remit the money when he sees my seal." **B**

"Your chief clerk may be dead by now," I reminded him.

460 "You're right!" moaned Tokubei. "My business will be under a new management and nobody will even remember my name!"

"And your wife will have remarried," said the old woman, with one of her chuckles. I found it hard to believe that the gentle young girl who had served us wine could turn into this dreadful harridan.[7]

---

7. **harridan:** spiteful old woman.

"Sending the message may be a waste of time," agreed the host.

"What waste of time!" cried Tokubei. "Why shouldn't I waste time? I've wasted fifty years already! Anyway, I've made up
470   my mind. I'm sending that message."

"I still think you shouldn't trust the priestess," said the host.

That only made Tokubei all the more determined to send for the money. However, he was not quite resigned to the amount. "Fifty gold pieces is a large sum. Surely the priestess can buy incense for less than that amount?" **C**

"Why don't you try giving her thirty gold pieces?" cackled the old woman. "Then the priestess will send you back thirty years, and your wife will only be middle-aged." **D**

IN OTHER WORDS Tokubei said he would send for more money. He did not know how much to send for. He had a lot of money, but he did not like to spend it. The host kept telling Tokubei not to trust the priestess. Tokubei did not listen.

While Tokubei was still arguing with himself about the exact
480   sum to send for, I decided to have a look at the bamboo grove. "I'm going for a walk," I announced, rising and picking up my sword from the floor beside me.

The host turned sharply to look at me. For an instant a faint, rueful smile appeared on his lips. Then he looked away.

Outside, I went straight to the clump of shoots in the bamboo grove. On the previous night—or what I perceived as the previous night—I had noticed that clump of bamboo shoots particularly, because I had been so hungry that I pictured them being cut up and boiled.

490   The clump of bamboo shoots was still in the same place. That in itself proved nothing, since bamboo could spring up anywhere, including the place where a clump had existed fifty years earlier. But what settled the matter in my mind was that the clump looked almost exactly the way it did when I had seen it

C YOUR TURN

Language Coach

Some words are spelled differently than they are **pronounced**. What word in this paragraph has a silent *g*?

_____

D YOUR TURN

Literary Focus

Does the old woman seem understanding of Tokubei's problem? How do you think her words here affect the **mood** of the story?

_____

_____

Reading Focus

Zenta notices important **details** in this paragraph. He sees that the bamboo looks the same as it did the night before. The plants grew an inch in one night, not in fifty years.

B **YOUR TURN**

Vocabulary

Something *consistent* is always the same. Re-read lines 499–506. Based on its context here, what do you think the word *inconsistency* means in line 499?

_____

_____

C **YOUR TURN**

Reading Focus

Analyzing **details** helps you to understand a story. Zenta notices something different about the paintings in the inn. Why are these details important?

_____

_____

D **READ AND DISCUSS**

Comprehension

Zenta seems to be realizing something about his experience. What is on Zenta's mind?

---

before, except that every shoot was about an inch taller. That was a reasonable amount for bamboo shoots to grow overnight. A

Overnight. Tokubei and I had slept on the ground here overnight. We had not slept here for a period of fifty years.

Once I knew that, I was able to see another inconsistency:
500 the door panels with the painted landscapes. The painting with the winter scene had been on the *right* last night and it was on the *left* this morning. It wasn't simply a case of the panels changing places, because the depressions in the panel for the handholds had been reversed. In other words, what I saw just now was not a pair of paintings faded and torn by age. They were an entirely different pair of paintings. B C

IN OTHER WORDS Zenta decided to look at the bamboo. The plants looked the same. They had grown an inch overnight. He and Tokubei had slept for one night, not fifty years. Then Zenta realized that the paintings had not aged. They were different paintings.

But how did the pretty young girl change into an old woman? The answer was that if the screens could be different ones, so could the women. I had seen one woman, a young girl,
510 last night. This morning I saw a different woman, an old hag.

The darkening of the thatched roof? Simply blow ashes over the roof. The grizzled-haired host of last night could be the same man who claimed to be his grandson today. It would be a simple matter for a young man to put gray in his hair and assume a stoop.

And the purpose of the hoax? To make Tokubei send for fifty pieces of gold, of course. It was clever of the man to accuse the shrine priestess of fraud and pretend reluctance to let Tokubei send his message. D

520 I couldn't even feel angry toward the man and his daughter—or mother, sister, wife, whatever. He could have killed me and taken my swords, which he clearly admired. Perhaps he was really a ronin and felt sympathetic toward another one.

When I returned to the house, Tokubei was looking resigned. "I've decided to send for the whole fifty gold pieces." **E** He sighed.

"Don't bother," I said. "In fact, we should be leaving as soon as possible. We shouldn't even stop here for a drink, especially not of wine."

530   Tokubei stared. "What do you mean? If I go back home, I'll find everything changed!"

IN OTHER WORDS Zenta realized the old woman and the young girl were different people. The young man had dressed up to look old. They made the house look old. They had played a trick on the two men to get Tokubei to send for more money. Zenta went back to the house and told Tokubei that they should leave.

"Nothing will be changed," I told him. "Your wife will be as young and beautiful as ever."

"I don't understand," he said. "Fifty years . . ."

"It's a joke," I said. "The people here have a peculiar sense of humor, and they've played a joke on us."

Tokubei's mouth hung open. Finally he closed it with a snap. He stared at the host, and his face became first red and then purple. "You—you were trying to swindle me!" **F** He turned
540 furiously to me. "And you let them do this!"

"I'm not letting them," I pointed out. "That's why we're leaving right now."

"Are you going to let them get away with this?" demanded Tokubei. "They might try to swindle someone else!"

"They only went to this much trouble when they heard of the arrival of a fine fat fish like you," I said. I looked deliberately at the host. "I'm sure they won't be tempted to try the same trick again."

"And that's the end of your story?" asked Matsuzo. "You and
550 Tokubei just went away? How did you know the so-called inn-keeper wouldn't try the trick on some other luckless traveler?"

E YOUR TURN

Language Coach

Sometimes English words are not spelled the way they are **pronounced**. What word in this sentence begins with a letter that is silent, or not pronounced?

_____

F YOUR TURN

Vocabulary

The word *swindle* helps show that Tokubei is angry. Underline the words that show it makes Tokubei angry. What do you think *swindle* means? Use a dictionary to help you.

_____

_____

B **YOUR TURN**

Reading Focus

Underline the interesting **detail** that the author reveals here. What does this tell you about the story?

_____

_____

C **YOUR TURN**

Reading Focus

In this section the author explains **details** about the farmer's wife's family. How is she related to the family in Zenta's story?

_____

_____

Zenta shook his head. "I didn't know. I merely guessed that once the trick was exposed, A they wouldn't take the chance of trying it again. Of course I thought about revisiting the place to check if the people there were leading an honest life."

IN OTHER WORDS Zenta told Tokubei that the innkeepers were playing a trick on them, and they left. Matsuzo could not believe that was the end of Zenta's story. Zenta did not think the family would play the trick on someone else.

"Why didn't you?" asked Matsuzo. "Maybe we could go together. You've made me curious about that family now."

"Then you can satisfy your curiosity," said Zenta, smiling. He held his cup out for more tea, and the farmer's wife came for-
560 ward to pour.

Only now she used both hands to hold the pot, and for the first time Matsuzo saw her left hand. He gasped. The hand had six fingers. B

"Who was the old woman?" Zenta asked the farmer's wife.

"She was my grandmother," she replied. "Having six fingers is something that runs in my family."

At last Matsuzo found his voice. "You mean this is the very house you visited? This is the inn where time was lost?"

"Where we *thought* we lost fifty years," said Zenta. "Perhaps
570 I should have warned you first. But I was almost certain that we'd be safe this time. And I see that I was right."

He turned to the woman again. "You and your husband are farmers now, aren't you? What happened to the man who was the host?"

"He's dead," she said quietly. "He was my brother, and he was telling you the truth when he said that he was a ronin. Two years ago he found work with another warlord, but he was killed in battle only a month later." C

Matsuzo was peering at the pair of sliding doors, which he
580 hadn't noticed before. "I see that you've put up the faded set of paintings. The winter scene is on the left side."

The woman nodded. "We sold the newer pair of doors. My husband said that we're farmers now and that people in our position don't need valuable paintings. We used the money to buy some new farm implements." **D**

She took up the teapot again. "Would you like another cup of tea?" she asked Matsuzo.

Staring at her left hand, Matsuzo had a sudden qualm. "I—I don't think I want any more."

590   Everybody laughed. **E**

IN OTHER WORDS Matsuzo wanted to see the family. The farmer's wife served tea. She had six fingers! The old woman was her grandmother. The man was her brother. They were all in the same inn! She and her husband became farmers. They sold the expensive paintings and put up the old paintings instead. They do not play tricks on people, and are hard working farmers.

Reading Focus

Matsuzo notices an important **detail** about the paintings. He sees that they are the old set that Zenta and Tokubei once saw.

E **YOUR TURN**

Literary Focus

The setting of the opening and closing of "The Inn of Lost Time" is very important. What does the **setting** here have in common with the setting of Zenta's story?

_____

_____

Skills Practice

The Inn of Lost Time

USE A VENN DIAGRAM

Authors provide many **details** to describe the **setting** of a story. You can use a Venn Diagram to compare these details.

DIRECTIONS: Write details in the Venn Diagram that show how the first and second days at the inn were different. List these details in the circle under the correct heading.

Then, write what details remained the same in the middle part of the diagram. These should be the details that convinced Zenta that he and his boss were the victims of a trick.

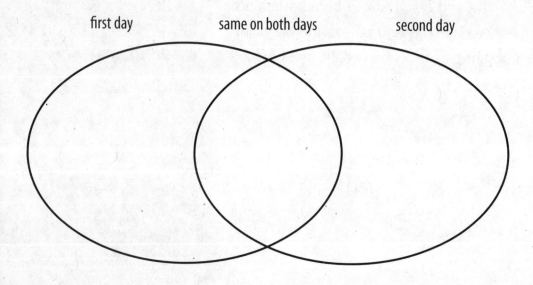

first day   same on both days   second day

The Inn of Lost Time

LITERARY FOCUS: SETTING AND MOOD

DIRECTIONS: Circle all of the words from the following list that apply to one of the **settings** in this story.

modern city	farmhouse	forest
library	grove	jungle
inn	winter	morning

READING FOCUS: ANALYZING DETAILS

DIRECTIONS: On the Preparing to Read page, you were instructed to keep a **details** chart. Review the **details** that you listed in your chart as you read "The Inn of Lost Time." Circle the details that help describe **mood**. Then, on the lines below, explain what the overall **mood** of the story was.

_____

_____

_____

_____

_____

Word Box

desolate

poignant

ruefully

grueling

traumatic

VOCABULARY REVIEW

DIRECTIONS: Draw a line from each word to its meaning.

desolate	very tiring
poignant	lonely; miserable
ruefully	emotionally painful
grueling	causing sadness or pain
traumatic	with embarrassment

Physical Science

INFORMATIONAL TEXT FOCUS: STRUCTURE AND PURPOSE OF A TEXTBOOK

Textbooks are full of useful information, but you have to know how to find it. Read the list of textbook elements below to learn about their uses.

- **Table of contents:** This is a list at the front of a book that tells what the book is about and shows its structure.

- **Headings:** These are words in large boldface type that are usually found at the beginning of a new section. Subheadings are smaller headings that divide big ideas into smaller topics.

- **Diagrams:** Graphs, charts, and outlines are diagrams that give information through visuals.

- **Captions:** The text found below photos and diagrams that explain what you are looking at.

- **Text styles:** Authors often use **boldfaced** and *italicized* text to draw your attention to key terms and ideas.

One way to better understand a textbook is by **taking notes**—writing down main ideas and important information. The headings in a textbook can help you take notes. As you read, write each main heading on a seperate note card. Take notes about the most important ideas under each heading. Look at the example below.

I What are Scientific Methods?

- Ways scientists solve problems

- List of steps to follow during experiments, or scientific tests

VOCABULARY

Work with a partner to practice using these words in complete sentences.

scientific methods (SAHY UHN TIF IK METH EDS) *n.:* series of steps followed to solve problems through scientific experiments.

observation (OB ZUR VEY SHUHN) *n.:* the process of getting information by using the senses.

hypothesis (HI POTH IH SIS) *n.:* possible explanation or answer.

necessarily (NEHS OH SAR UH LEE) *adv.:* unavoidably.

INTO THE TEXT

You use textbooks everyday in your classes at school. Textbooks tell us about many different subjects. Textbook writers try to organize a textbook in such a way that the book is easy to read and understand.

SKILLS FOCUS

Informational Text Skills
Understand the structure and purpose of a textbook; create notes to enhance comprehension of a text.

TEXTBOOK CHAPTER

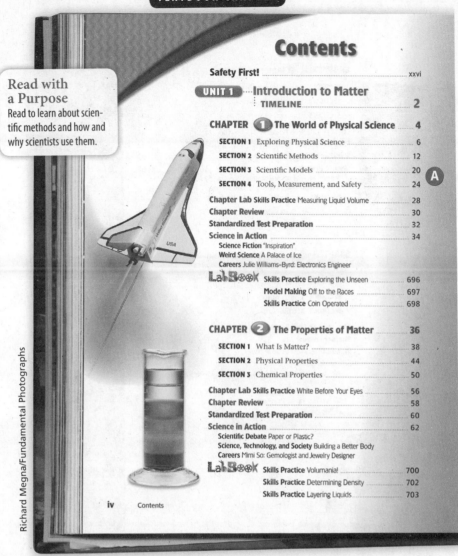

Read with a Purpose
Read to learn about scientific methods and how and why scientists use them.

Contents

A **HERE'S HOW**

Reading Focus

I can see from the **table of contents** that the first chapter is about physical science. I also see that it is broken into smaller sections.

IN OTHER WORDS The table of contents outlines the material covered in the textbook. Unit 1 will focus mainly on "The World of Physical Science" and "The Properties of Matter."

Reading Focus

Check the **table of contents** for Chapter 3. What is the second section of Chapter 3 called?

_____

_____

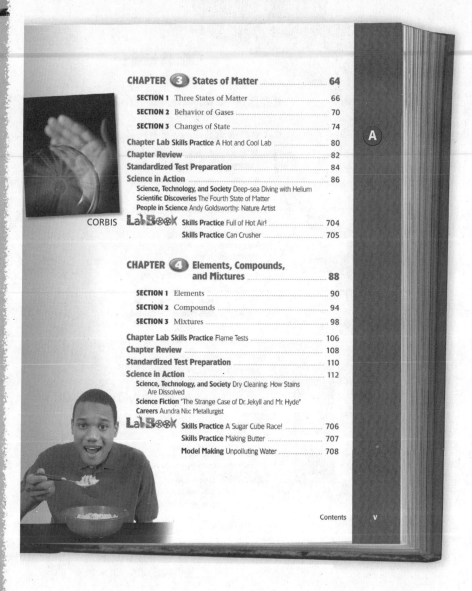

IN OTHER WORDS The table of contents continues on this page. Here, chapters three and four are laid out.

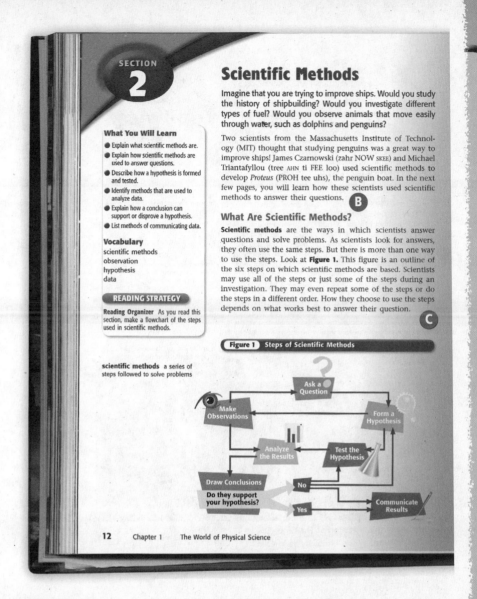

Scientific Methods

Imagine that you are trying to improve ships. Would you study the history of shipbuilding? Would you investigate different types of fuel? Would you observe animals that move easily through water, such as dolphins and penguins?

Two scientists from the Massachusetts Institute of Technology (MIT) thought that studying penguins was a great way to improve ships! James Czarnowski (zahr NOW SKEE) and Michael Triantafyllou (tree AHN ti FEE loo) used scientific methods to develop *Proteus* (PROH tee uhs), the penguin boat. In the next few pages, you will learn how these scientists used scientific methods to answer their questions. **B**

What Are Scientific Methods?

Scientific methods are the ways in which scientists answer questions and solve problems. As scientists look for answers, they often use the same steps. But there is more than one way to use the steps. Look at **Figure 1.** This figure is an outline of the six steps on which scientific methods are based. Scientists may use all of the steps or just some of the steps during an investigation. They may even repeat some of the steps or do the steps in a different order. How they choose to use the steps depends on what works best to answer their question. **C**

What You Will Learn

● Explain what scientific methods are.
● Explain how scientific methods are used to answer questions.
● Describe how a hypothesis is formed and tested.
● Identify methods that are used to analyze data.
● Explain how a conclusion can support or disprove a hypothesis.
● List methods of communicating data.

Vocabulary

scientific methods
observation
hypothesis
data

READING STRATEGY

Reading Organizer As you read this section, make a flowchart of the steps used in scientific methods.

scientific methods a series of steps followed to solve problems

Figure 1 Steps of Scientific Methods

Ask a Question

Make Observations

Form a Hypothesis

Analyze the Results

Test the Hypothesis

Draw Conclusions
Do they support your hypothesis?

No

Yes

Communicate Results

B **READ AND DISCUSS**

Comprehension

What is the author setting us up for? **Follow-up:** How do James Czarnowski and Michael Triantafyllou fit into that equation?

C **HERE'S HOW**

Vocabulary

By reading the first paragraph, I know that *scientific methods* are "series of steps followed to solve problems."

IN OTHER WORDS Two scientists named James Czarnowski and Michael Triantafyllou wanted to improve how ships and ship engines work. To do so, they used scientific methods, or series of specific steps that scientists follow when doing experiments. This is explained under the heading "What Are Scientific Methods?" Figure 1 is a diagram that outlines the steps of scientific methods. Notice that "Figure 1" is boldfaced in the text to draw attention to it.

A YOUR TURN

Vocabulary

The word *observation* means "the process of getting information by using the senses." Underline the sentence in this paragraph that gives a clue to the meaning of *observation*.

B YOUR TURN

Reading Focus

What do the **heading** and subheading on this page tell you?

_____

_____

_____

_____

C YOUR TURN

Reading Focus

What does Figure 3 tell you? Which textbook element is Figure 3?

_____

_____

_____

_____

Asking a Question

Asking a question helps focus the purpose of an investigation. Scientists often ask a question after making many observations. **Observation** is any use of the senses to gather information. Noting that the sky is blue or that a cotton ball feels soft is an observation. Measurements are observations that are made with tools, such as the ones shown in **Figure 2**. Keep in mind that observations can be made (and should be accurately recorded) at any point during an investigation.

✔ **Reading Check** What is the purpose of asking questions? *(See the Appendix for answers to Reading Checks.)*

A Real-World Question

Czarnowski and Triantafyllou, shown in **Figure 3**, are engineers, scientists who put scientific knowledge to practical use. Czarnowski was a graduate student at the Massachusetts Institute of Technology. He and Triantafyllou, his professor, worked together to observe boat propulsion (proh PUHL shuhn) systems. Then, they investigated how to make these systems work better. A propulsion system is what makes a boat move. Most boats have propellers to move them through the water.

Czarnowski and Triantafyllou studied the efficiency (e FISH uhn see) of boat propulsion systems. *Efficiency* compares energy output (the energy used to move the boat forward) with energy input (the energy supplied by the boat's engine). From their observations, Czarnowski and Triantafyllou learned that boat propellers are not very efficient.

A

Figure 2 *Stopwatches and rulers are among the many tools used to make observations.*

observation the process of obtaining information by using the senses

Figure 3 *James Czarnowski (left) and Michael Triantafyllou (right) made observations about how boats work in order to develop Proteus.*

B **C**

Republished with permission of The Globe Newspaper Company, Inc. Photo by Barry Chin.

Section 2   Scientific Methods   **13**

IN OTHER WORDS The first step in any experiment is asking a question—deciding what the purpose of the experiment is. For instance, Czarnowski and Triantafyllou hoped to research a typical ship's propulsion (how it moves) and efficiency (how well it uses energy). There are photos of both scientists, with captions that tell the reader who each man is.

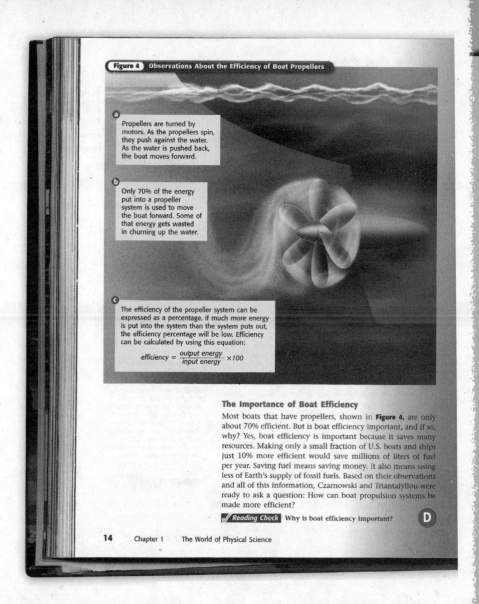

Figure 4 Observations About the Efficiency of Boat Propellers

a Propellers are turned by motors. As the propellers spin, they push against the water. As the water is pushed back, the boat moves forward.

b Only 70% of the energy put into a propeller system is used to move the boat forward. Some of that energy gets wasted in churning up the water.

c The efficiency of the propeller system can be expressed as a percentage. If much more energy is put into the system than the system puts out, the efficiency percentage will be low. Efficiency can be calculated by using this equation:

$$efficiency = \frac{output\ energy}{input\ energy} \times 100$$

The Importance of Boat Efficiency

Most boats that have propellers, shown in **Figure 4**, are only about 70% efficient. But is boat efficiency important, and if so, why? Yes, boat efficiency is important because it saves many resources. Making only a small fraction of U.S. boats and ships just 10% more efficient would save millions of liters of fuel per year. Saving fuel means saving money. It also means using less of Earth's supply of fossil fuels. Based on their observations and all of this information, Czarnowski and Triantafyllou were ready to ask a question: How can boat propulsion systems be made more efficient?

✔ **Reading Check** Why is boat efficiency important? **D**

14　Chapter 1　　The World of Physical Science

D READ AND DISCUSS

Comprehension

Now what have we learned about Czarnowski and Triantafyllou? **Follow-up:** Why is this such an important question?

IN OTHER WORDS After asking a question, the next step is to propose a hypothesis—an educated guess that attempts to answer the question. Czarnowski observed, or noticed, that penguins swim very quickly and seemingly easily. He hypothesized, or guessed, that ships would be more energy-efficient if their propulsion systems were more like a penguin's style of swimming. The diagram shows the penguin's style of swimming and makes it easy for readers to understand.

Vocabulary

Can you think of a synonym for *hypothesis*? Remember that a synonym is a word with nearly the same definition as another word.

Comprehension

How does this new information add to what we know about the scientific method? **Follow-up:** How do these steps fit in with the two men's hypothesis?

HERE'S HOW

Reading Focus

I think that the scientific method is a little like a textbook's **table of contents**. Both provide structure and a series of steps to follow.

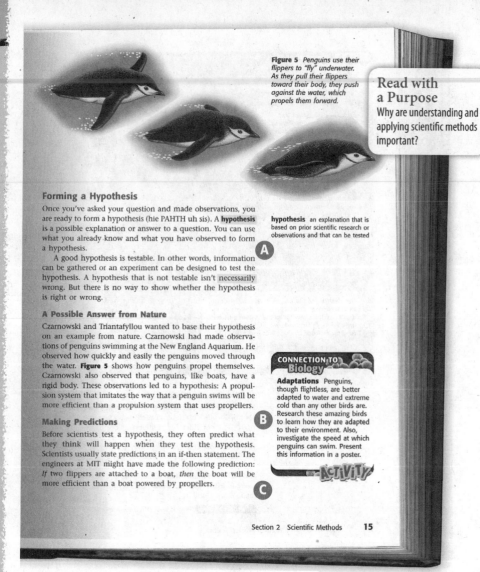

Figure 5 *Penguins use their flippers to "fly" underwater. As they pull their flippers toward their body, they push against the water, which propels them forward.*

Read with a Purpose
Why are understanding and applying scientific methods important?

Forming a Hypothesis

Once you've asked your question and made observations, you are ready to form a hypothesis (hie PAHTH uh sis). A **hypothesis** is a possible explanation or answer to a question. You can use what you already know and what you have observed to form a hypothesis.

A good hypothesis is testable. In other words, information can be gathered or an experiment can be designed to test the hypothesis. A hypothesis that is not testable isn't necessarily wrong. But there is no way to show whether the hypothesis is right or wrong.

hypothesis an explanation that is based on prior scientific research or observations and that can be tested

A Possible Answer from Nature

Czarnowski and Triantafyllou wanted to base their hypothesis on an example from nature. Czarnowski had made observations of penguins swimming at the New England Aquarium. He observed how quickly and easily the penguins moved through the water. **Figure 5** shows how penguins propel themselves. Czarnowski also observed that penguins, like boats, have a rigid body. These observations led to a hypothesis: A propulsion system that imitates the way that a penguin swims will be more efficient than a propulsion system that uses propellers.

Making Predictions

Before scientists test a hypothesis, they often predict what they think will happen when they test the hypothesis. Scientists usually state predictions in an if-then statement. The engineers at MIT might have made the following prediction: *If* two flippers are attached to a boat, *then* the boat will be more efficient than a boat powered by propellers.

CONNECTION TO Biology

Adaptations Penguins, though flightless, are better adapted to water and extreme cold than any other birds are. Research these amazing birds to learn how they are adapted to their environment. Also, investigate the speed at which penguins can swim. Present this information in a poster.

ACTIVITY

Section 2   Scientific Methods   **15**

Physical Science **115**

IN OTHER WORDS Before testing hypotheses, scientists make predictions about their expected results. Czarnowski and Triantafyllou tested their hypothesis by building a boat that moves with a propeller system. Figure 4 illustrates how the propellers push water backward to make the boat move forward.

Applying Your Skills

Physical Science

INFORMATIONAL TEXT FOCUS: STRUCTURE AND PURPOSE OF A TEXTBOOK

1. Which question can you answer by reading the **table of contents** for *Physical Science*?

   A. Where will I find information about organizing scientific data?

   B. What is the scientific definition of *efficiency*?

   C. How is the design of the *Proteus* different from the design of other boats?

2. Which of the following text features would explain the parts and significance of a **diagram**?

   A. heading

   B. table of contents

   C. caption

3. What details appear in **boldface** type in *Physical Science*?

   A. main ideas and chapter summaries

   B. names of scientists and inventors

   C. vocabulary words and references to figures

Word Box

scientific methods

observation

hypothesis

necessarily

VOCABULARY REVIEW

DIRECTIONS: Match each vocabulary word in the first column with the phrase it best describes in the second column. Write each letter on the correct blank.

_____ **1.** scientific methods

_____ **2.** observation

_____ **3.** hypothesis

_____ **4.** necessarily

a. using the senses to get information

b. an educated guess

c. steps followed while conducting scientific experiments

d. unavoidably

Collection 1

VOCABULARY REVIEW

DIRECTIONS: Match the vocabulary word with the letter of the correct definition.

_____ **1.** battered

_____ **2.** eerie

_____ **3.** desolate

_____ **4.** scientific method

_____ **5.** observation

_____ **6.** reveal

_____ **7.** structure

a. lonely; miserable

b. badly dented

c. strange and frightening

d. the process of getting information by using the senses

e. steps followed while conducting experiments

f. how something is organized

g. make known

DIRECTIONS: Write three complete sentences using each of the following words: *outcome*, *ruefully*, and *convinced*.

1. _____

_____

2. _____

_____

3. _____

_____

Language Review

Collection 1

LANGUAGE COACH: ORAL FLUENCY

Sometimes you cannot tell how to pronounce English words just by looking at the way they are spelled. For example, the last syllable of *palate* does not sound like *late*.

DIRECTIONS: Examine the words below. Circle the words that do not sound the way they are spelled.

colonel   kernel   seen   scene   campaign   think   whole   hole

WRITING ACTIVITY

A summary gives the most important points of a reading passage.

DIRECTIONS: Write a summary of one of the stories or articles you read in this collection, following these guidelines:

1. Begin with a sentence stating the main idea.

2. Identify the title of the piece early in the summary, and use quotation marks to set it off.

3. Include two or three additional sentences identifying the main points the writer uses to support the main idea.

_____

_____

_____

_____

_____

_____

_____

_____

_____

Characters

Literary and Academic Vocabulary for Collection 2

LITERARY VOCABULARY

characterization (KAR IHK TUHR Y ZAY SHUHN) *n.:* The way a writer creates and reveals character.

Good characterization in a story can make every character seem real.

motivation (MOH TIH VAY SHUHN) *n.:* why people act the way they do.

Kelly's motivation for playing basketball was that she wanted to be like her mother, who had played in college.

inferences (IHN FREHN SUHZ) *n.:* guesses based on what you see or know.

You can make inferences about a character's personality by looking at the way he or she acts.

ACADEMIC VOCABULARY

incident (IHN SUH DUHNT) *n.:* something that has happened; an event or occurrence.

There was one incident in the story in which the main character was pushed and then spilled milk in the cafeteria.

factor (FAK TUHR) *n.:* something that has an influence on something else.

One factor to think about when you read a story is why the main character acts the way he or she does.

interact (IHN TUHR AKT) *v.:* behave toward one another.

It is important to look at how characters interact with each other throughout a story.

response (RIH SPAHNS) *n.:* a reply or reaction.

When something bad happens to a character in a story, it is important to look at that character's response to the event.

A Retrieved Reformation

Based on the story by O. Henry

LITERARY FOCUS: MOTIVATION

What makes people do the things they do? In stories, as in life, a person's **motivation,** or reason for acting a certain way, is not always clear. To analyze motivation as you read, ask yourself, "What clues tell me why this person did that?" As you read this story, think about some questions you might want to ask the main character to understand his motivation.

READING FOCUS: MAKING CONNECTIONS

To **make connections** in a story, think about what you already know and how it relates to what you are reading. You might connect what you read to something that you have experienced, or have read before. For example, you might make a connection between this story and a movie you have seen. To help make connections as you read, fill in a chart like the one below.

The Character	Did this	It reminded of . . .	And helped me understand . . .
Warden	lectured Jimmy	a movie I saw where the warden spoke to a prisoner	the warden wants to help Jimmy lead an honest life
Jimmy			

VOCABULARY

retrieved (REH TREEVHD) *v.:* gotten or taken back.

reformation (REH FUHR MAY SHUHN) *n.:* the state of being changed.

warden (WAWR DUHN) *n.:* person in charge of a prison.

burglar (BUHR GLUHR) *n.:* someone who breaks into buildings to steal items.

INTO THE STORY

The author of this story is O. Henry, whose real name was William Sidney Porter. Before he became famous, Porter served three years in a Texas prison for stealing money from a bank where he worked. To help support his young child at home, he started writing short stories for magazines while he was in prison. We know he based the main character of this story, Jimmy Valentine, on a real thief he met in prison.

SKILLS FOCUS

Literary Skills
Understand motivation.

Reading Skills
Make connections from a text.

A RETRIEVED REFORMATION

Based on the story by O. Henry

© Ingram Publishing/Getty Images

A guard came to the prison shoeshop. Jimmy Valentine was carefully sewing shoes. The guard took him to the front office. There the warden handed Jimmy his papers. Jimmy had been in prison for nearly ten months. Now his friends had convinced the governor to free him.

"Now, Valentine," said the warden. "You're not a bad guy at heart. Stop breaking into safes, and live a lawful life." **A**

At a quarter past seven on the next morning Jimmy stood in the warden's outer office. On his way out, he got a railroad ticket
10 and a five-dollar bill. The warden gave him a cigar, and they shook hands. Mr. James Valentine walked out into the sunshine.

Jimmy went straight to a restaurant. There he used his freedom to enjoy a chicken and a bottle of wine. This was followed by a cigar that was better than the one the warden had given him. From there he took a train to a little town near the state line. **B**

Jimmy went to Mike Dolan's café, got his key, and went upstairs. Everything in his room was just as he had left it. There on the floor was still Ben Price's collar button. It had been torn from that famous detective's shirt when he had fought with
20 Jimmy to arrest him. **C**

A **READ AND DISCUSS**

Comprehension

What does the conversation between Jimmy and the warden tell us about Jimmy?

B **HERE'S HOW**

Literary Focus

I know that Jimmy just got out of prison. I can guess his **motivation** here as he goes to the restaurant. Jimmy probably has not had a good meal in a long time. Because of that, the first thing he does is go out to eat.

C **HERE'S HOW**

Language Coach

People like newscasters and actors need to speak **fluently**, or easily and smoothly. I can practice pronouncing words properly by reading out loud with a partner. When I finish reading this story, I can go back and read my favorite parts out loud.

Copyright © Information TK

A READ AND DISCUSS

Comprehension

How does this new information add to what we already know about Jimmy?

B READ AND DISCUSS

Comprehension

What is Jimmy up to now?

C HERE'S HOW

Vocabulary

I have never seen the word *dandy* before. By reading the surrounding sentences, I still cannot figure out what the word means. I think it is important, though, since Ben Price uses it to describe the main character, Jimmy. I decided to look it up in my dictionary. *Dandy* means "a man who pays attention to how he looks." This tells me that Jimmy dresses nicely, and cares about the way he looks.

D HERE'S HOW

Reading Focus

I can **make connections** to understand why Ben Price wants to make sure Jimmy does not get out of prison early. I know that Ben had arrested Jimmy before he went to prison. Ben thinks Jimmy has gone back to stealing.

Jimmy slid back a panel in the wall and dragged out a dusty suitcase. He opened it. Here was the finest set of burglar's tools in the East. It was made of special steel, with the latest designs in tools. It even had two or three things Jimmy had invented himself. The set had cost him over nine hundred dollars. **A**

In half an hour Jimmy went downstairs. He was now dressed in good clothes. He carried his suitcase in his hand.

A week after the release of Valentine, a safe was robbed in Richmond, Indiana. There was no clue about who the thief was.

30 Only eight hundred dollars was stolen. Two weeks later another safe in Logansport was opened. Fifteen hundred dollars in cash was stolen. That began to interest the police. Then an old bank safe in Jefferson City was robbed of five thousand dollars. The losses were now high enough to send the case to Ben Price. **B**

Ben Price said, "Dandy Jim Valentine's stealing again. **C** Yes, I guess I want Mr. Valentine. The next time he'll do his prison sentence without getting out early." **D**

Ben Price knew Jimmy's habits. He had learned them while working on an earlier case. Once people heard that Ben Price was

40 trying to catch the thief, other people with safes felt better.

One afternoon Jimmy Valentine and his suitcase got out of a train in Elmore, Arkansas. Jimmy, who looked like an athletic young man just home from college, went down the sidewalk toward the hotel.

A young lady crossed the street, passed him at the corner, and entered a door with a sign saying "The Elmore Bank." Jimmy Valentine looked into her eyes. He forgot he was a thief. She blushed slightly. Young men with Jimmy's style and good looks were rare in Elmore.

50 Jimmy grabbed a boy who was sitting on the steps of the bank. Jimmy began to ask him questions about the town. Soon the young lady came out. She paid no attention to the young man with the suitcase, but kept walking.

"Isn't that young lady Polly Simpson?" asked Jimmy, trying to trick the boy.

STYLE BOOK-FALL & WINTER
S. D. BROADHURST CO.
1919   1920
Mt. Olive, N. C.

Peters DIAMOND BRAND SHOES

Peters Shoe Co's Diamond Brand St. Louis Peters DIAMOND BRAND SHOES

"Naw," said the boy. "She's Annabel Adams. Her pa owns this bank."

Jimmy went to the Planters' Hotel. He signed in as Ralph D. Spencer, and rented a room. He leaned on the desk and told the clerk that he had come to Elmore to go into business. How was the shoe business, now, in the town? Was there an opening?

The clerk said that there wasn't a real shoe store in town. Other stores sold some shoes. Business in general was fairly good. He hoped Mr. Spencer would decide to locate in Elmore. He would find it a pleasant town to live in, and the people very friendly. **E**

Mr. Spencer thought he would stop over in the town a few days and think about it. He said he would carry up his suitcase himself. It was rather heavy.

Mr. Ralph Spencer was the new identity that replaced Jimmy Valentine's real self. All because of love, Mr. Spencer stayed in Elmore and opened a shoe store. He made many friends. And he met Miss Annabel Adams and became more and more in love with her. **F**

By the end of a year Mr. Ralph Spencer had won the respect of the community. His shoe store was doing well. He and

E READ AND DISCUSS

Comprehension

What is going on?
Follow-up: What do Jimmy's conversations with the people in Elmore tell us about him?

F HERE'S HOW

Literary Focus

I remember that words like "because" can be clues to a character's **motivation** in a story. Here, it helps me understand that love is the thing that motivates Jimmy to change his ways.

Annabel were engaged to be married in two weeks. Mr. Adams, the country banker, liked Spencer. Annabel loved him and was proud of him. He was as much at home in her family as if he were already part of it. A

One day Jimmy sat down in his room and wrote this letter. He mailed it to the safe address of one of his old friends in St. Louis:

Dear Old Pal:

I want you to be at Sullivan's place, in Little Rock, next Wednesday night. I want to give you my little kit of tools. I know you'll be glad to get them. You couldn't get one like it for a thousand dollars. I quit the old business a year ago. I've got a nice store. I'm making an honest living. I'm going to marry the finest girl on earth two weeks from now. I wouldn't touch a dollar of another man's money now for a million. After I get married I'm going to sell my store and go West, where there won't be so much danger of being found. I tell you, Billy, she's an angel. She believes in me. I wouldn't do another crime for the whole world. Be there, for I must see you. I'll bring along the tools with me.

Your old friend,
Jimmy B

On the Monday night after Jimmy wrote this letter, Ben Price arrived in Elmore in a horse-drawn buggy. He walked around town in his quiet way until he found out what he wanted to know. From across the street, he got a good look at Ralph D. Spencer.

"Going to marry the banker's daughter are you, Jimmy?" said Ben to himself, softly. C

The next morning Jimmy ate breakfast at the Adamses'. He was going to Little Rock that day to order his wedding suit and buy something nice for Annabel. That would be the first time he had left town since he came to Elmore. It had been more than a year now since those last thefts, and he thought he could safely go away.

After breakfast the family went downtown together, including Mr. Adams, Annabel, Jimmy, and Annabel's married sister with her two little girls. The girls were five and nine years old. First they came by the hotel where Jimmy still rented a room. He took his suitcase. Then they went on to the bank. Outside stood Jimmy's horse and buggy with a driver.

Everyone went inside the banking room. Jimmy set his suitcase down.

120 The Elmore Bank had just put in a new safe. Mr. Adams was very proud of it and wanted everyone to see it. It had a new kind of door. It fastened with three solid steel bolts thrown together with a single handle, and it had a time lock. Mr. Adams proudly explained how it worked to Mr. Spencer. The two children, May and Agatha, were delighted by the shining metal and funny clock and knobs.

While they were busy, Ben Price walked into the bank. He told the teller that he didn't want anything. He was just waiting for a man he knew.

Suddenly there was a scream. May, the older girl, had been
130 playing and shut Agatha inside the safe. She had then pushed the bolts and turned the knob of the combination.

The old banker ran to the handle. He tugged at it for a moment. "The door can't be opened," he groaned.

Agatha's mother screamed again, wildly.

"Hush!" said Mr. Adams, raising his shaking hand. "Agatha!" he called as loudly as he could. "Listen to me." They could just hear the child screaming in the dark safe.

"My darling!" cried the mother. "She will die of fright! Open the door! Oh, break it open! Can't you men do something?" **D**

140 "There isn't a man nearer than Little Rock who can open that door," said Mr. Adams. "Spencer, what shall we do? That child can't stand it long in there. There isn't enough air, and, besides, she'll go into fits from fright."

Agatha's mother was really scared now. She beat the door with her hands. Somebody wildly suggested dynamite. Annabel turned to Jimmy. **E**

D **READ AND DISCUSS**

Comprehension

What is going on? **Follow-up:** What mood has the author created for us?

E **YOUR TURN**

Reading Focus

When you **make connections** in a text, you should think about what you already know. Does this story remind you of another story you have read? Does it remind you of a movie or television show? Explain your answer.

_____

_____

_____

_____

_____

_____

_____

A READ AND DISCUSS

Comprehension

What does it mean that "Ralph D. Spencer went away, and Jimmy Valentine took his place"?

B YOUR TURN

Vocabulary

The word *reformation* means "the state of being changed." Based on what you have read, do you think that Jimmy has gone through a *reformation*? Why or why not?

_____

_____

_____

_____

C YOUR TURN

Literary Focus

Earlier in this story Ben was highly **motivated** to capture Jimmy. Why do you think he pretends not to know him in the bank?

_____

_____

_____

D READ AND DISCUSS

Comprehension

How do things turn out for Jimmy?

"Can't you do something, Ralph—*try*, won't you?"

He looked at her with an odd smile.

"Annabel," he said, "give me that rose you are wearing."

150 Hardly believing that she heard him right, she unpinned the rose from her dress, and placed it in his hand. Jimmy stuffed it into his vest pocket. He threw off his coat and pulled up his shirt sleeves. Ralph D. Spencer went away, and Jimmy Valentine took his place. **A**

"Get away from the door, all of you," he ordered.

He set his suitcase on the table, and opened it out flat. From that time on he seemed to be unaware of anyone else. He laid out the shining tools swiftly, whistling softly. The others watched him as if under a spell.

160 In a minute Jimmy's drill was cutting smoothly into the steel door. In ten minutes he threw back the bolts and opened the door. **B**

Agatha, frightened but safe, was gathered into her mother's arms.

Jimmy Valentine put on his coat, and walked toward the front door. As he went he thought he heard a faraway voice call "Ralph!" But he never paused.

At the door a big man stood somewhat in his way.

"Hello, Ben!" said Jimmy, still with his strange smile. "Found 170 me at last, have you? Well, let's go. I don't know that it makes much difference, now."

And then Ben Price acted rather strangely.

"Guess you're mistaken, Mr. Spencer," he said. "Don't believe I recognize you. Your buggy's waiting for you, ain't it?" **C**

And Ben Price turned and strolled down the street. **D**

Comprehension Wrap-Up

1. Why does Ben Price let Jimmy walk away?

2. What factors lead to Jimmy changing his criminal ways and becoming a better person?

Applying Your Skills

A Retrieved Reformation

LITERARY FOCUS: MOTIVATION

DIRECTIONS: Answer the following questions.

1. What is Jimmy's **motivation** at the beginning of the story?

_____

_____

2. What is Jimmy's motivation after he gets out of jail?

_____

_____

3. What is Jimmy's motivation when he gets to Elmore?

_____

_____

READING FOCUS: MAKING CONNECTIONS

DIRECTIONS: Review what you know about Ben and Jimmy, then answer the question below.

1. What is the connection between the two men? _____

_____

_____

_____

_____

VOCABULARY REVIEW

DIRECTIONS: Now that you know the meanings of the words *retrieved* and *reformation*, re-write the title of this story in your own words.

A Retrieved Reformation: _____

_____

The Wise Old Woman *and* Mrs. Flowers

LITERARY FOCUS: CHARACTERS AND GENRES

No matter what kind of story we read, we meet new **characters**. We learn who the characters are, what actions they take, and what their **motivations**, or reasons, are for doing things. Authors writing in different **genres**, or types of literature, may use different styles to create similar characters. For example, "The Wise Old Woman" is the fictional genre of folk tale. *Mrs. Flowers* is the nonfiction genre called autobiography.

Folk tales are told to teach a lesson. The characters may not seem as real as characters in other genres. They represent, or stand for, traits like kindness or cruelty, to help readers learn the lesson. An autobiography is a story that a real person tells about his or her life. The characters are real people.

READING FOCUS: COMPARING CHARACTERS

As you read, **compare**, or see what is the same, in the two stories. You can compare the main characters. You can also compare how the characters act in the selections.

VOCABULARY

Practice saying these words out loud. Then, with a partner, use these words in complete sentences.

impressed (IHM PREHST) *v.:* gained the respect of someone.

recite (RIH SYT) *v.:* say from memory.

INTO THE FOLK TALE AND AUTOBIOGRAPHY

"The Wise Old Woman" is a Japanese folk tale. The author, Yoshiko Uchida, grew up as a Japanese American in California. As an adult, she went to Japan to learn about her family's history and culture. This story is one of many stories she collected on that trip.

"Mrs. Flowers" is an excerpt from Maya Angelou's autobiography. When she was young, Angelou and her brother went to live with their grandmother, who owned a general store. This piece is about that experience.

SKILLS FOCUS

Literary Skills
Understand characters and genres.

Reading Skills
Compare and contrast characters.

THE WISE OLD WOMAN

Based on the folk tale retold by Yoshiko Uchida

Many long years ago, a cruel young lord ruled over a small village in the hills of Japan.

"I have no use for old people in my village," he said. "They are not useful. They cannot work. I order that anyone over age 71 must be sent away from the village and left in the mountains to die."

"What a terrible law! What a cruel and unfair lord we have," the people of the village whispered. But the lord punished anyone who disobeyed him. So villagers who turned 71 were tearfully

10   carried into the mountains, never to return. **A**

As time passed, there were fewer old people in the village. Soon none were left at all. Then the young lord was happy.

"What a fine village of young, healthy, and hard-working people I have," he bragged. "Soon it will be the finest village in all of Japan."

Now, there lived in this village a kind young farmer and his mother. The two of them lived happily together. However, as the years went by, the mother grew older. Before long she turned 71. **B**

20   "If only I could somehow trick the cruel lord," the farmer thought. But everyone knew that his mother was 71. **C**

"The Wise Old Woman" from *The Sea of Gold and Other Tales from Japan*, adapted by Yoshiko Uchida. Copyright © 1965 by Yoshiko Uchida. Reproduced by permission of **Bancroft Library, University of California, Berkeley.**

A **READ AND DISCUSS**

Comprehension

What has the author told us so far? **Follow-up**: What do the villagers think of this new law?

B **HERE'S HOW**

Literary Focus

In the **genre** of folk tales, characters represent different things. The young son is said to be kind. I think he and his mother represent kindness. As I read, I will try to figure out what other characters represent.

C **HERE'S HOW**

Reading Focus

The author uses certain words to show differences between the ruler and the son. I have circled adjectives on this page that describe the characters, so that I can easily **compare** them.

A READ AND DISCUSS

Comprehension

What is going on with this mother and son?

B HERE'S HOW

Literary Focus

I see that the son in this folk tale seems very upset about the trip up the mountain. His mother does not seem very worried. I think the son is **motivated** by his kindness.

C READ AND DISCUSS

Comprehension

What is the son's plan to save his mother?

D READ AND DISCUSS

Comprehension

What is happening in the village now?

The farmer knew that if he did not take his mother away to the mountains soon, the lord would send his soldiers. The soldiers would throw them both into a dark jail to die a terrible death.

Then one day the mother said, "Well, my son, the time has come for you to take me to the mountains. We must hurry before the lord sends his soldiers for you." She did not seem worried. **A**

"Forgive me, dear mother," the farmer said sadly. The next morning he lifted his mother to his shoulders. They set off on the steep path toward the mountains. Up and up he climbed. The son walked slowly. He did not want to leave his old mother in the mountains. Soon, he heard his mother breaking off small twigs from the trees that they passed.

"Mother, what are you doing?" he asked.

"Do not worry," she answered gently. "I am just marking the way so you will not get lost returning to the village."

The son stopped. "Even now you are thinking of me?" he asked.

The mother nodded. "Of course, my son," she replied. "You will always be in my thoughts."

At that, the young farmer said, "Mother, I cannot leave you in the mountains to die all alone. We are going home. No matter what the lord does to punish me, I will never leave you again." **B**

So they waited until the sun had set. Then, in the dark, they returned quietly to their little house. The farmer dug a deep hole in the floor of his kitchen. He made a small room where he could hide his mother. From that day, she spent all her time in the secret room. The farmer carried meals to her there. The rest of the time, he worked in the fields and acted as though he lived alone. In this way, for almost two years he kept his mother safely hidden. No one in the village knew that she was there. **C**

Then one day there was a loud noise among the villagers. Lord Higa of the town beyond the hills threatened to take over their village and make it his own.

"Only one thing can save you," Lord Higa announced. "Bring me a box containing one thousand ropes made of ashes and I will spare your village." **D**

© Victoria & Albert Museum, London, UK/Bridgeman Art Library

The cruel young lord quickly gathered together all the wise men of his village. He said, "Surely you can tell me how to meet Lord Higa's demands so our village can be saved."

But the wise men shook their heads. "It is impossible to make even one rope from ashes," they answered. "How can we ever make one thousand?"

"Fools!" the lord cried angrily. "What good is your wisdom if you cannot help me now?"

He offered a great reward of gold to any villager who could help him save their village.

But all the people whispered, "It is an impossible thing. Ashes crumble at the touch of the finger. How could anyone ever make a rope from them?" They shook their heads and sighed, "We will be defeated by another cruel lord." **E** **F**

The young farmer wondered what would happen to his mother if a new lord even worse than their own came to rule over them.

His mother saw the sad look on his face. She asked, "Why are you so worried?"

So the farmer told her of the demand made by Lord Higa. His mother did not seem bothered at all. Instead she laughed softly and said, "That is not such an impossible task. All one has to do is soak ordinary rope in salt water and dry it well. When it is

E **READ AND DISCUSS**

Comprehension
What do the villagers think of the proposal by Lord Higa?

F **HERE'S HOW**

Language Coach
I know that the *g* in *sigh* is silent. I will practice pronouncing this word until I can say it **fluently**, or smoothly.

YOUR TURN

Reading Focus

The ruler **compares** the young farmer to the wise men of the village. But to whom is he *really* comparing the wise men, to himself or the young farmer's mother?

B READ AND DISCUSS

Comprehension

How have things changed since Lord Higa first made his demand?

C READ AND DISCUSS

Comprehension

Now what is going on with the evil lord?

D READ AND DISCUSS

Comprehension

How does this new situation connect to Lord Higa's first demand?

E HERE'S HOW

Vocabulary

I know that *impressed* means "gained the respect of someone." When it says, "he was *impressed*," that means that the young man earned the ruler's respect.

burned, it will hold its shape and there is your rope made of ashes! Tell the villagers to hurry and find one thousand pieces of rope."

"Mother, you are wonderfully wise," said the farmer. He rushed to tell the young lord what he must do.

"You are wiser than all the wise men of the village," the lord said when he heard the farmer's solution. **A** He gave the farmer many pieces of gold. The thousand ropes were quickly made and the village was saved. **B**

In a few days, however, there was another great noise in the village. A few days later Lord Higa had sent another threat. "This time you will fail and then I will defeat your village," he said. "Bring me a drum that sounds without being beaten."

"That is not possible," said the people of the village. "How can anyone make a drum sound without beating it?"

This time the wise men held their heads in their hands and cried, "It is hopeless. Lord Higa will defeat us all." **C**

The young farmer hurried home. "Mother, Mother, we must solve another problem or Lord Higa will take over our village!" He quickly told his mother about the drum.

His mother, however, smiled and answered, "This is easy. Make a drum with sides of paper and put a bumblebee inside. As it tries to escape, it will buzz and beat itself against the paper and you will have a drum that sounds without being beaten."

The young farmer was amazed at his mother's wisdom. "You are much wiser than any of the wise men," he said. Then he hurried to tell the young lord how to meet Lord Higa's new order. **D**

When the lord heard the answer, he was very impressed. **E** "Surely a young man like you cannot be wiser than all my wise men," he said. "Tell me who has helped you solve all these difficult problems?"

The young farmer could not lie. "My lord," he began slowly, "for the past two years I have broken the law of the land. I have kept my elderly mother hidden beneath the floor of my house. It is she who solved your problems and saved the village."

90

100

110

He trembled as he spoke, for he feared the lord's anger.
Surely now the soldiers would throw him into the dark dungeon.
But when he looked at the lord, he saw that the young ruler was
not angry at all. At last the lord saw how much wisdom and

120 knowledge old people possess.

"I have been very wrong," he said finally. "I must ask the
forgiveness of your mother and of all my people. Never again will
I order that the old people of our village be sent to the mountains
to die. Rather, they will be treated with respect and honor. They
will share the wisdom of their years." **F**

And so it was. From that day, the villagers were no longer
forced to leave their parents in the mountains. The village
became once more a happy, cheerful place in which to live. The
terrible Lord Higa stopped sending his impossible demands

130 and no longer threatened to defeat them. He too was impressed.
"Even in such a small village there is much wisdom," he declared,
"and its people should be allowed to live in peace."

And that is exactly what the farmer and his mother and all
the people of the village did. **G**

Comprehension Wrap-Up

1. What characteristics do older people have that make them
   so important to a community?

F YOUR TURN

Literary Focus
Considering what you know
about the folk tale **genre**,
what lesson do you think this
story is trying to teach us?

_____

_____

_____

_____

_____

_____

G READ AND DISCUSS

Comprehension
How do things turn out for
the farmer and his mother?
Follow-up: How do things
turn out for the ruler and
the villagers?

MRS. FLOWERS

from I Know Why the Caged Bird Sings
Based on the autobiography by Maya Angelou

For almost a year, I hung around the house, the Store, the school, and the church, sad and unhappy. I felt like an old biscuit, one that nobody wanted. Then I met the lady who saved me from my deep sadness. **A**

Mrs. Bertha Flowers was a gentlewoman.[1] She showed me the best that any person can be. **B**

I'll never forget that special summer afternoon when she stopped at the Store to buy groceries. Another Negro woman her age would have carried her own groceries home. But Momma said,
10 "Sister Flowers, I'll send Bailey[2] up to your house with these things."

Mrs. Flowers smiled her slow, beautiful smile that made me feel warm and loved. "Thank you, Mrs. Henderson," she said. "I'd prefer Marguerite, though." My name was beautiful when she said it. "I've been meaning to talk to her." Momma and Mrs. Flowers gave each other a grown-up look.

Mrs. Flowers walked in front along the rocky path. The thin fabric of her flowered dress floated gently in the breeze. She said, without turning her head, "I hear you're doing very good school-work, Marguerite. But it's all written work. The teachers say that
20 you do not talk." The path became wider here. We could walk together. I stayed back. **C**

"Come and walk along with me, Marguerite." I had to give in and walk beside her. She said my name so nicely.

"Now no one is going to make you talk," said Mrs. Flowers. "But keep in mind, it is only people who talk to one another. It is

---

1. **gentlewoman:** a woman who is polite, considerate, and dignified.
2. Bailey is the author's younger brother.

Excerpt (retitled "Mrs. Flowers") adapted from *I Know Why the Caged Bird Sings* by Maya Angelou. Copyright © 1969 and renewed © 1997 by Maya Angelou. Retold by Holt, Rinehart and Winston. Reproduced by permission of **Random House, Inc.**

A · YOUR TURN

Language Coach

Being aware of and correctly pronouncing silent letters is important for building **oral fluency**. In English, words like *build* and *guitar* have a silent *u* sound. Which word has a silent *u* in this paragraph?

B · HERE'S HOW

Literary Focus

I know the **genre** of this nonfiction selection is autobiography. This tells me that the characters are based on real people. I will keep reading to see what else I can learn about Mrs. Flowers.

C · HERE'S HOW

Reading Focus

I will begin by **comparing** Mrs. Flowers and Marguerite. So far I know that they live in the same area and they both seem friendly.

---

the one thing that makes us different from animals." That was a new idea to me. I would need time to think about it. **D**

"Your grandmother says you read a lot. That's good, but not good enough. Words need a person's voice to fill them with meaning."

I memorized the part about a person's voice filling words with meaning. It seemed so true.

Mrs. Flowers said she was going to give me some books. I was to take good care of them. I was to read them aloud. I was to read each sentence in as many different ways as possible.

The sweet smell of vanilla met us as she opened the door of her house.

"I made tea cookies this morning. I planned to invite you for cookies and lemonade. I wanted to talk with you."

She took the grocery bags from me and disappeared through the kitchen door. I looked around the room. Photographs looked down from the walls. The white, freshly ironed curtains moved with the wind. I wanted to gather up the whole room and take it to Bailey. He would help me figure it out.

"Have a seat, Marguerite. Over there by the table." She carried a plate covered with a tea towel. She said she had not baked cookies for a long time. I was sure her cookies would be perfect, just as she was perfect.

The cookies were flat and round. They were a light brown on the edges, and butter-yellow in the center. With the cold lemonade they were all I ever wanted to eat. I remembered my manners and took little bites off the edges. She said she had made them just for me, and she had some left in the kitchen. I could take these home to my brother. So I pushed one whole cookie in my mouth. I wanted to keep it there. Not swallow it. It was a dream come true. **E** **F**

As I ate, Mrs. Flowers began the first of "my lessons in living." She said that I must not put up with ignorance. I must be understanding of illiteracy.[3] I was to understand that people who were not able to go to school sometimes knew more than college

---

3. **illiteracy** (IH LIH TUHR UH SEE): lack of ability to read; lack of learning or education.

D READ AND DISCUSS

Comprehension
What is Mrs. Flowers up to?

E READ AND DISCUSS

Comprehension
What is the author saying with all of this?

F YOUR TURN

Reading Focus
Compare Marguerite's situation now with lines 1–4.

_____

_____

_____

_____

60 professors. She wanted me to listen carefully when all people spoke. I was to listen for plain sense[4] and wise words. **A**

I finished the cookies. She brought a thick, small book from the bookcase. I had already read *A Tale of Two Cities*. She opened the first page and began to read.

"It was the best of times, it was the worst of times. . . ." Her voice seemed to sing the words. I wanted to look at those pages. Were the words the same that I had read? Or were they changed into music?

"How do you like that?"

70 It came to me that she expected me to answer her question. The sweet vanilla taste was still on my tongue. Her reading was a wonder in my ears. I had to speak.

I said, "Yes, ma'am." That was all I could say.

"Take this book of poems and memorize one for me. Next time you pay me a visit, I want you to recite."[5]

On that first day, I ran down the hill and I didn't stop running until I reached the Store.

I was liked. What a difference it made. I was respected. Not as Mrs. Henderson's grandchild or Bailey's sister but for just

80 being me. Marguerite Johnson. **B**

I did not ask why Mrs. Flowers began to pay attention to me. It did not occur to me that Momma might have asked her to talk to me. All I cared about was that Mrs. Flowers made tea cookies for me. She read to me from her favorite book. It was enough. It proved that she liked me. **C** **D**

---

4. **sense** (SEHNS): meaning.
5. **recite** (RIH SYT): say from memory.

Applying Your Skills

The Wise Old Woman *and* Mrs. Flowers

COMPREHENSION WRAP-UP

1. Talk about the relationship between Mrs. Flowers and Marguerite in "Mrs. Flowers."

LITERARY FOCUS: CHARACTERS AND GENRES

1. What are some differences between the literary **genres** of the folk tale and the autobiography?

   _____

   _____

   _____

2. Did you notice any similarities between the genres? Write your answer below.

   _____

   _____

READING FOCUS: COMPARING CHARACTERS

DIRECTIONS: Look at the chart that you kept as you read "The Wise Old Woman" and "Mrs. Flowers." Even though the stories are examples of two different genres of literature, you can still make **comparisons** between the **characters**. Which characters from the different stories acted in similar ways? Which characters were the most alike?

_____

_____

_____

VOCABULARY REVIEW

DIRECTIONS: Fill in the blanks with the correct word from the Word Box.

Word Box
impressed
recite

1. Martin tried very hard, and he _____ the girl that he liked.

2. Chris had to get up in front of the whole class and _____ lines of poetry from his book.

Preamble to the Constitution, Bill of Rights, *and* Don't Know Much About Liberty

INFORMATIONAL TEXT FOCUS: COMPARING TEXTS: TREATMENT, SCOPE, AND ORGANIZATION

Two or more works that talk about the same topic can be very different. Pay attention to the following to find similarities and differences between different pieces of informational writing:

- **Treatment:** The treatment of a topic is the way it is presented. One treatment, for example, might be serious. The author might try not to show any personal feelings about the topic, and just report the facts. This would be an **objective** discussion of key ideas. Another treatment might be funny and playful. The author may include many statements that show his or her own ideas about a subject. This would be a **subjective** discussion.

- **Scope:** When the treatment covers many different parts of a topic, we say it has a **broad scope**. When the treatment only covers a few parts, we say it has a **limited scope**.

- **Organization:** The order in which an author presents ideas is different between texts. Two of the most common forms of organization are to list events in the order they happen, or to list them in the order of importance.

VOCABULARY

Working with a partner, use the following words in sentences.

preamble (PREE AM BUHL) *n.:* an introductory statement.

Constitution (KAHN STUH TOO SHUN) *n.:* written document that guides a nation.

liberty (LIH BUHR TEE) *n.:* freedom.

amendment (UH MEHND MEHNT) *n.:* official change to a law.

due process (DOO PRAW SES) *n.:* set of rules followed in court cases.

majority (MUH JAWR UH TEE) *n.:* larger part of something.

minority (MUH NAWR UH TEE) *n.:* smaller part of something.

SKILLS FOCUS

Informational Text Skills
Find similarities and differences between texts in the treatment, scope, or organization of ideas.

PREAMBLE TO THE CONSTITUTION OF THE UNITED STATES OF AMERICA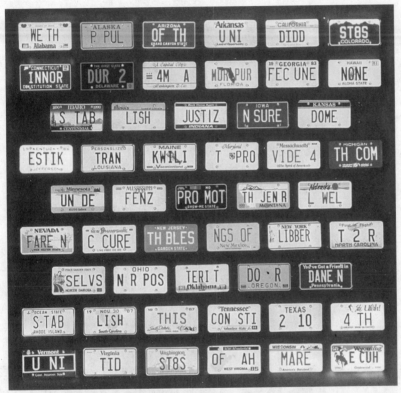

Based on the Constitution of the United States of America

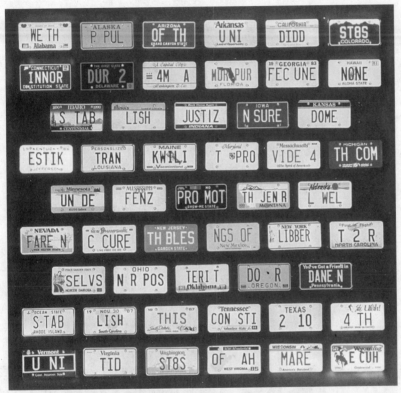

Smithsonian American Art Museum, Washington, DC, U.S.A./Art Resource, NY

We the People of the United States, in order to form a more united country, set up justice, make sure we have peace, defend against danger, support the well-being of the people, and keep the blessing of liberty for ourselves and our children, do make this Constitution for the United States of America legal. **B**

Comprehension Wrap-Up

1. Talk about the Preamble. How does it help us understand the main sections of the Constitution? Why do you think the writers of the Constitution included a Preamble?

A **HERE'S HOW**

Vocabulary

I am not sure what the word *preamble* means in the title of this piece. It is in the title, so it must be important. I checked my dictionary, and *preamble* means "an introductory statement." I remember that the prefix *pre-* means "before." That can help me remember that the *Preamble* to the U.S. Constitution is the statement that comes before the main part of the Constitution.

B **READ AND DISCUSS**

Comprehension

What does the Preamble tell us?

THE BILL OF RIGHTS: AMENDMENTS 1–10 OF THE CONSTITUTION

Based on the Constitution of the United States of America

A READ AND DISCUSS

Comprehension

What has the author given us here? **Follow-up:** Why do you think the writers of the Constitution included a way to change it?

At the time they accepted the Constitution, the leaders of the states said that they wished to prevent misunderstandings and the misuse of its powers. Therefore, they added amendments to increase public confidence in the government and help it function smoothly.

The Senate and House of Representatives of the United States of America have agreed to suggest these amendments to the states. When three quarters of the states approve them, they will become part of the Constitution. **A**

Amendment I

10   Congress may not make laws establishing an official religion for the country, or keep people from following their religion freely. It may not limit freedom of speech, or of the press. It may not keep people from gathering together in peace or asking the government to fix problems. **B**

Amendment II

People need to be able to defend their safety and freedom. Their right to keep and use weapons will not be taken away.

Amendment III

Citizens cannot be forced to let soldiers stay in their homes, except by special laws during a war.

Amendment IV

The government cannot search or take anything from people's
20   bodies, houses, papers, and other property without a good reason. Such searches can take place only with probable cause, or a good reason, supported by evidence. Any people or things that will be searched or taken must be clearly described. **C**

Amendment V

Except in the army and during a war, people can be put on trial for a crime only with an indictment, or official accusation, from a grand jury. People cannot be tried for the same crime twice. No one will be forced to be a witness against himself in a criminal case. No one's life, liberty, or property can be taken away without a trial under the due process of law. **D** Private property can be
30   taken for public use only if the owner is paid a fair price.

B **HERE'S HOW**

Reading Focus

The First Amendment deals with five major freedoms. I would say it has a **broad scope**.

C **HERE'S HOW**

Reading Focus

I can see that in these first four amendments, the writers of the Constitution are focusing on how the government can treat people. This **organization** suggests to me that they wanted to make sure the government treated people fairly.

D **HERE'S HOW**

Vocabulary

The phrase *due process* sounds to me like "do process." I read that *due process* involves following certain rules in court cases. I can easily remember what this means if I think of it as "the way courts do process cases."

Reading Focus

The first four amendments focused on how the government treats people. You can contrast them with the next four. What do amendments V–VIII talk about and how are they **organized**?

_____

_____

_____

_____

Reading Focus

The last two amendments seem to be different from the others. I think these last two have a **broader scope**. They just say that citizens have other rights that the Constitution does not mention.

Reading Focus

The Bill of Rights deals with the rights of citizens. What are some words you would use to describe the **treatment** of rights in this document?

_____

_____

Amendment VI

People accused of crimes have the right to a speedy and public trial, by a fair jury. The trial should take place in the state and legal area where the crime was committed. The accused person has the right to know the charges and the reasons for them. People accused of crimes have the right to find and question witnesses, and to get help from a lawyer.

Amendment VII

Cases involving money should be decided by a jury. A case that has been decided by a jury can be brought to court again only in ways that follow the law.

Amendment VIII

40 Courts cannot order unfairly large sums of money to keep people in jail before a trial or punish them for crimes. They also cannot order cruel or unusual punishments for crimes. **A**

Amendment IX

The listing of certain rights in the Constitution does not mean that people do not have other rights. The people may have other rights not listed in this Constitution.

Amendment X **B**

State governments, and citizens, keep any powers that are not clearly given to the United States government by this Constitution. **C**

Comprehension Wrap-Up

1. Talk about the Bill of Rights and the many ways we see and hear it in action every day.

Don't Know Much About
★★★ LIBERTY ★★★

Americans Are Clueless When It Comes to the First Amendment

from Weekly Reader Senior

Illustrations by Chris Murphy.

When it comes to the First Amendment, most Americans don't know their rights from their wrongs! **A**

Only one in 1,000 Americans can list all five freedoms protected by the First Amendment to the U.S. Constitution, according to a recent survey. (Just in case you're one of those 999 people who can't, the rights are freedom of religion, freedom of speech, freedom of the press, freedom of assembly, and freedom to petition.) **B**

One in seven people could name one of the five First Amendment freedoms, and one in five people could name two, according to the McCormick Tribune Freedom Museum in Chicago, which sponsored the survey.

Although Americans failed the First Amendment pop quiz, they passed the Bart Simpson section of the survey with flying colors. More than half of the respondents could name at least two of the main characters of *The Simpsons*. Twenty-two percent could name all five. **C**

A **HERE'S HOW**

Language Coach

An **antonym** is a word that has the opposite meaning of another word. There are two words that are antonyms in this sentence. They are *rights* and *wrongs*.

B **HERE'S HOW**

Vocabulary

I am not sure what *freedom to petition* is. When I look up *petition* in the dictionary, I see that it means "a formal request." That must mean that freedom of petition is my right to make requests.

C **READ AND DISCUSS**

Comprehension

What does it tell us about Americans that they know more about a TV show than about the First Amendment?

IN OTHER WORDS The article begins by sharing the results of a study performed by a museum in Chicago. The study found that most Americans cannot name the five freedoms that make up of the First Amendment of the Constitution. (These five freedoms are the freedom of religion, freedom of speech, freedom of press, freedom of assembly, and freedom to petition.) The study also found that most Americans can, however, name at least two of the characters from the television show *The Simpsons*.

From "Don't Know Much About Liberty" by Chris Murphy from *Weekly Reader Senior Edition*, April 21, 2006. Copyright © 2006 by **Weekly Reader Senior**; Illustrations copyright © 2006 by **Chris Murphy**. All rights reserved. Reproduced by permission of the publisher and illustrator.

Reading Focus

Re-read how the study asked Americans questions about the First Amendment and *The Simpsons*. What two words could you use to describe the **treatment** of the topic in this article?

_____

_____

Reading Focus

In the second paragraph of this article, the author listed the rights of the First Amendment. Here the author explains *why* these rights were included in the amendment. Does this **organization** help you understand the information better than just reading the freedoms? Why?

_____

_____

Those findings made Gene Policinski, executive director of the First Amendment Center, want to eat his shorts (as Bart Simpson would say). "These are such basic freedoms, and they're in our lives every day," he told *Senior Edition*. "All we have to do is look around." **A**

No matter how old you are or what state you live in, you exercise First Amendment freedoms every day, Policinski says. When you turn on the television, you can choose the show you want to watch. If you disagree with a law, you can write a letter to your state representative. If you don't like something the government is doing, you can say so without getting in trouble. **B**

That's exactly what the nation's founders hoped to achieve when they ratified, or approved, the Bill of Rights in 1791. The Bill of Rights is the first 10 amendments to the Constitution. The founders wanted Americans to have control over their daily lives and a say in how the government is run.

Here's why the founders included each freedom:

1 Freedom of religion

The Colonists came to America in search of religious freedom. They wanted to worship without fear of punishment. The nation's founders included this clause to make sure Congress could neither establish a national religion nor stop people from practicing their chosen religion.

2 Freedom of speech

The Colonists' rocky relationship with Great Britain made them determined to prevent their new government from abusing its power. This clause ensures that the government can't stop people from saying almost anything they want to say—even if it's unpopular or critical of the president.

IN OTHER WORDS The article continues by explaining why it is very important that more Americans get to know the five freedoms. The nation's founders added the Bill of Rights to the Constitution in 1791 because they wanted all Americans to have control over their own lives. You use all five freedoms on a regular basis. For example, freedom of religion allows you to follow any religion you want, without being afraid of the government. Freedom of speech allows you to say anything you want without fear that the government will make you stop.

3 Freedom of the press

The nation's founders feared that if the government controlled the nation's newspapers, it could violate the Constitution without anyone finding out. This clause allows U.S. newspapers, magazines, and other media to report on whatever they want, as long as they don't print false information or invade people's privacy.

4 Freedom of assembly

Majority may rule in the United States, but the nation's founders wanted to make sure minority voices were still heard. This clause gives Americans the right to protest or parade publicly in support of any cause—no matter how controversial—as long as they do it peacefully. **C**

5 Freedom to petition the government for a redress of grievances

The Colonists started the American Revolution (1775–1783) because they had little voice in Great Britain's government. This clause requires that the government listen to what citizens have to say, whether it be through letter writing or lawsuits. **D**

Read with a Purpose What basic rights are protected by the Constitution and the Bill of Rights?

Comprehension Wrap-Up

1. In what ways do we see the freedoms in action every day?

IN OTHER WORDS Freedom of the press is another right included in the First Amendment. Newspapers and other news organizations can report pretty much anything they want, as long as it is true and respectful of people's privacy. Freedom of assembly means that people can gather together to show how they feel about something. The government will never interfere unless these people become violent. The final freedom, the freedom to petition, means that the government needs to listen to everything its citizens want to tell it.

C   YOUR TURN

Vocabulary

Re-read the first sentence in this paragraph. If *majority* means the "larger part of something," what do you think *minority* means? (Hint: Words beginning with *min-* often have to do with "least" or "small," such as *minimum* and *minor*.)

_____

_____

D   READ AND DISCUSS

Comprehension

What does the information about why each amendment was created tell us about life before they were written?

Preamble to the Constitution, Bill of Rights, *and* Don't Know Much About Liberty

USE A COMPARE AND CONTRAST CHART

DIRECTIONS: Complete the following chart to compare and contrast the **treatment**, **scope**, and **organization** of the three texts.

	Preamble to the Constitution	Bill of Rights	Don't Know Much About Liberty
Treatment			
Scope			
Organization			

Applying Your Skills

Preamble, Bill of Rights, and Don't Know Much About Liberty

COMPREHENSION WRAP-UP

1. In what ways do we see the five freedoms in action every day?

INFORMATIONAL TEXT FOCUS: COMPARING TEXTS

DIRECTIONS: Choose the letter that *best* answers each question.

1. Which of the following best describes the **treatment** of the topics in the Bill of Rights?

   A. serious

   B. slanted

   C. funny

   D. false

2. Which text has the **broadest scope**?

   A. Preamble

   B. Bill of Rights

   C. "Don't Know Much About Liberty"

   D. scope is the same for all three

3. Which of the following best describes the **organization** of the last paragraph of "Don't Know Much About Liberty?"

   A. time order

   B. point-by-point order

   C. order of importance

   D. all of the above

4. Which text adds some humor to its mostly serious **treatment**?

   A. Preamble

   B. Bill of Rights

   C. "Don't Know Much About Liberty"

   D. all of the above

VOCABULARY REVIEW

DIRECTIONS: Complete the paragraph below by filling in the blanks with the correct words from the Word Box. Not all of the words will be used.

Word Box

preamble

Constitution

liberty

amendment

due process

majority

minority

The (1) _____ to the Constitution explains why the document was written. It shares the authors' feelings about the topic of (3) _____ and Britain's government. The document also makes sure that every American can be heard by their government. This includes the (4) _____, the larger part of the population, and the (5) _____, the smaller part of the population.

Skills Review

Collection 2

VOCABULARY REVIEW

DIRECTIONS: Write words from the Word Box in the blanks to complete the passage. Not all words will be used.

Word Box

- amendment
- burglar
- constitution
- dandy
- due process
- factor
- impress
- liberty
- interact
- preamble
- recite
- reformation
- response
- retrieve
- warden

In *The Retrieved Reformation*, Jimmy was in prison for being a (1) _____. The (2) _____ of the prison advised him to give up his criminal life. The first thing Jimmy did with his new (3) _____ was to get something good to eat. The rights of criminals like him are protected by the Bill of Rights, the first ten (4) _____ of the (5) _____.

When you encounter unfamiliar words, look at **context clues**—the words surrounding the unfamiliar word. Context clues might help you figure out the meanings of the unfamiliar words.

DIRECTIONS: Practice identifying context clues. Read each of the following sentences. Then, underline the context clue provided for each boldface word.

1. The teacher was **impressed** when the student gave the correct answer to the question.

2. Because Jimmy Valentine liked to dress well, everyone called him **Dandy** Jimmy Valentine.

3. Mrs. Flowers wanted me to practice so that I could **recite** the poem to her.

4. No one's life, liberty, or property can be taken away without a trial under the **due process** of law.

5. When Jimmy **retrieved** the tools from his suitcase, it almost gave away his past as a thief.

6. The was one **factor** above all others that had the greatest influence on the jury members.

Language Review

Collection 2

LANGUAGE COACH: ANTONYMS

DIRECTIONS: Antonyms are words that have opposite meanings. Match the words in the left column with their antonyms in the right column. Write the letters on the correct blanks.

_____ **1.** retrieved	**a.** hot
_____ **2.** wrong	**b.** short
_____ **3.** cold	**c.** lost
_____ **4.** tall	**d.** fast
_____ **5.** slow	**e.** right

ORAL LANGUAGE ACTIVITY

DIRECTIONS: With a partner, take on the roles of two characters who came in contact with one another in one of the readings in this collection. Such pairs might include Ben and Jimmy from *A Retrieved Reformation*, the young man and his mother from *The Wise Old Woman*, or Marguerite and Mrs. Flowers from *Mrs. Flowers.* To help yourselves, re-read passages that reveal something about the motivations of the characters. Then make up your own dialogue between the two characters, explaining their motivation for their actions in the story. Practice saying the dialogue out loud and present it to the class.

Collection

3

Theme

© Jon Feingersh/Masterfile

Literary and Academic Vocabulary for Collection 3

LITERARY VOCABULARY

theme (THEEM) *n.*: what a story tells us about life.

The theme of the story was looking ahead and making changes.

universal or recurring themes *n.*: themes that can be found in many different stories from many different time periods.

Love is a universal theme in poetry, song, and literature.

generalization (JEH NUH RUH LY ZAY SHUHN) *n.*: a broad statement based on several smaller examples.

After reading the story, I was able to make a few generalizations about Sioux culture.

ACADEMIC VOCABULARY

convey (KUHN VAY) *v.*: communicate; express.

The author tried to convey that his main character was in a great deal of pain.

significant (SIHG NIHF UH KUHNT) *adj.*: meaningful; important.

Thinking about significant events in a story may help you find the theme.

indicate (IHN DIH KAYT) *v.*: point out; suggest.

The author does not always clearly indicate the theme of a story.

consequence (KAHN SUH KWEHNS) *n.*: result of something that happened.

Every action in a story can have a possible consequence.

The Medicine Bag

Based on the story by Virginia Driving Hawk Sneve

LITERARY FOCUS: CHARACTER AND THEME

Theme is what a story has to tell us about life. Often, you can find out what the theme of a story is by paying close attention to the main **character** of a story. By seeing how the main character changes throughout a story, we can learn something about life. For example, in the movie *Rocky*, we see the main character change his ways. By the end of the movie, we learn that by working hard and being a good person, we can achieve our goals in life.

READING FOCUS: MAKING GENERALIZATIONS

A **generalization** is a broad statement based on several smaller examples. When you make a generalization, you look at different pieces of information and make a statement about them. For example, when you finish reading "The Medicine Bag," you might make a generalization about how people are affected by their culture. In some cases, making generalizations can help you see the theme of a story. As you read, take notes about Martin's actions and think about your own experiences to help make generalizations.

VOCABULARY

Practice saying these words out loud.

Sioux (SOO) *n.*: an American Indian tribe most common on the Great Plains of the American West.

reservation (REH ZUR VAY SHUN) *n.*: a confined area of land where some American Indian tribes live apart from other cultural groups.

vision (VIH ZHUN) *n.*: a dream that shows someone spiritual wisdom.

INTO THE STORY

Some cultures and families mark the passage into adulthood with a ritual. These traditions are called rites of passage. In Sioux culture, a teenage boy becomes a man by going off by himself to find spiritual power through a dream. Sometimes he also finds a special object believed to protect him or give him power. This object is called *medicine*, although it is not like the medicine you take when you get sick. The object is treated as something holy. It is passed down from generation to generation.

SKILLS FOCUS

Literary Skills
Understand character; understand theme.

Reading Skills
Make generalizations about theme.

THE MEDICINE BAG

Based on the story by Virginia Diving Hawk Sneve

© Marilyn "Angel" Wynn/NativeStock

My younger sister Cheryl and I always bragged about our Sioux Indian grandpa, Joe Iron Shell. **A** Our friends lived in the city and only knew about Indians from movies and TV. They liked our stories. When we came home after visiting Grandpa, we always had exciting stories to tell.

We never showed our friends Grandpa's picture. We knew that the stories we told didn't go with the real thing. Grandpa was old. He wasn't tall and strong-looking like TV Indians. His gray hair hung in clumps on his neck, not in braids. He lived all by himself in a tiny house on the Rosebud Reservation in South Dakota, not in a tepee. So when Grandpa came to visit us, I was embarrassed. **B**

One day I heard a lot of dogs barking on our street. About a block away I saw a crowd of little kids yelling. The dogs were growling around someone who was walking down the middle of the street.

I watched the group as it slowly came closer. In the center of the strange parade was a man wearing a tall black hat. Sometimes

10

A ⟨ HERE'S HOW ⟩

Vocabulary

I see the word *Sioux* in the first line of the story. I am not sure what it means. By reading the sentence, I think I can get a better understanding. *Sioux* is followed by the word "Indian." I think that the *Sioux* are an American Indian tribe. I checked my dictionary, and found that I was right! The *Sioux* are an American Indian tribe from the Great Plains in the West. Joe Iron Shell is part of this tribe.

B ⟨ READ AND DISCUSS ⟩

Comprehension

What do you know about the lives of the narrator and his sister? **Follow-up:** Why does the narrator tell his friends about his grandfather but never show them his picture?

Adapted from "The Medicine Bag" by Virginia Driving Hawk Sneve. Retold by Holt, Rinehart and Winston. Reproduced by permission of **Virginia Driving Hawk Sneve.**

A (READ AND DISCUSS)

Comprehension

What does Martin's reaction to Grandpa's arrival tell you about his attitude towards Grandpa?

B (READ AND DISCUSS)

Comprehension

How does the narrator's attitude towards Grandpa's clothing add to what you know about his thoughts towards Grandpa?

C (HERE'S HOW)

Reading Focus

I notice that Mom does not hug Grandpa out of respect for Sioux culture. But it is okay for Cheryl to hug him because she is a child. From this, I can **make a generalization**. In Sioux culture, public affection between adults is not proper. However, it is okay between adults and children.

20 he stopped to look at something in his hand and at the houses on either side of the street. "Oh, no!" I whispered. "It's Grandpa!" **A**

I yelled at the dogs to get away, and they ran off. The kids ran to the curb and watched me and the old man.

"Grandpa," I said. I reached for his beat-up old tin suitcase. But he set it down right in the street and shook my hand.

"Hau, Takoza,[1] Grandchild," he greeted me in Sioux.

I stood there with everyone watching. Grandpa's big black hat had a sad-looking old feather. His wrinkled black suit hung like a sack over his body. He wore a bright-red satin shirt with a beaded western tie. His outfit looked out of place in the city.

30 "Hi," I said. I felt like crying. I couldn't think of anything to say. I just picked up Grandpa's suitcase and led him up the driveway to our house. **B**

Mom was standing on the steps. She looked as if she couldn't believe what she saw. Then she ran to us.

"Grandpa," she gasped. "How in the world did you get here?"

She didn't hug Grandpa. I remembered that showing affection is not proper in the Sioux culture. It would embarrass him.

"Hau, Marie," he said. He shook Mom's hand. She smiled.

We helped him up the steps, and Cheryl came running out

40 of the house. She looked so happy to see Grandpa that I was embarrassed about how I felt.

"Grandpa!" she yelled happily. "You came to see us!"

Grandpa smiled and stretched out his arms to my ten-year-old sister. She was still young enough to be hugged. **C**

"Wicincala,[2] little girl," he said. Then he fainted.

Mom and I carried him inside. While Mom called the doctor, I tried to make Grandpa feel better. He was so skinny that his coat slipped off easily. I loosened his tie and opened his shirt collar. I found a small pouch hanging from a leather string

50 around his neck. I left it alone.

Mom came back with a bowl of water. "The doctor thinks Grandpa got too hot," she said. She wiped his face with water. Mom said, "Oh, Martin. How do you think he got here?"

---

1. **Takoza:** Sioux word for "grandchild."
2. **Wicincala:** Sioux word for "little girl"

We found out after the doctor came. Dad got home from work just as the doctor was leaving. Grandpa was sitting up in bed. "You're okay," my dad told him. "The doctor said you just got too tired and hot after your long trip." Grandpa relaxed and told us about his trip. Soon after our visit Grandpa decided that he wanted to see where we lived. Besides, he felt lonely after we left. **D**

60   I knew everybody felt as bad as I did—especially Mom. She was all Grandpa had left. Even though she had married a white man and we lived in the city, Mom made sure that every summer we spent a week with Grandpa.

    I never thought that Grandpa would be lonely. But he was, and so he came to see us. He had ridden on buses for two and a half days. When he arrived in the city, he was tired from sitting for so long, but he set out to find us.

    A nice police officer helped him get a bus to our street. After Grandpa got off the bus, he started walking. But he couldn't

70 see the house numbers on both sides when he walked on the sidewalk, so he walked in the middle of the street. That's when all the little kids and dogs followed him.

    I was proud of Grandpa. He was eighty-six years old and had never been away from the reservation before, but he had the courage to travel here alone. **E** **F**

    Dad said, "We are honored to have you with us. I am sorry that we did not bring you home with us this summer."

    Grandpa was pleased. "Thank you," he answered. "But do not feel bad that you didn't bring me with you. I would not have

80 come then. It was not time." To the Sioux, a thing would be done when it was the right time to do it. That's just the way it was. **G**

    "Also," Grandpa went on, looking at me, "I have come because it is soon time for Martin to have the medicine bag."

    We all knew what that meant. Grandpa thought he was going to die. It was his family's custom to pass the medicine bag, along with its history, to the oldest male child.

    "Even though the boy has a white man's name," he continued, "the medicine bag will be his."

D **READ AND DISCUSS**

Comprehension

What has happened?

E **READ AND DISCUSS**

Comprehension

What does Martin think about Grandpa now?

F **YOUR TURN**

Vocabulary

Grandpa has never left the *reservation* before. Based on the context of the word in this sentence, what is a *reservation*?
(a) An agreement to save a seat for someone.
(b) A doubt about something.
(c) Land where some American Indian tribes live.

G **HERE'S HOW**

Literary Focus

The narrator keeps explaining Grandpa's behavior and statements by pointing out that they follow Sioux culture. This tells me that Grandpa takes the traditions of his culture very seriously. I know that main **characters** often reveal the **theme** of a story, I think that the theme of this story involves traditions and culture.

A READ AND DISCUSS

Comprehension
What is the medicine bag?
Follow-up: Why does Martin
have mixed feelings about
taking the medicine bag?

B YOUR TURN

Literary Focus
Grandpa says that he dressed
up in his Sioux clothes because
he knew Martin's friends were
coming. How do Grandpa's
actions here connect to the
theme of the story?

The medicine bag was the dirty leather pouch I had found
90 around his neck. I could imagine the jokes my friends would
make if they saw it. But I knew I would have to take it. **A**

Grandpa was tired. "Not now, Martin," he said. "It is not
time. Now I will sleep."

So that's how Grandpa came to be with us for two months.
My friends kept asking to come see him, but I was afraid they
would laugh at Grandpa—and at me. Nothing bothered Cheryl
about bringing her friends to see Grandpa. Every day, little girls
or boys crowded around the old man as he sat outside.

Grandpa would smile and answer their questions. He'd tell
100 them stories of brave warriors, ghosts, and animals. The kids listened in silence. Those little guys thought Grandpa was great.

Finally, one day after school, my friends came home with
me. When we got to my house, Grandpa was sitting outside.
He had on his red shirt and a leather vest that was covered with
beads. He had on soft, beaded Indian shoes. His old black hat
had been brushed, and the feather was standing straight up. His
silver hair lay over the red shirt collar.

I stared just as my friends did. I heard one of them say
quietly, "Wow!"

110 Grandpa looked up. When his eyes met mine, they twinkled
as if he were laughing inside. He nodded to me. My face got all
hot. I could tell that he had known all along that I was afraid he'd
embarrass me in front of my friends.

"Hau, hoksilas boys," he greeted, and held out his hand.

My buddies all shook his hand. They were so polite I almost
laughed.

"You look fine, Grandpa," I said as the guys sat down.

"Yes," he agreed. "When I woke up this morning, it seemed
the right time to dress in the good clothes. I knew that my grand-
120 son would be bringing his friends." **B**

"You guys want some lemonade or something?" I offered.
No one answered. They were listening to Grandpa. He was telling
how he'd killed the deer from which his vest was made.

Grandpa did most of the talking while my friends were there. I was so proud of him and amazed at how polite my buddies were. When it was suppertime and they had to leave, they shook Grandpa's hand again and said to me:

"Martin, he's really great!"

"Yeah, man! Don't blame you for keeping him to yourself."

130 "Can we come back?" **C**

But after they left, Mom said, "No more visitors for a while, Martin. Grandpa likes having company, but it tires him."

That evening Grandpa called me to his room before he went to sleep. "Tomorrow," he said, "it will be time to give you the medicine bag."

I was scared, but I answered, "OK, Grandpa."

All night I had weird dreams about thunder and lightning on a high hill. From a distance I heard the slow beat of a drum. **D** When I woke up in the morning, I felt as if I hadn't

140 slept at all. After school, I ran home.

Grandpa was in his room, sitting on the bed. The shades were down. I sat on the floor in front of Grandpa, but he didn't even look at me. After what seemed a long time, he spoke. **E**

"I sent your mother and sister away. What you will hear today is only for a man's ears. What you will receive is only for a man's hands." I felt shivers down my back.

"My father in his early manhood," Grandpa began, "made a holy journey to find a spirit guide for his life. You cannot understand how it was in that time, when the Sioux were first made

150 to stay on the reservation. There was a strong need for guidance from the Great Spirit. But too many of the young men were filled with sadness and hate. They thought it was hopeless to search for a vision when they had to live on a reservation. **F** But my father held to the old ways.

"He carefully prepared for his trip and then he went alone to a high hilltop to pray. After three days he had his holy dream. In it he found the white man's iron. He did not understand his vision of finding something belonging to the white people. In that time they were the enemy. When he came down from the

C **READ AND DISCUSS**

Comprehension

What is Martin learning from Grandpa's visit?

D **YOUR TURN**

Reading Focus

Martin says he had "weird dreams." Make a **generalization** about how you think his American Indian culture may have shaped these dreams.

_____

_____

_____

E **READ AND DISCUSS**

Comprehension

Why do you think Martin enters Grandpa's room and just sits there in the dark, not doing anything until Grandpa talks to him?

F **HERE'S HOW**

Language Coach

Many English words have silent letters. For example, the word *thought* in line 152 has the silent letters *gh*. Being aware of silent letters is important for building **oral fluency**.

160 hill, he found the remains of a campfire and the broken shell of an iron kettle. This was a sign from his dream. He took a piece of the iron for his medicine bag. He had made it of elk skin years before.

"He returned to his village, where he told his dream to the wise old men of the tribe. They gave him the name Iron Shell, but they did not understand the meaning of the dream. Iron Shell kept the piece of iron with him at all times. He believed it protected him. **A**

"Then Iron Shell was taken away to a live at a white man's 170 school. He was angry and lonesome for his parents and the young girl he had married. At first Iron Shell did not try to learn. One day it was his turn to work in the school's blacksmith shop. As he walked in, he knew that he was there to learn and work with the white man's iron.

"Iron Shell worked as a blacksmith when he returned to the reservation. All his life he treasured the medicine bag. When he was old, he gave it to me."

Grandpa covered his face with his hands. His shoulders were shaking with quiet sobs. I 180 looked away until he began to speak again.

"I kept the bag until my son, your mother's father, left us to fight in the war across the ocean. I gave him the bag, for I believed it would protect him in battle. But he did not take it with him. He was afraid that he would lose it. He died in a faraway place." **B**

Again Grandpa was still. I felt his sadness around me.

"My son," he went on, "had only 190 a daughter. It is not proper for her to know of these things." **C**

He unbuttoned his shirt, pulled out the leather pouch, and lifted it over his head. He held it in his hand and turning it over and over.

© Jerry Jacka Photography

"In the bag," he said as he opened it, "is the broken shell of the iron kettle, a pebble from the hill, and a piece of a holy plant. After the bag is yours, you must put a piece of the holy plant within and never open it again until you pass it on to your son."

200   I somehow knew I should stand up. Grandpa slowly got up too. He stood in front of me, holding the bag in front of my face. I waited for him to put it over my head.

But he placed the soft leather bag in my right hand and closed my other hand over it. He said, "It would not be right to wear it in this time and place, where no one will understand. Put it away until you are on the reservation. Wear it when you get the holy plant." **D**

Grandpa turned and sat on the bed. He leaned his head against the pillow. "Go," he said, "I will sleep now."

210   "Thank you, Grandpa," I said softly. I left with the bag in my hands.

That night Mom and Dad took Grandpa to the hospital. Two weeks later I stood alone on the reservation and put the holy plant in my medicine bag. **E**

Comprehension Wrap-Up

1. Knowing what we do about Martin, how do you think he will handle the honor of having the medicine bag?

D READ AND DISCUSS

Comprehension

Based on what we know about Martin, what will he think of Grandpa's orders not to wear the bag on a daily basis?

E READ AND DISCUSS

Comprehension

What does Martin's putting the holy plant in his medicine bag let us know about Grandpa?

The Medicine Bag

USE A CONCEPT MAP

Remember that recognizing details about **characters** and the things they experience can help you identify the **theme** of a story. A concept map like the one below can help you organize details about characters to figure out the theme. Use the concept map below to help you recall some important details about characters in "The Medicine Bag."

Under each character's name in the circles, write down details about that character. You can use this information to draw conclusions about what the theme of the story is.

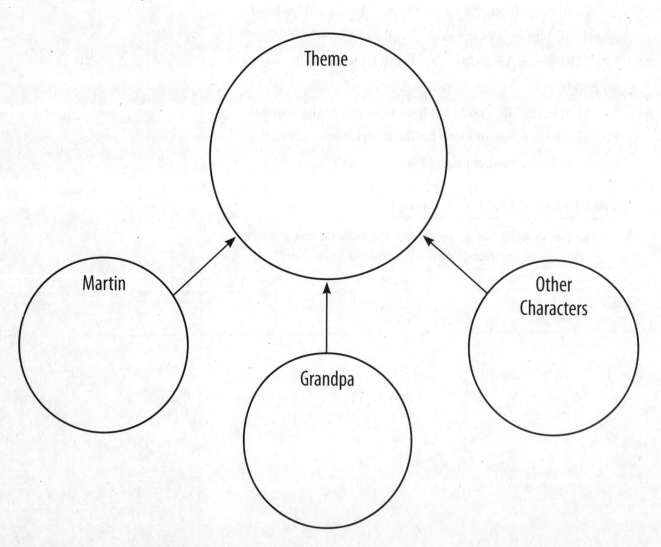

Applying Your Skills

The Medicine Bag

LITERARY FOCUS: CHARACTER AND THEME

DIRECTIONS: Answer the following questions.

1. Who is the main **character** of this story? _____

2. In your own words, explain what the **theme** of this story is. _____

_____

_____

_____

READING FOCUS: MAKING GENERALIZATIONS

DIRECTIONS: Circle the **generalizations** below that can be made based on what you learned from "The Medicine Bag."

1. Grandpa was a kind man.

2. Martin was a bad person because he was embarrassed by his Grandpa.

3. The Sioux culture has different views about men and women.

4. A person's culture can have a great effect on his or her everyday life.

5. Because the Sioux culture looks down on adults hugging each other, it can be said that they are not a caring people.

6. The Sioux care greatly about past generations.

VOCABULARY REVIEW

DIRECTIONS: Fill in blanks with the correct word from the Word Box.

Word Box
Sioux
reservation
vision

1. Grandpa's father had a _____ of finding an iron.

2. Before making the trip to see his family, Grandpa lived on a _____.

3. The _____ are an American Indian tribe from the Great Plains.

Preparing to Read

A Shot At It, How I Learned English, *and* Ed McMahon Is Iranian

LITERARY FOCUS: THEMES ACROSS GENRES

A **theme** can teach us a lesson about life. Authors writing in different **genres**, or types of literature, may use different styles to reflect the same theme. For example, writers of poetry may use words that rhyme. Autobiography and essay writers may tell about a personal experience.

The selections you are about to read represent different genres. Even so, they all have a similar theme.

READING FOCUS: COMPARING THEMES

To identify a selection's **theme**, think about its title, the problems the characters face, and how the problems are solved. As you read, write down notes to **compare**, or find what is similar, about the theme of each selection.

VOCABULARY

guidance counselor (GUY DUHNS KOWN SUH LUHR) *n.:* A trained person who helps students plan for the future.

transfixed (TRANS FIHKSD) *adv.:* staring without moving.

terrorist (TEHR UHR IHST) *n.:* someone who uses violence to scare people into doing what he or she wants.

Literary Skills
Analyze themes across genres.

Reading Skills
Articulate and discuss themes and connections that cross cultures; compare and contrast themes.

INTO THE SELECTIONS

The first selection is from Esmeralda Santiago's autobiography. She was born in Puerto Rico and moved to Brooklyn, New York, when she was thirteen. Her life changed when she went to the School of Performing Arts.

Gregory Djanikian lived in Egypt as a young boy and moved to Pennsylvania when he was six. His poem tells the story of the first time he played baseball.

Mariam Salari was born in the United States. Her father was Iranian. Her essay takes place during the Iran Hostage Crisis, when anti-American Iranians had taken 52 people hostage at the U.S. Embassy in Iran. Some Americans began to express anger towards all people of Iranian heritage.

A SHOT AT IT

Based on an excerpt from *When I Was Puerto Rican*
by Esmeralda Santiago

When I was in the ninth grade we moved, so I had to change schools. In my first week at Public School 33 I was given lots of tests. The tests showed that I couldn't speak English very well, but I read and wrote it at the tenth-grade level. **A**

One morning, my guidance counselor, Mr. Barone, called me to his office.

"So," he said, "what do you want to be when you grow up?" **B**

"I don't know." Since we had come to Brooklyn, I had not thought about the future much.

10 He looked through some papers and asked, "Do you have any hobbies?" I didn't know what he meant. He waved his hands and explained, "things you like to do after school."

"Ah, yes." I tried to imagine what I did that might count as a hobby. "I like to read."

A **READ AND DISCUSS**

Comprehension
How is the author starting things off?

B **HERE'S HOW**

Vocabulary
I am not sure what a *guidance counselor* is. I have heard the word *guide* before, though. It means "to give advice," or "help." I will read ahead to try to better understand the context of the term. Mr. Barone asks, "What do you want to be when you grow up?" This tells me that a *guidance counselor* is someone who helps students with their plans for the future.

Literary Focus

The counselor talks about getting Esmeralda into a good school so that she has "a shot at" going to college. I can tell from the context that the phrase "a shot at" means "a chance." I think getting into college and making changes may be **themes** of this autobiography.

Comprehension

What is happening in Mr. Barone's office?

"Yes, we know that," he said. "One of the tests we gave you tells us what kinds of things you might be good at. The tests show that you would be good at helping people. You can go to a high school to prepare for a career in nursing. You would also do well in teaching."

I frowned. He looked at the papers again.

Mr. Barone leaned over the papers on his desk. "Why don't you think about it and get back to me," he said. He closed the folder with my name on it. "You're a smart girl, Esmeralda. Let's try to get you into a good school so that you have a shot at college." **A**

A few days later, I was in Mr. Barone's office again.

I thought of the night before, when Mami had called us into the living room. On the television were "fifty of America's most beautiful girls."

"Aren't they lovely?" Mami said. The girls floated by the camera, twirled, and disappeared behind a screen. An announcer called out their names, ages, and states.

"I want to be on television," I said.

"Oh, then you want to be an actress," said Mr. Barone. He reached for a book. "I only know of one school that trains actresses, but we've never sent them a student from here."

Performing Arts, the write-up said, was a public school for students wishing to pursue a career in theater, music, and dance.

"It says here that you have to try out," Mr. Barone said. "Have you ever performed in front of other people?"

"I was a speaker in my school show in Puerto Rico," I said. "And I recite poetry. There, not here."

He closed the book. "Let me call them and find out exactly what you need to do. Then we can talk some more." **B**

I left his office strangely happy. I knew that something good had just happened.

"I'm not afraid." Every day I walked home from school repeating those words. I couldn't imagine that anything good happened in the dark hallways and behind the locked doors I passed.

92   A Shot At It

I decided I had to get out of Brooklyn. Mami had chosen this as our home. I had to go along with her because I was a child who had no choice. But I didn't want to. **C**

"How can people live like this?" I shouted once. I wanted to feel grass under my feet instead of cement.

"Like what?" Mami asked. She looked around our apartment. The kitchen and living room were covered with sagging lines of drying laundry.

"Everyone on top of each other," I said. "No room to do any-

60 thing. No air."

"Do you want to go back to Puerto Rico, to live with no electricity and no toilets?"

"I hate my life!" I yelled. "Then do something about it," she yelled back.

When Mr. Barone showed me the listing for Performing Arts High School, I knew what to do.

"The try-outs are in less than a month. You have to perform a speech from a play. If you do well, and your grades here are good, you might get into the school."

70 Mr. Barone took charge of preparing me. He chose a speech from a play called *The Silver Cord*. It took place in a New York living room around 1905.

I was to play Christina, a young married woman. In my speech, Christina was arguing with her mother-in-law. **D** I learned the sounds of all the words in the speech from Mr. Gatti, the English teacher.

"We don't have time to study the meaning of every word," Mr. Gatti said. "Just make sure you say every word correctly." **E**

Then I went to see Mrs. Johnson, who taught Home

80 Economics.

"Sit," she said. "No, not like that. Float down to the chair with your knees together." She showed me, and I copied her. "That's better. What do you do with your hands? Put your hands on your lap, and leave them there."

I sat stiff while Mrs. Johnson and Mr. Barone asked me questions they thought the people at Performing Arts would ask.

C YOUR TURN

Literary Focus

How do Esmeralda's feelings connect to the **theme** of taking "a shot at" going to college?

_____

_____

_____

_____

D HERE'S HOW

Language Coach

My teacher says that the **origin** of the word *arguing* is the Latin word *arguere*, which means "to make clear." This makes sense, because when you *argue*, you try to make your point clear to another person.

E HERE'S HOW

Reading Focus

I notice that Esmeralda will be playing a character that is totally different from herself. This seems to fit in with the **theme** of change. I can **compare** Esmeralda to the character that she plays.

A YOUR TURN

Reading Focus

This is the same question Mr. Barone asked earlier. **Compare** Esmeralda's answer here with her answer in line 14. Why is her answer different now? How does it connect to the **theme** of the story?

_____

_____

_____

B YOUR TURN

Literary Focus

Mr. Barone says, "I think we have a shot at this." What is he talking about? How does this point to the **theme** of the story?

_____

_____

_____

_____

C READ AND DISCUSS

Comprehension

How does Mami help Esmeralda prepare for her audition? **Follow-up:** How does Mami seem to feel about the School for the Performing Arts?

"Do you have any hobbies?" Mr. Barone asked. Now I knew what to answer.

"I enjoy dancing and the movies." **A**

90   "Why do you want to come to this school?"

"I would like to study at Performing Arts because it is an excellent school and so that I may be trained as an actress."

"Very good!" Mr. Barone said. He and Mrs. Johnson had worked on my answer to this question. He twinkled his eyes. "I think we have a shot at this." **B**

Mrs. Johnson said, "Wear a dress that is very simple in dark colors."

Mami bought me a red wool dress, my first pair of stockings, and new shoes. The night before, she rolled up my hair in curlers. For once, I was allowed to wear makeup.

100   We set out for the try-out on a cloudy January morning.

"Why couldn't you choose a school close to home?" Mami said. The trip took one hour each way by subway. But Mami was proud of me. And she seemed excited that I would be leaving the neighborhood and meeting new people. **C**

Three women sat behind a long table in a classroom. The desks and chairs had been pushed against a wall. I entered and floated down to the chair in front of them. I put my hands on my lap and smiled.

110   I had dreamed of this moment for several weeks. I wanted to impress the women. Then I would be accepted into Performing Arts and leave Brooklyn every day.

But at that moment, I forgot my English and Mrs. Johnson's lessons on how to behave. As I tried to answer the women's questions, I waved my hands. I formed words with my fingers because the words would not leave my mouth.

"Why don't you let us hear your speech now?" one woman asked softly.

I closed my eyes and breathed deeply. Then I walked to the
120   middle of the room and began my speech.

Mr. Gatti had reminded me to speak slowly, but I said my whole three-minute speech in just one minute.

"Thank you, dear," she said. "Could you wait outside for a few moments?"

In the hall, a couple of girls my age sat next to their mothers, waiting their turn. They looked up as I came out. Mami stood up. She looked as scared as I felt.

"What happened?" she asked.

"Nothing," I said. If I began telling her about it, I would start
130   crying in front of the other people. "I have to wait here a minute." **D**

"Did they say anything?" she asked.

"No. I'm just supposed to wait."

We leaned against the wall. Across from us there were newspaper clippings about former students. On the ragged edge, someone had written "P.A." and the year the actor, dancer, or musician had graduated. I tried to picture myself in a clipping, with "P.A. '66" across the top.

The door opened. One woman poked her head out and led me back into the room. I met a girl named Bonnie, who went to
140   the school.

The woman said, "Without using words, I want you and Bonnie to pretend you are sisters decorating a Christmas tree."

Bonnie looked a lot like Juanita Marín, an old friend from Puerto Rico. We decided where the Christmas tree would be.

D READ AND DISCUSS

Comprehension
What happened in the audition?

A YOUR TURN

Literary Focus

In her first role, Esmeralda played Christina, a girl much different from herself. Here, Esmeralda's real life seems to help her in her audition with Bonnie. How might this connect to the **theme** of change in this memoir?

_____

_____

_____

_____

B READ AND DISCUSS

Comprehension

What is the author letting us know in the section titled "One of These Days?"

Then we sat on the floor. We pretended we were taking decorations out of boxes and hanging them on the branches.

My family never had a Christmas tree, but once I had helped Papi put colored lights around a bush on our land. We hung the wire with tiny red bulbs until we ran out. Then Papi
150 added another cord to it. We kept going until the bush looked like it was on fire.

Before long I forgot that the tree didn't exist and Bonnie was not my sister. Then she pretended to hand me a very special decoration. Just before I took it, she made like it fell to the ground and shattered. I was scared that Mami would come in and yell at us. When I began to pick up the tiny pretend pieces, a voice broke in. "Thank you." **A**

Bonnie got up, smiled, and went out.

One of the women stretched her hand out for me to shake.
160 "We will let your school know in a few weeks. It was very nice to meet you."

On the way home Mami kept asking what had happened. I kept saying, "Nothing." I was upset. I had practiced for hours. Mami had bought me new clothes and shoes, and she took the day off from work. After all that, I had failed the try-out and would never get out of Brooklyn.

One of These Days

Ten years after my graduation from Performing Arts, I visited the school. I had a scholarship to Harvard University. One
170 woman from my try-out had become my favorite teacher. **B**

"I remember your try out," she said when I visited.

I had forgotten the skinny girl with curled hair, red dress, and lively hands. But she hadn't. She told me that the women had asked me to leave so that they could laugh. It was so funny to see a fourteen-year-old Puerto Rican girl spitting out a speech about a mean mother-in-law at the turn of the century. The words were impossible to understand because I spoke so fast.

"We liked the courage it took to stand in front of us and do what you did," she said.

180 "So you mean I got into the school because I had guts?" We both laughed.

"Are any of your sisters and brothers in college?"

"No, I'm the only one, so far."

"Do you ever think about how far you've come?" she asked.

"No." I answered. "I never stop to think about it. It might mess up the future." **C**

"Let me tell you another story, then," she said. "The first day of your first year, you were absent. We called your house. I asked to speak to your mother, and you translated what she said. She

190 said she really needed you to go somewhere with her to translate. At first you wouldn't tell me where, but then you said you were going to the welfare office. You were crying. I told you that other students in this school received welfare too. The next day you were here. And now you are about to graduate from Harvard."

"I'm glad you made that phone call," I said.

"And I'm glad you came to see me." Her warm hug surprised me.

"Thank you," I said.

I walked the halls of the school and found the room where

200 my life had changed. It was across from the science lab. A few doors down newspaper clippings of famous graduates still hung on the wall. Someone still wrote the letters "P.A." followed by the graduating year along the edges.

"P.A. '66," I said to myself. "One of these days." **D**

Comprehension Wrap-Up

1. Can we learn a lesson from Esmeralda Santiago's memoir?

Literary Focus

I know a **theme** of this autobiography is looking to the future. When she was young, Esmeralda looked past her school and her life in Brooklyn. She worked hard to get into Performing Arts. Here, this theme of looking ahead comes up once again.

D (HERE'S HOW)

Reading Focus

Once again, I see the **theme** of looking ahead. As I read the next two selections, "How I Learned English" and "Ed McMahon is Iranian," I will remember this theme of change. I will try to **compare** the theme of "A Shot At It" with the themes of the other selections.

HOW I LEARNED ENGLISH

By Gregory Djanikian

It was in an empty lot
Ringed by elms and fir and honeysuckle.
Bill Corson was pitching in his buckskin jacket,
Chuck Keller, fat even as a boy, was on first,
His t-shirt riding up over his gut,
Ron O'Neill, Jim, Dennis, were talking it up
In the field, a blue sky above them
Tipped with cirrus.[1]
    And there I was,
Just off the plane and plopped in the middle
Of Williamsport, Pa., and a neighborhood game,
Unnatural and without any moves,
My notions of baseball and America
Growing fuzzier each time I wiffed.[2] **A**

5

10

A **READ AND DISCUSS**

Comprehension

What is happening in this scene? **Follow-up:** The narrator uses words like "wiffed" to describe his experience playing baseball. What do light and playful words like this tell us about the narrator?

IN OTHER WORDS Some boys are playing baseball in an empty lot. The setting is Williamsport, Pennsylvania. The author has just immigrated there. This is the first time he has played baseball. He knows little about the game or about the United States. He moves very little during the game, missing the ball a lot because he does not know what to do.

So it was not impossible that I,
Banished to the outfield and daydreaming
Of water, or a hotel in the mountains,
Would suddenly find myself in the path
Of a ball stung by Joe Barone.
I watched it closing in
Clean and untouched, transfixed[3]

15

20

---

1. **cirrus:** high, wispy clouds.
2. **wiffed:** missed the ball.
3. **transfixed:** staring without moving.

"How I Learned English" from *Falling Deeply into America* by **Gregory Djanikian.** Copyright © 1989 by Gregory Djanikian. First published in *Poetry*, 1986. Reproduced by permission of the author.

Courtesy of Bill Goff , Inc.

By its easy arc before it hit

My forehead with a thud.

    I fell back.

25   Dazed, clutching my brow.

Groaning, "Oh my shin, oh my shin,"

And everybody peeled away from me

And dropped from laughter, and there we were,

All of us writhing on the ground for one reason

30   Or another. **B** **C**

IN OTHER WORDS The boys make the author play in the outfield, where he is least likely to have a ball hit to him. As he daydreams, he does not notice a ball hit by Joe Barone coming towards him. When he does see it, he just stares and stands still as it hits him in the forehead. He grabs his forehead in pain and incorrectly calls it his "shin." This mistake makes the other boys laugh.

B YOUR TURN

Literary Focus

What do you think this story's **theme** is? How does it **compare** to the theme of "A Shot At It"?

_____

_____

_____

_____

_____

C READ AND DISCUSS

Comprehension

Why are the boys laughing?

A **READ AND DISCUSS**

Comprehension
Why does the author say that his laughing and Joe's helping him up were so important?

B **READ AND DISCUSS**

Comprehension
What kind of boy is the narrator?

Someone said "shin" again,

There was a wild stamping of hands on the ground,

A kicking of feet, and the fit

Of laughter overtook me too,

35 And that was important, as important

As Joe Barone asking me how I was

Through his tears, picking me up

And dusting me off with hands like swatters, **A**

And though my head felt heavy,

40 I played on till dusk

Missing flies and pop-ups and grounders

And calling out in desperation things like

"Yours" and "take it," but doing all right,

Tugging at my cap in just the right way,

45 Crouching low, my feet set,

"Hum baby" sweetly on my lips. **B**

IN OTHER WORDS As the other boys laugh over the author's mistaken use of the word "shin" for "forehead," he starts to laugh as well. This was an important step towards making friends with the other boys. Joe Barone, whose ball hit the author, feels bad about it and helps the author stand up. As the boys play baseball the rest of the day, the author starts to learn how to play the game and use the same words as the other boys.

Comprehension Wrap-Up

1. Talk about what it may be like to be the new person in a group of people that already know each other. Would it be easy or hard to laugh at yourself in an embarrassing situation, like the narrator does in this poem?

ED MCMAHON IS IRANIAN

Based on the essay by Mariam Salari

© Douglas C. Pizac/AP Photo

It was a normal afternoon. My mother and I were arranging things in our new Florida home. My little brother was napping.

Then the doorbell rang. As my mom opened the door, there was a huge explosion. BANG!

A splash of red paint had stained our front door. The stains on the door marked us as terrorists, as bad guys. **A** My mom slammed the door shut and called my father at work. I remember being scared and not knowing what had happened. I could tell that my mom was very frightened. That scared me even more.
10 She tried to tell me that everything was all right. She asked me to go to my room and take a nap. Then the police came, and she told them what had happened. **B**

When Dad came home, I didn't know what to say. There was a strange silence in the air. After dinner I went to my dad. I curled up next to him in his big brown leather chair.

"Daddy, who did that thing today?" I asked

My father looked to my mom for help in answering, but she was quiet. I could tell that he was looking for a good answer for his five-year-old daughter. "Someone did this because they
20 were mad at the Iranians who are holding fifty-two Americans as prisoners."

A HERE'S HOW

Vocabulary

I can see that the root word for *terrorist* is *terror*. I know that *terror* means "fear." If *terrorists* are the "bad guys," the main goal of a *terrorist* is probably to scare people with violence.

B HERE'S HOW

Language Coach

My teacher says that the **origin** of the word *police* is the Latin word *politia*, which means "a civil organization." This seems to make sense.

"Ed McMahon Is Iranian" by Mariam Salari from *A World Between: Poems, Short Stories & Essays*. Copyright © 1999 by **Mariam Salari**. Reproduced by permission of the author.

A (READ AND DISCUSS)

Comprehension
What has happened?

B (YOUR TURN)

Reading Focus
Mariam says that she is not a real American, even though she was born in the United States. How do her feelings **compare** to the **themes** of "A Shot At It" and "How I Learned English?"?

_____

_____

_____

_____

_____

_____

_____

_____

C (READ AND DISCUSS)

Comprehension
What effect does Father's joke have on Mariam?
Follow-up: Why do you think she enjoys the joke years later, even though she knows it is a trick?

"Mad at us? We didn't do anything."

"No, we did not, but they think it is our fault." **A**

"I hate being Iranian. I'm not going to make any friends at my new school. They will all hate me. I don't want to be Iranian. I wish I were American."

"You are an American, Mariam. You were born in this country."

"No, I wish I were a *real* American. No one here is an Iranian." **B**

30 My parents looked at each other for a painful second. Then my dad looked up at the television. The *Tonight Show* was on, starring Johnny Carson and Ed McMahon.[1]

My father suddenly answered me, "You are wrong. There are many Iranians in the USA."

I looked up. "Like who?" I asked.

He pointed to the fat man on the screen. "Him, Ed Mac MA Hohn is Iranian."

Through my tears, I looked at the fat man on the TV. He was an Iranian? For whatever reason, I let myself believe it.

40 Of course my dad's accent would have made any name sound Iranian, but that didn't matter to me.

For years I honestly believed that Ed McMahon was Iranian. I would tell everyone that Ed was Iranian. Ed promoted a popular mail-in prize contest. Every time one of those letters came in the mail, I thought Ed had sent it to us because he knew we were Iranians, too. Of course, every time Ed was on television my dad would say, "Look, there's Ed Mac MA Hohn. He's Iranian."

Now, eighteen years later, Ed Mac MA Hohn is a little joke in our house. My dad still likes to make celebrities' names sound

50 Iranian and try to trick us. I still like to let him do it. **C**

Comprehension Wrap-Up

1. Talk about Father's trick on Mariam. Why do you think he played this trick?

_____

1. For thirty years, Ed McMahon [MIHK MAN] was Johnny Carson's sidekick on the popular late-night television series *The Tonight Show*. He is not Iranian.

Applying Your Skills

A Shot At It, How I Learned English, and Ed McMahon Is Iranian

LITERARY FOCUS: THEMES ACROSS GENRES

DIRECTIONS: Using the choice list to the right, complete the table below. Identify the title, **genre** name, and write a short description of the work in that genre.

Choice list:
A Shot At It

account of an immigrant boy's first baseball game

autobiography of a Puerto Rican girl who moves to Brooklyn and is helped by her guidance counselor

essay

How I Learned English

memoir

Title	Description	Genre
		memoir
How I Learned English		
	true story of a father's attempt to make a girl feel better about her culture after her family is marked as terrorists	

READING FOCUS: COMPARING THEMES

DIRECTIONS: Write a brief paragraph **comparing** the **themes** of the three selections you just read.

_____

_____

_____

_____

VOCABULARY REVIEW

DIRECTIONS: Write two sentences that meet the following requirements:

1. Write a sentence about a news report that uses the word *terrorist*.

_____

2. Write a sentence about a surprise party that uses the word *transfixed*.

_____

Lewis and Clark: Into the Unknown

Based on the magazine article by The World Almanac

INFORMATIONAL TEXT FOCUS: CAUSE-AND-EFFECT ORGANIZATION

Writing that follows a **cause-and-effect organization** explains how or why one thing leads to another. Magazine and news articles usually give information about causes and effects.

A **cause** is a reason that an action or reaction takes place. You can ask yourself "Why?" to find out the causes of an event.

The **effect** is a result of a cause. You can ask yourself, "What happened as a result?" to find out the effects of a cause.

A cause often has more than one effect. An effect may have several causes. Sometimes, one effect can make other effects happen. As you read, take note of causes and effects.

VOCABULARY

experts (EHK SPURTZ) *n.:* people highly trained in a skill or area of study.

corps (KAWR) *n.:* a group of people with special training; a military unit.

INTO THE ARTICLE

In 1800, Spanish leaders made a secret deal with France to give France a huge section of land in North America. This land was called the Louisiana Territory. It included the city of New Orleans, which led into the Mississippi River.

The United States did not want France to take control of this land or of the Mississippi River. So, in 1803, the United States bought the Louisiana Territory from France and paid about 3 cents an acre for 828,000 square miles of land. This deal, called the Louisiana Purchase, doubled the size of the United States. Since neither Spain nor France had done much with the land, very little was known about it. Most of it had never even been explored or mapped by Europeans. Meriwether Lewis and William Clark led a group that explored, mapped, and wrote down information about the land for the U.S. government. They found an amazing new place filled with plants, animals, and people, unknown to the rest of the world until then.

SKILLS FOCUS

Informational Text Skills
Identify and understand cause-and-effect organization.

Lewis and Clark: Into the Unknown

Based on the magazine article by The World Almanac

What did the unknown land beyond the great river look like? What strange animals might be living there? In 1802, Thomas Jefferson, America's third president, was thinking about these questions. At the time, the Mississippi River formed the western border of the United States. No one knew much about the land beyond.

Jefferson believed moving west was best for the country. So the United States made a deal with France to buy the huge land area between the Mississippi River and the Rocky Mountains. The president wanted Americans to get excited about this new
10 land, called the Louisiana Territory. A successful trip to the West, he thought, might create that kind of excitement. **A** **B**

Explorers would bring back information. They would talk to and make friends with Native Americans. And just maybe, they might find the Northwest Passage. If it really existed, this waterway to the Pacific Ocean could improve trade.

Forming the Group

Jefferson needed somebody brave and smart to lead this group. He chose his own secretary, Meriwether Lewis. The president had Lewis study with experts to get ready for the trip. Since there would be no doctors, Lewis needed to know medicine.
20 He had to be able to find his way by the stars. He also needed to know plant and animal science.

Lewis was excited. But he did not want to lead alone. He asked a friend named William Clark to be the second leader. In 1803, the two headed to the city of St. Louis. They brought along a slave named York, who had been with Clark since

A READ AND DISCUSS

Comprehension

What did President Thomas Jefferson do that changed the country?

B HERE'S HOW

Reading Focus

President Jefferson thought the country should move west. This is a **cause**. The **effect** of this cause is that the United States bought land from France. He thought that a successful trip to this new land would have the effect of getting the country excited.

A **HERE'S HOW**

Language Coach

I notice that in the word *corps* (kawr) the *ps* is silent. The dictionary tells me that *corps* comes from French. So, there may be other French words that also have a silent *ps* in them.

B **READ AND DISCUSS**

Comprehension

Why was the Corp of Discovery formed?
Follow-up: What was the big deal about being chosen as leader?

C **YOUR TURN**

Reading Focus

What was the **cause** of Lewis and Clark meeting with Native American tribes? What **effects** came out of these meetings?

childhood. They hired and trained nearly four dozen more men as members of their group, called the Corps of Discovery. **A** They even brought a dog named Seaman. **B**

Strange Places and New Faces

On March 10, 1804, Lewis and Clark went to the ceremony that
30   made the Louisiana Purchase official. In late spring, their group started up the Missouri River in boats. They passed a small French town on May 25. One of the group members wrote in his diary that this tiny village was "the last settlement of whites on this river." From then on, almost everyone the group met was Native American.

The explorers knew they could not go across the land without help from Native Americans. Lewis and Clark set up meetings with tribes along the way. Many native peoples welcomed them, but there were problems with a few tribes. **C**

Welcome Helpers

40   In late October, the explorers began building a winter fort near the Mandan and Hidatsa[1] Indians in what is now North Dakota. During their stay, Lewis and Clark learned that they needed horses to cross the mountains. The tribes told them the

---

1.   **Hidatsa** [HEH DAHT SAH]

Shoshone[2] might give them the animals, if they could make a deal.

Lewis and Clark found a Shoshone woman to help them. Sacagawea[3] had been captured by the Hidatsa years earlier. Lewis and Clark hired her and her husband, a French Canadian fur trapper, to translate for them. When the group started
50 traveling in spring, Sacagawea, her husband, and their new baby son went along.

Sacagawea's ability to speak Shoshone was very helpful. She helped the group get horses. That was not all, however. The tribes the explorers met were sometimes fearful. But when they saw Sacagawea and her baby son, they felt better. Surely a woman and infant wouldn't be with a war party, they thought. **D**

D (READ AND DISCUSS)

Comprehension

What problem did Lewis and Clark have? **Follow-up:** How did Sacagawea help Lewis and Clark?

E (READ AND DISCUSS)

Comprehension

How did things turn out for the explorers when their trip was done?

To the Pacific Ocean

Lewis and Clark's group faced many problems. They ran into grizzly bears and paddled their canoes through dangerous rapids. At one point, they spent a month walking their canoes
60 around a waterfall. Once they lost their way in the mountains and nearly starved.

They did not find the Northwest Passage. But Lewis and Clark did find the country's rich western plants and animals. In their journals, they described 178 new plants and 122 new animals. With courage and luck, the group made it all the way to what is today Oregon. Then they made it home again to tell their amazing story. **E**

Comprehension Wrap-Up

1. Discuss the kinds of character traits you think these explorers had to have in order to complete their trip.

2. **Shoshone** [SHOH SHOH NEE]
3. **Sacagawea** [SAHK UH JUH WEE UH]

Skills Practice

Lewis and Clark: Into the Unknown

USE A CAUSE-AND-EFFECT MAP

Remember that **causes** are why something happened. **Effects** are the results of causes. One cause may have many effects. One effect may have many causes.

DIRECTIONS: Fill in the following cause-and-effect map to show the causes and effects of Lewis and Clark's journey.

Causes

1. President Jefferson buys the Louisiana Territory.
2.
3.

Corps of Discovery

Effects

1.
2.
3.

Applying Your Skills

Lewis and Clark: Into the Unknown

INFORMATIONAL TEXT: CAUSE-AND-EFFECT ORGANIZATION

DIRECTIONS: Circle the letter of the *best* answer for each question below.

1. Which of these questions can you ask to help identify the **cause** of an event?

   A. What happened as a result?

   B. Why did it happen?

   C. How did it change things?

   D. What happened next?

2. Which of following statements about **cause and effect** is true?

   A. All effects have at least five causes.

   B. No effects have more than one cause.

   C. Many effects have more than one cause.

   D. Most effects do not have a specific cause.

VOCABULARY REVIEW

DIRECTIONS: A *synonym* is a word or phrase that means the same thing as another word. Fill in the following chart with as many words or phrases that you can think of that are synonyms for your vocabulary terms.

Vocabulary Term	Synonyms
experts	
corps	

Lewis and Clark Revisited

Based on the magazine article by The World Almanac

INFORMATIONAL TEXT FOCUS: COMPARISON-AND-CONTRAST ORGANIZATION

Many articles **compare** and **contrast** two or more topics. Comparing involves finding things that are alike. Writers may use words like "both" to compare things. Contrasting involves finding things that are different. Writers may use words like "but" and "however" to contrast things. There are two common ways that writers compare and contrast information:

Block method: The writer first talks about all of the features of the first subject. Then, the writer talks about all of the features of the second subject. For example, a writer comparing Presidents Jefferson and Lincoln may write about Jefferson first, then Lincoln second.

Point-by-point method: The writer discusses one feature or point at a time, explaining how that feature appears in each subject. For example, to compare Jefferson and Lincoln, a writer might begin by talking about their educations. After comparing their educations, the writer will move on to another feature, such as their political beliefs.

VOCABULARY

Write each of these words on a separate index card. On the back of each card, write the definition for the word on the front.

reenactment (REE EHN AKT MUHNT) *n.:* a performance of an event that already happened.

expedition (EK SPUH DIH SHUHN) *n.:* a journey taken for a certain purpose.

satellite (SAH TUH LYT) *n.:* an object that orbits the Earth or another larger object in space.

SKILLS FOCUS

Informational Text Skills
Identify and understand compare-contrast organization.

INTO THE ARTICLE

The following article compares a modern-day reenactment of the Lewis and Clark expedition to the actual historical event. Reenactments bring the past to life both for those involved and for those who watch.

LEWIS AND CLARK REVISITED

Based on the magazine article by The World Almanac

James Woodcock/Billings Gazette/AP Photo

Lewis and Clark Revisited

President Thomas Jefferson's directions to Meriwether Lewis over 200 years ago were clear. Jefferson told Lewis to find and map a waterway to the Pacific Ocean. He also told Lewis to meet with native people along the way, and write down what he learned. When Lewis and the rest of his group set out to explore the Louisiana Purchase, however, most details about the land and its waterways were unknown.

Two hundred years after that brave journey, the Army Corps of Engineers put together a "journey of rediscovery" called
10   the Discovery Expedition. **A** About 177 people traveled the Lewis and Clark trail. Around ten people stayed with it from start to finish.

While Lewis and Clark had a peace-making and trade mission, the new group's goals were mainly educational. In Lewis and Clark's time, two-thirds of the U.S. population lived within 50 miles of the Atlantic Ocean. Now, Americans are spread across the entire land. Details about the trail are on the Internet. The new trip was like a play acted out by people who enjoyed history. **B**

A HERE'S HOW

Vocabulary

I see that *explorers* and *expedition* both begin with the prefix *ex-*. One of the meanings of this prefix is "out of" or "outside." In this article, both *explorers* and *expedition* have to do with studying things outside.

B READ AND DISCUSS

Comprehension

What has the author told us about the Discovery Expedition? **Follow-up:** How did the two journeys differ?

A   HERE'S HOW

Reading Focus

I have underlined the sentence in this paragraph that shows the writer is about to **compare** the two trips.

B   YOUR TURN

Reading Focus

This paragraph **contrasts** the two journeys. Write one difference between them on the lines below.

_____

_____

_____

_____

_____

C   YOUR TURN

Vocabulary

Re-read this paragraph. Use context clues to write a definition for the word *threatened*, on the lines below. Use a dictionary to check your answer.

_____

_____

Starting Out

20   Leaders of the Discovery Expedition tried to recreate the first trip as much as possible. They did make some changes, though. For example, Lewis crossed the Ohio River with a boat using oars, poles, sails, and ropes. On the new trip, the person playing Lewis had a motorboat.

<u>The new crew had supplies just like the originals, as much as possible.</u> Lewis and Clark brought medicines of their times, including pills that had gun powder in them. The first explorers covered themselves with animal fat to fight mosquitoes. **A**

Lewis and Clark made their first winter camp in Camp Wood, Illinois. Because the Mississippi River has moved east since then, the new group placed their camp two miles from the 30 original location. The original Corps of Discovery did not spend the cold months in video meetings with schools around the nation, as the new group did. Those on the modern trip ate some deer meat and salt pork, but they also enjoyed pizza and donuts donated by visitors. **B**

Meeting Along the Way

Lewis and Clark met friendly Native Americans and picked up some of their customs. They traded their military uniforms for deerskin clothing, buffalo robes, and soft leather shoes. The Mandan and Hidatsa tribes helped them pass the winter. The 40 tribes gave them maps for the trip ahead. But other tribes threatened the group. **C**

The new group felt some of that. Some Indian chiefs welcomed them. One group held a fake peace council in Nebraska. But another tribe came out in protest. They said that the journey brought back bad feelings about the government's treatment of them after Lewis and Clark's trip.

Changes to the Land

The Missouri River area called the Missouri Breaks, wrote one reporter, "still looks almost exactly as Lewis and Clark found it

200 years ago." But other places have changed much more. **D**

50 Many dams and other water projects have left marks. So has pollution from farms and industry.

Forests have been heavily cut and logged. There were 20 million acres of old-growth forest in Oregon and Washington. Now there are 2.3 million, according to one study.

Lewis and Clark recorded meeting a lot of wildlife, including killing 40 grizzlies. Today, these bears are dying out. There were as many as 100,000 from the Great Plains to the Pacific. Now they number about 1,000.

When Lewis and Clark's group first ate salmon in Oregon,
60 Clark drew a picture of the fish. There were about 30 million fish then. Today that number is closer to 300,000. **E**

A Longer Human Reach

Lewis and Clark's crew finished in September 1806, in St. Louis. In their day, that city's population was about 1,000. Today, wrote one reporter, "that's fewer than attend a lot of high school football games."

D (HERE'S HOW)

Reading Focus

The use of the word "but" in this sentence tells me that the next lines will **contrast**, or show differences between, the two journeys.

E (READ AND DISCUSS)

Comprehension

What other things do we learn about the two journeys?

© Robin Loznak/Great Falls Tribune/AP Photos

Reading Focus

How did the outcomes of the two trips **compare** to one another?

_____

_____

_____

_____

_____

_____

Reading Focus

Did the author use the **block method** or the **point-by-point method** in this article?

_____

_____

Reading Focus

The author finishes this story by **comparing** and **contrasting** mapmaking during both journeys. Why do you think the author includes this comparison?

_____

_____

_____

_____

_____

Lewis and Clark returned with important knowledge about the United States and the people who lived there. The new group also did much of what they had hoped to do. They increased excitement about this key journey in our country's history. **A B**

70

Maps Then and Now

The mapmaking tools of Lewis and Clark's time were called the octant and the sextant. These tools helped people figure out longitude and latitude using the sun, the moon, or a star. Lewis and Clark's group marked space by using tools that measured quarter miles. On water, they measured distance by throwing a chain ahead in the water and keeping track of the time it took to meet it.

Today, mapmaking is high tech. Satellites photograph the Earth, and computers analyze the pictures. Maps are created digitally from that information. Global Positioning System satellites

80 can even locate your position using beamed signals. **C**

Comprehension Wrap-Up

1. Why would so many people take part in a reenactment? What do you think they could gain from such an adventure?

© North Wind Picture Archives

Applying Your Skills

Lewis and Clark Revisited

INFORMATIONAL TEXT FOCUS: COMPARISON-AND-CONTRAST ORGANIZATION

DIRECTIONS: Fill in the following Venn Diagram to **compare** and **contrast** the journeys of the Corps of Discovery and the Discovery Expedition. Write things that are the same where the two ovals overlap, and write things that are different in the oval with the correct title.

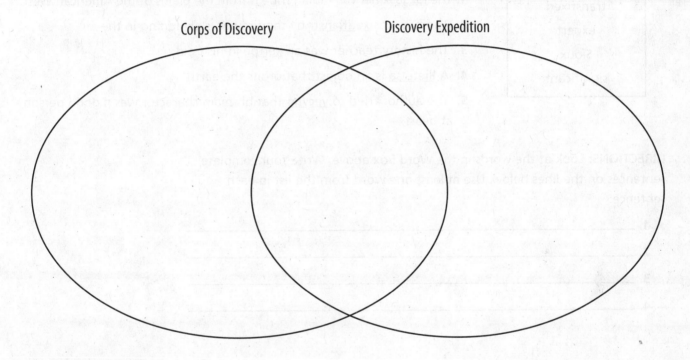

Corps of Discovery   Discovery Expedition

VOCABULARY REVIEW

DIRECTIONS: Fill in the blanks with the correct words from the Word Box. Not all words will be used.

Word Box

reenactment

expedition

satellite

1. The Discovery _____ was a _____ of Lewis and Clark's journey with the Corps of Discovery.

2. Today, mapmakers have many different tools to help them, such as a _____, which sends information from space.

Skills Review

Collection 3

Word Box

- reservation
- satellite
- vision
- convey
- transfixed
- expert
- Sioux
- significant

VOCABULARY REVIEW

DIRECTIONS: Somehow, the underlined word in each sentence got scrambled! Use the Word Box to the left to help you unscramble the correct vocabulary word in each sentence. Write the unscrambled vocabulary word above the scrambled word.

1. The <u>ioxuS</u> American Indian tribe is from the plains of the American West.

2. The boy was <u>xedfianstr</u> by the fireworks exploding in the air.

3. The history teacher was an <u>xertpe</u> in his field.

4. A <u>llietetsa</u> is an object that orbits the earth

5. The author tried to <u>yecvno</u> that his main character was a good person at heart.

DIRECTIONS: Look at the words in the Word Box above. Write four complete sentences on the lines below. Use at least one word from the list in each sentence.

1. _____

2. _____

3. _____

4. _____

Language Review

Collection 3

LANGUAGE COACH: WORD ORIGINS

DIRECTIONS: In French, the ending sounds of certain words are dropped, or not pronounced. Review the following terms from your reading and circle the one in which the last two letters are silent.

expedition   cirrus   transfixed   experts   corps

WRITING ACTIVITY

DIRECTIONS: Write a paragraph in which you identify the common **theme** of "A Shot At It," "How I Learned English," and "Ed McMahon is Iranian." Give examples from the selections that reveal the theme. In addition to the word *theme*, use the following words in your paragraph: *idea* or *meaning*, *conflict*, and *character*.

_____

_____

_____

_____

_____

_____

_____

_____

Style

Literary and Academic Vocabulary for Collection 4

LITERARY VOCABULARY

dialect (DY UH LEHKT) *n.:* a way a language is spoken in a particular place or among a particular group of people.
The dialect of people from New York is different than the dialect of people from Texas.

conclusion (KUN KLOO SHUN) *n.:* final thought or judgment about something.
After reading the story, I drew the conclusion that the author was strongly against using computers. He always used a typewriter instead.

paraphrase (PEAR A FRAYZ) *v.:* restate a text in your own words.
When I paraphrase an article, I can better understand what the writer is saying.

ACADEMIC VOCABULARY

distinctive (DIHS TIHNGK TIHV) *adj.:* special; different from others.
As a unique author, he writes with a distinctive style.

establish (EHS TAB LIHSH) *v.:* bring about; set up.
She practiced writing frequently to establish her style.

impact (IHM PAKT) *n.:* strong effect.
The writer's word choice had a big impact on the story.

impression (IHM PREHSH UHN) *n.:* idea or mental image.
I had the impression that the writer wanted to shock readers with the surprise ending.

The Tell-Tale Heart

Based on the story by Edgar Allan Poe

LITERARY FOCUS: IRONY

Irony is a literary term. It is used to describe when what the characters and readers expect to happen differs from what actually happens. "The Tell-Tale Heart" is a scary story, and Edgar Allan Poe's use of irony makes it even scarier. Look for all three types of irony in Poe's short story:

- **Verbal irony**: Saying the opposite of what is meant.

- **Situational irony**: When something happens that is the opposite of what was expected.

- **Dramatic irony**: When the reader knows something that a character does not know.

READING FOCUS: PARAPHRASING A TEXT

Poe is known for writing with very confusing language. One way to better understand Poe is to pause every now and then and **paraphrase**. When you paraphrase, you restate what you have read in your own words. Doing so makes a difficult story easier to understand. One example is provided below.

Original Text	Paraphrase
"It was his eye! One of his eyes looked like a vulture's. It was a pale blue eye with a film over it. His glance made my blood run cold."	He had a creepy blue eye, and I felt scared every time he looked at me.

VOCABULARY

Work with a partner to practice using these words in complete sentences.

shrieked (SHREEKD) *v.*: screamed (in a high pitch).

corpse (KAWRPS) *n.*: a dead body.

chatted (CHAT TED) *v.*: spoke in a relaxed manner.

INTO THE STORY

Edgar Allan Poe is famous for his horror and mystery stories. His life was short and tragic. Many of Poe's stories deal with dark themes. Poe is known for writing about the darkness in the human heart and mind.

SKILLS FOCUS

Literary Skills
Understand irony.

Reading Skills
Paraphrase material from a text.

THE TELL-TALE HEART

Based on the story by Edgar Allan Poe

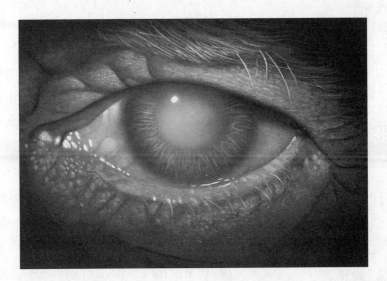

True! I had been very, very nervous, and I still am. But why do you call me insane? The disease has improved my senses, particularly my hearing. I heard everything in heaven and in earth—and even in hell. See how calmly I can tell you the whole story. **A**

I can't say how I came up with the idea, but once I'd thought of it, I could think of nothing else. I loved the old man. He had never hurt or insulted me. I didn't want his gold.

It was his eye! One of his eyes looked like a vulture's.[1] It was a pale blue eye with a film[2] over it. His glance made my blood run cold. So I decided to kill him and get rid of the eye forever.

Now this is the point. You think I am crazy. You should have seen how carefully I made plans! I hid my feelings well. Shortly before I killed the old man, I was kinder to him than I'd ever been. **B**

About midnight every night for a week, I turned the door-knob—oh, so gently! Then, I made an opening for my head. In the opening, I put a lantern with the light covered. Next, I stuck my head through the opening. I moved very, very slowly because I didn't want to wake up the old man.

10

---

1. **vulture** (VUHL CHUHR): large bird that eats the flesh of dead animals.
2. **film**: a thin coating.

A (**READ AND DISCUSS**)

Comprehension

This paragraph is a bit confusing. What have we learned so far?

B (**HERE'S HOW**)

Literary Focus

I would not expect the narrator to be nice to someone he is planning to kill. I think this is an example of **irony**.

A **HERE'S HOW**

Reading Focus

To better understand the text, I can **paraphrase** this paragraph: I opened my lantern to see the eye. Every night, the eye was closed. I could not kill the man until I saw his eye.

B **READ AND DISCUSS**

Comprehension

How are things looking for the narrator now?

C **YOUR TURN**

Reading Focus

Paraphrase lines 42–43.

_____

_____

_____

_____

D **YOUR TURN**

Literary Focus

Why is it **ironic** that the narrator feels terrified, as well?

_____

_____

_____

_____

20 It took me an hour to get my head where I could see him. Ha! Would a madman have been as wise as this? Then, I carefully opened the lantern cover so I could see the vulture eye. But every night, the eye was closed. I could not kill him until I saw his Evil Eye. **A**

Every morning, I asked how he had slept. So you see, he would have to have been a smart man to suspect me. On the eighth night, I was so still that a watch's minute hand moves faster than my hand. Before this moment, I had never felt how powerful and wise I was. The old man moved on the bed suddenly, as if he had been startled.[3]

30 Now, you may think that I drew back, but I knew that he could not see the door opening in the dark. Finally, I had my head in. My thumb slipped on the lantern's cover. The old man cried out, "Who's there?" **B**

I kept still for a whole hour. During that time the old man sat up in bed, listening. Then, I heard a groan of terror. At midnight on many nights, I have made that sound. I pitied the old man, but my heart chuckled.

I knew that he had been lying awake since the first noise. He had been growing more and more afraid. But there was no

40 escape. The presence of Death made him _feel_ my head in the room.

I waited for a long time, very patiently. I aimed the light only on the old man's vulture eye. It was wide open. **C**

Now, I have told you that I am not mad. Rather, my senses are too sharp. So I began to hear a low, dull, quick sound, like a watch wrapped in cotton. I knew _that_ sound too well. It was the beating of the old man's heart. It made me even angrier, like a drumbeat makes a soldier braver.

I held the light on the eye, but the sound of the heart grew

50 quicker and louder. He _must_ have been terrified![4] The noise terrified me, too. **D** I thought the heart would burst. And now I became afraid that a neighbor might hear the sound.

---

3. **startled** (STAHR TLD): surprised and frightened.
4. **terrified** (TEH RUH FYD): filled with great fear.

©Culver Pictures, Inc.

With a loud yell, I leaped into the bedroom. The old man shrieked only once. **E** In an instant, I dragged him to the floor and pulled the heavy bed over him. Then, I smiled because the deed[5] was done.

But, for a while, the heart beat on with a muffled[6] sound. Finally, it stopped. The old man was dead. I held my hand over his heart for many minutes but felt no heartbeat. He was stone

60   dead. His eye would trouble me no more.

Do you still think I'm mad? Consider how I hid the body. First, I cut up the corpse. **F** Next, I took up three boards from the bedroom floor and hid the body parts there. There were no bloodstains. I had caught all the blood in a tub. When I finished, it was four o'clock. I answered a knock at the door with nothing to fear. **G**

Three police officers entered. The officers had come because a neighbor had reported a shriek in the night.

I smiled. What did I have to fear? I said I had shrieked

70   from a dream. Saying the old man was away, I let them search the house. Then, I led them to *his* bedroom and brought chairs. I wanted them to rest *here*. I put my own chair over the place where I'd buried the old man.

---

5. **deed:** an act.
6. **muffled** (MUH FUHLD): covered up; made less loud.

E   HERE'S HOW

Vocabulary

I think that *shrieked* means "screamed." My teacher also tells me that a *shriek* is "a high pitched scream."

F   YOUR TURN

Vocabulary

What is a *corpse*? Circle the word in line 61 that gives you a clue about the meaning of *corpse*.

G   READ AND DISCUSS

Comprehension

The narrator gives a detailed description of how he handled the body and the crime scene. What point is he trying to make?

My *manner*[7] had convinced the officers. We all chatted happily, but soon, I felt myself get pale. **A** **B** My head ached, and my ears seemed to ring. I kept talking, but the feelings got worse. Soon, I realized the noise was *not* within my ears.

I am sure that I now grew *very* pale. I talked faster and louder, but the sound grew. *It sounded like a watch wrapped in cotton.* I gasped for breath. The officers didn't hear the noise. I talked faster; the noise grew.

I stood up and paced the floor, waving my arms as I argued about nothing. But the noise steadily grew. I dragged my chair over the floorboards, but the noise arose over all and grew louder and louder and *louder*!

Still the officers chatted and smiled. Was it possible they could not hear it? Almighty God!—no, no! They heard! They suspected! They *knew!* They were making a cruel joke of my horror! Anything was better than their knowing smiles. I could bear it no more. I felt I must scream or die! And now! Again—listen! louder! louder! *louder*!

"Villains!"[8] I shrieked. "Pretend no more! I admit the deed! Tear up the floorboards! Here! Here! It is the beating of his hideous[9] heart!" **C** **D**

Comprehension Wrap-Up

1. Discuss whether you think the narrator is mad or very wise.

2. What is the role of the old man's beating heart?

3. How does Poe's language and attention to detail help set the mood to this story?

---

7. **manner:** way of behaving.
8. **villains** (VIH LUHNZ): wicked people.
9. **hideous** (HIH DEE UHS): very ugly; disgusting.

Applying Your Skills

The Tell-Tale Heart

LITERARY FOCUS: IRONY

DIRECTIONS: Review the different types of **irony** discussed on the Preparing to Read page. Then provide one example of each type of irony from the story in the chart below.

Verbal irony	Situational irony	Dramatic irony
1.	2.	3.

READING FOCUS: PARAPHRASING A TEXT

DIRECTIONS: Practice **paraphrasing** by restating the sentences below from "The Tell-Tale Heart" in your own words.

Original Text	My Paraphrase
Line 61: "Do you still think I'm mad? Consider how I hid the body."	1.
Lines 89–91: "I could bear it no more. I felt I must scream or die. And now! Again—listen! louder! louder! *louder*!	2.

VOCABULARY REVIEW

DIRECTIONS: Fill in the blanks with the correct words from the Word Box.

Word Box

shrieked

corpse

chatted

1. The narrator felt confident that no one could find the old man's _____ where he hid it.

2. The old man and the narrator _____ over breakfast every morning.

3. The narrator _____ with rage as he attacked the old man.

Raymond's Run

Based on the story by Toni Cade Bambara

LITERARY FOCUS: LITERARY DEVICES: DIALECT

Dialect is a way of speaking that is typical of a certain place or a certain group of people. For example, if you live in New York, you might think that people in Texas have a different way of speaking English. They might think that you sound different, too! You are both noticing differences in dialect. Everyone speaks a dialect of some kind. Even if your dialect is close to standard English, it will probably still show regional or group difference. When you read this story, pay attention to Squeaky's dialect.

READING FOCUS: ANALYZING DETAILS

The story's main character, Squeaky, speaks fast and has a lot to say. If you read the story quickly, you may miss some of her points. You can prevent this by **analyzing details**. When you analyze details, you look closely at parts of a text as you read. This helps you understand what is really being said. As you read, keep a chart like the one below.

Text	Analysis
"There is no track meet that I don't win the first place medal. I'm the swiftest thing in the neighborhood."	Squeaky is very fast. She is also very proud of her running.

VOCABULARY

Work with a partner to practice using these words in complete sentences.

chicken (CHIK UHN) *adj.*: cowardly.

break (BREYK) *n.*: a chance.

fly (FLAHY) *v.*: go really fast.

INTO THE STORY

Toni Cade Bambara grew up in New York City. "Raymond's Run" takes place in Harlem, a part of New York City. Bambara's stories tell about the people of Harlem and the way of life in the big city.

SKILLS FOCUS

Literary Skills
Understand dialect.

Reading Skills
Analyze details.

RAYMOND'S RUN

Based on the story by Toni Cade Bambara

HRW Photo by Debra LaCappola and Charles Meier

I don't have to work around the house like some girls. All I have to do is mind my brother Raymond, which is enough. **A**

Raymond needs looking after because he's not quite right. A lot of rude people have lots to say about Raymond, but they have to say it to me. I'd much rather knock you down than talk, even though I'm small and have a squeaky voice. That's how I got my name. Squeaky. If things get rough, I run. I'm the fastest thing on two feet. **B**

There is no track meet that I don't win the first-place medal.

10 **C** I'm the swiftest thing in the neighborhood. That goes for Gretchen, too. She says that she is going to win the first-place medal this year. What a joke. No one can beat me.

I'm walking down Broadway practicing my breathing. Raymond pretends he's driving a stagecoach.[1] That's OK by me. So long as he doesn't stop my breathing exercises. I'm serious about my running.

---

1. **stagecoach:** in the early days of our country, a coach, or carriage, that carried passengers and mail and was pulled by horses.

"Raymond's Run" adapted from *Gorilla, My Love* by Toni Cade Bambara. Copyright © 1971 by Toni Cade Bambara. For on-line information about other Random House, Inc. books and authors, see the Internet website at http://www.randomhouse.com. Retold by Holt, Rinehart and Winston. Reproduced by permission of **Random House, Inc.**

A HERE'S HOW

Language Coach

Mind is a word with **multiple**, or more than one, meanings. I have heard the word *mind* as a noun meaning "brain" before. However, in line 2 it is used as a verb. In this case, I think *mind* means "to take care of."

B HERE'S HOW

Reading Focus

By **analyzing details** in the first two paragraphs, I learn that Squeaky is fast and caring. She looks out for her brother and she is not afraid to stand up for him.

C HERE'S HOW

Literary Focus

I like this story because it is as if I can hear Squeaky's voice. Take line 9, for example. In standard English, I might write: "I win first-place medals in all track meets." But, the way Squeaky says it makes her seem like a real person talking in a real **dialect**.

A **READ AND DISCUSS**

Comprehension

Why does Squeaky talk about running so much?

B **YOUR TURN**

Literary Focus

Underline the word in this sentence that is part of Squeaky's **dialect**. Then rewrite the whole sentence in standard English.

_____

_____

_____

C **HERE'S HOW**

Vocabulary

Squeaky uses a lot of slang. For example, she uses the word *chicken* in line 29 to mean "cowardly."

D **READ AND DISCUSS**

Comprehension

How does this scene with the three girls add to what we know about Squeaky?

E **YOUR TURN**

Reading Focus

By **analyzing details**, what can you say about Squeaky and Raymond's relationship?

_____

_____

_____

Some people act like things come easy to them. Take Cynthia Procter. She just won the spelling bee for the millionth time. "A good thing you got 'receive,' Squeaky," she says. "I would
20 have got it wrong. I forgot to study." I could kill people like that. I stay up all night studying the words for the spelling bee. And I practice running whenever I can. **A**

So I'm walking down Broadway breathing out and in. Along come Gretchen and her two buddies. Mary Louise used to be a friend of mine. Rosie is as fat as I am skinny. She has a big mouth about Raymond. But there's not much difference between herself and Raymond. She can't afford to throw stones. So they are coming up Broadway and the street ain't that wide. **B** I could let them pass, but that's chicken. **C** As they get to me,
30 they slow down. I'm ready to fight.

"You signing up for the May Day races?" smiles Mary Louise. Only it's not a real smile.

"You're not going to win this time," says Rosie. I've beat her up many times for insults[2] smaller than that.

"I always win because I'm the best." I say it straight at Gretchen. Gretchen smiles, but it's not a smile. They all look at Raymond bringing his stagecoach to a stop.

"What grade you in now, Raymond?"

"You got anything to say to my brother, Mary Louise
40 Williams? You just say it to me."

"You his mother?" Rosie says back to me.

"That's right, fatso. If anybody says another word, I'll be their mother." They stand there. Gretchen stands first on one leg and then the other. She's about to say something but doesn't. She walks around me looking me up and down. Then she keeps walking, and her two buddies follow her. **D** Me and Raymond smile at each other. **E** He says, "Gidyap." I keep on walking and doing my breathing exercises.

I take my time getting to the park on May Day. The track
50 meet is the last thing on the program.[3] The biggest thing on the

---

2. **insults** (IHN SUHLTS): rude or impolite words or actions.
3. **program** (PROH GRAM): the order of events.

128 Raymond's Run

program is the May Pole dancing.[4] I can do without that, thank you. Who wants to be dancing around a May Pole? Getting all dirty and sweaty, acting like a fairy or flower in a new white dress and shoes. You should be yourself. For me that means being a poor black girl who can't afford fancy shoes and a dress. **F**

I was once a strawberry in a nursery school play. I danced with my arms over my head. As expected, my mother and father came dressed up and clapped. You'd think they'd know better. I am not a strawberry. I do not dance. I run. That is what I am all about. So I always come late to the May Day program. I get my number pinned on. Then, I lay in the grass till they call out the fifty-yard dash.

I put Raymond in the little swings on the other side of the fence. Then here comes Mr. Pearson, dropping things all over the place. "Well, Squeaky," he says, checking my name off the list. He hands me number seven and two pins.

"Hazel Elizabeth Deborah Parker." I tell him to write it down on his list.

"Going to give someone else a break this year?"

I look at him real hard. Is he joking? I should lose the race on purpose? Grown-ups got a lot of nerve sometimes. I pin on number seven and stomp away. **G**

The man on the loudspeaker announces the fifty-yard dash. Gretchen is at the starting line. I get into place. I see Raymond on the other side of the fence. He is bending down with his fingers on the ground. Just like he knew what he was doing.

---

4. **May Pole dancing:** dancing around a tall pole decorated with ribbons and flowers to celebrate May Day, a springtime festival that often features sports and games.

F READ AND DISCUSS

Comprehension
How does Squeaky's description of the May Pole dancing add to our image of her?

G YOUR TURN

Vocabulary
Re-read lines 68–71. What do you think the word *break* means in line 65?

_____

_____

_____

A HERE'S HOW

Vocabulary

The word *fly* in line 78 can mean "an insect" or "go really fast." Here I think it means "go really fast" because Squeaky is telling how fast she is running.

B READ AND DISCUSS

Comprehension

What is happening with Squeaky, Gretchen, and the race results?

C HERE'S HOW

Literary Focus

Squeaky is talking in **dialect** when she says, "I'm the baddest thing around." In this dialect, *bad* means "good."

D YOUR TURN

Reading Focus

After the race, Squeaky begins to rethink what is important to her. What can you say about Squeaky by **analyzing details** in this paragraph?

_____

_____

_____

_____

_____

_____

I spread my fingers in the dirt and crouch on my toes. I am telling myself, Squeaky you must win. You are the fastest thing in the world. At the sound of the pistol, I am off. I fly past the
80 other runners. **A** My arms pump up and down. I glance to my left. No one. To the right, a blurred Gretchen. On the other side of the fence, Raymond is running. His arms are down to his side and the palms tucked up behind him. It's the first time I ever saw that. I almost stop to watch my brother Raymond on his first run. But I keep going and tear past the white ribbon.

I lean down to catch my breath. Here comes Gretchen. She's gone past the finish line and is coming back. She's taking it slow, breathing in steady. I sort of like her a little for the first time. "In first place . . . ," the man on the loudspeaker pauses. I stare at Gretchen. She stares back. We both are wondering who won. **B**
90 Raymond is yanking at the fence. Then like a dancer or something, he starts climbing up nice and easy. I notice how smoothly he climbs hand over hand. I remember how he looked running with his arms down to his side. It came to me that Raymond would make a very fine runner. And now I'm smiling. I'm thinking it doesn't matter who wins the race. I'd rather be a coach with Raymond as my champion. After all, with a little more study I can beat Cynthia at the spelling bee. And everyone says I'm the baddest thing around. **C** I've got a roomful of ribbons and medals and awards. But what has Raymond got to call his own? **D**
100 I'm laughing out loud by this time. Raymond jumps down from the fence. He runs over with his arms down to the side. No one before him has this running style. My brother Raymond, a great runner. The man on the loudspeaker is announcing, "In first place—Miss Hazel Elizabeth Deborah Parker. In second place— Miss Gretchen P. Lewis." I look at her and I smile. Because she's good, no doubt about it. Then she smiles. We stand there with this real smile of respect between us. We don't practice real smiling every day. Maybe we are too busy being flowers or fairies or strawberries instead of something honest and worthy of
110 respect . . . you know . . . like being people.

Raymond's Run

LITERARY FOCUS: LITERARY DEVICES: DIALECT

DIRECTIONS: In the chart below, rewrite the phrases of Squeaky's **dialect** in standard English.

Squeaky's Dialect	My Translation
Lines 25–27: "[Rosie] has a big mouth about Raymond. But there's not much difference between herself and Raymond. She can't afford to throw stones."	1.
Line 42–43: "That's right, fatso. If anybody says another word, I'll be their mother."	2.

READING FOCUS: ANALYZING DETAILS

DIRECTIONS: Using the **details** you analyzed while reading the story, write a short paragraph telling what you learned about Squeaky and her brother.

_____

_____

_____

_____

VOCABULARY REVIEW

DIRECTIONS: Fill in the blanks with the correct words from the Word Box.

Word Box

chicken

break

fly

As the runners lined up for the race, Squeaky was ready to

(1) _____; she planned to run as fast as possible. Despite

what Mr. Pearson had asked, she did not plan on giving anyone a

(2) _____. When she saw Raymond running along the

fence, Squeaky thought about stopping to watch him, but she did not want

to be called (3) _____ for not finishing the race.

from Ray Bradbury Is on Fire!, The Flying Machine, *and* The Dragon

LITERARY FOCUS: LITERARY CRITICISM: BIOGRAPHICAL APPROACH

Writers often take a **biographical approach**, or draw on their own backgrounds, to create a story. The setting may be a place they visited on vacation. The characters may be based on people they know. The themes of a story also sometimes reflect ideas important to the author. For example, it is easy to see how Ray Bradbury's interest in technology influences the stories you are about to read.

READING FOCUS: DRAWING CONCLUSIONS

Drawing conclusions means making judgments about something. When you read, you draw conclusions about the text using the evidence the author presents to you. Imagine reading a story set in New York City that includes the names of actual streets and stores. After reading, you will probably draw the conclusion that the author is very familiar with New York City.

VOCABULARY

With a partner, practice using these words in complete sentences.

bamboo (BAM BOO) *n.:* a type of woody grass.

criticize (KRIH TIH SYZ) *v.:* to consider and then judge something or someone, often negatively.

gird (GUHRD) *v.:* secure; make fast.

INTO THE STORIES

During more than 70 years of writing, author Ray Bradbury has created more than 700 works. His stories usually involve fantasy, mystery, and magic. A theme running throughout his work is that science and technology should help, not hurt, human beings. The first selection is taken from an interview with Bradbury. The next two selections are short stories: a fairy tale set in China long ago and a graphic story about two knights.

SKILLS FOCUS

Literary Focus
Understand a biographical approach to literary criticism.

Reading Focus
Draw conclusions.

from RAY BRADBURY IS ON FIRE!

Based on the interview by James Hibberd

Today, writer Ray Bradbury continues to complain about modern inventions. He is a science-fiction writer who's also afraid of technology. He famously claims to have never driven a car. Bradbury finds accident rates way too high. He also saw a deadly car

© Jean-Claude Amiel/Kipa/Corbis

10 accident when he was a teenager. He does not like the Internet. He doesn't even like computers. **A**

Bradbury's label as a science-fiction writer is incorrect. He makes fun of technologies that replace active thinking and contact between people. He does not care much about science or science-fiction. Bradbury is the author of more than thirty books, six hundred short stories, and many poems, essays, and plays. In his work, Bradbury supports things that are human and real. There is simply no easy label for a writer who mixes poetry and myths with fantasy and technology to create exciting tales that

20 also criticize society. **B** There is no bookstore section for an author whose stories appeal to twelve-year-olds, but who also stuns adult readers with his powerful understanding of human life. **C**

One secret to the huge amount Bradbury writes is that his ideas of play and work are the same. When asked, "How often do you write?" Bradbury replies, "Every day of my life." He says you have to be "in love" with your work. Otherwise, "you shouldn't do it."

A READ AND DISCUSS

Comprehension

What strikes you as interesting in this description of Ray Bradbury?

B HERE'S HOW

Vocabulary

I have heard *criticize* used many times, usually in a negative way. While *criticize* does mean "to find fault with," it can also mean "to consider something or someone and then judge them." Through his writing, Bradbury tries to make readers look closely at society.

C HERE'S HOW

Literary Focus

I know that Ray Bradbury does not like science that much, even though he writes about it a lot. He seems to be more interested in how science affects people. I will keep this **biographical** information in mind as I read his stories. Maybe I will be able to find this idea in one of the stories that follow this interview.

A HERE'S HOW

Language Coach

I know that the *w* is silent in the word *writer*. Other words like *wrap* and *wrist* are also pronounced with a silent *w*. Learning pronunciations like these is important for building **oral fluency**.

B READ AND DISCUSS

Comprehension

What is Bradbury saying about his manner of working?

C YOUR TURN

Reading Focus

Re-read lines 53–56. What **conclusion** could you draw about what Bradbury thinks of people who do not read?

_____

_____

_____

_____

_____

_____

D READ AND DISCUSS

Comprehension

What is the value of reading for Bradbury?

I phoned Bradbury's Los Angeles home for a 9:00 A.M.

30 interview. He told me he'd already written a short story.

James Hibberd. **What makes a great story?**

Ray Bradbury. If you're a storyteller, that's what makes a great story.

James Hibberd. **You've been critical of computers in the past. But what about programs that aid creativity? Do you think using a word processor handicaps a writer?** **A**

Ray Bradbury. There is no one way of writing. Pad and pencil, wonderful. Typewriter, wonderful. It doesn't matter what you use. In the last month I've written a new screenplay with a pad and

40 pen. There's no one way to be creative. Any way will work. **B**

James Hibberd. **What's an average workday like for you?**

Ray Bradbury. Well, I've already got my work done. At 7:00 A.M., I wrote a short story.

James Hibberd. **How long does that usually take?**

Ray Bradbury. Usually about a morning. If an idea isn't exciting you shouldn't do it. I usually get an idea when I'm getting up, and by noon it's finished. As quickly as you can, you react to an idea. That's how I write short stories. They've all been done in a single morning.

50 **James Hibberd.** **There's so much competition for a young person's attention nowadays. For the record, why is reading still important?**

Ray Bradbury. Are you kidding? You can't have a civilization without that, can you? If you can't read and write you can't think. You've got to be able to look at your thoughts on paper and discover what a fool you were. **C** **D**

Comprehension Wrap-Up

1. How do the descriptions "afraid of technology" and "science-fiction writer" affect our understanding of Bradbury?

2. Describe Bradbury's thoughts on why reading is important.

THE FLYING MACHINE

Based on the story by Ray Bradbury

In the year A.D. 400, the Emperor Yuan lived near the Great Wall of China. The land he ruled was green with rain. The country was at peace. His people were not too happy or too sad. **A**

Early in the year, a servant ran to Emperor Yuan. The servant cried, "Oh, Emperor, it is a miracle!"

"Let me guess," said the Emperor. "The sun has risen and a new day is here. Or the sea is blue. *That* is the finest of all miracles."

"Your Highness, a man is flying. I saw him in the air, flying with wings. It looked like a dragon in the heavens with a man in

10 its mouth. But it was a dragon made of paper and bamboo."

"You have just woken up from a dream," said the Emperor.

"I have seen what I have seen!" said the servant. "Come, and you will see it too."

They walked across a field of grass, over a small bridge, and up a tiny hill.

"There!" said the servant.

And in the sky, very high up, was a man. He was wearing bright papers and bamboo sticks that made wings and a beautiful tail. He was flying around like a large bird or a young dragon. **B**

20 The man called down to them, "I fly, I fly!"

The servant waved. "Yes, *yes!*"

The Emperor Yuan did not move. Instead he looked at the Great Wall of China in the faraway hills. **C** For many years, that wonderful wall had protected them from enemy armies and kept the peace.

"Tell me," he said to his servant, "has anyone else seen this flying man?"

"I am the only one, Your Highness," said the smiling servant.

The Emperor watched another minute. Then he said, "Call

30 him down to me."

A READ AND DISCUSS

Comprehension

What has the author told us about this Emperor and his people?

B YOUR TURN

Vocabulary

Bamboo is "a type of woody grass." Lines 17–19 explain that the man is able to fly using a machine made of only paper and bamboo. Knowing what you do of paper, what do you think is a quality of bamboo?

_____

_____

C HERE'S HOW

Reading Focus

I can tell that the Emperor is not as happy as his servant is about the flying man. I can **draw this conclusion** because I am told that the Emperor does not move when he sees the man. The Emperor looks away. I wonder why he is not excited. As I continue reading, I will have to look for details that answer this question.

A YOUR TURN

Reading Focus

What **conclusion** can you draw about how well the flying man understands the Emperor's reaction to the flying machine? Underline the evidence that supports this conclusion.

_____

_____

_____

_____

B READ AND DISCUSS

Comprehension

What does the conversation between the Emperor and the flying man tell us about the Emperor's thoughts?

C YOUR TURN

Literary Focus

In "Ray Bradbury Is on Fire!" you read that Bradbury is "a science-fiction writer who's also afraid of technology." How does this **biographical** information connect to what the Emperor says here?

_____

_____

_____

_____

"Come down! The Emperor wishes to see you!" called the servant. He had to shout.

The flying man landed. He came proudly to the Emperor. Tripping over his outfit, the flier bowed before the old man. **A**

"What have you done?" asked the Emperor.

"I have flown in the sky, Your Highness," replied the man.

"You have told me nothing at all." The Emperor reached out a hand to touch the pretty paper and the birdlike wings of the invention.

40   "Is it not beautiful, Your Highness?"

"Yes, too beautiful."

"It is the only one in the world!" smiled the man. "And I am the inventor."

"Who else knows of this?"

"No one. Not even my wife. She thought I was making a kite. I rose in the night and walked to the cliffs far away. And when the morning breezes blew and the sun rose, I leaped from the cliff. I flew! But my wife does not know."

"Good for her, then," said the Emperor. "Come along." **B**

50   They walked back to the great house. The Emperor, the servant, and the flier paused within the huge garden.

The Emperor clapped his hands. "Guards!"

The guards came running.

"Hold this man. And call the executioner," said the Emperor. The executioner came running with a sharp silver ax.

"What's this!" cried the flier. "What have I done?" He began to cry.

"Here is the man who has made a certain machine," said the Emperor. "Yet he does not know what he has created. He

60 only wanted to create, without knowing why or what this thing will do." **C**

The Emperor turned to a nearby table. On it sat a machine that he himself had created. It looked like a garden of metal and jewels. The Emperor took a tiny golden key from around his neck. He put the key into the tiny machine and wound it up.

©Christie's Images/Corbis

The machine began to move. The birds sang in tiny metal trees, wolves walked through little forests, and tiny people listened to the tiny birds.

"Isn't it beautiful?" said the Emperor. "If you asked me what
70 I have done here, I could answer you. I have made birds sing. I have made forests hum. I have set people to walking in this forest, enjoying the songs. That is what I have done."

"But Emperor!" cried the flier. He dropped to his knees. "I have done the same thing! I have found beauty. I have soared like a bird. I cannot say how beautiful it is up there, in the sky, with the wind around me. The sky smells wonderful! And how free one feels! *That* is beautiful, Emperor!" **D**

"Yes," said the Emperor sadly. "I know it must be true. I felt my heart move with you in the air. But there are times when one
80 must lose a little beauty to save other beauty. I do not fear you, but I fear another man. Some other man will see you and build a thing of bright papers and bamboo like this. But the other man will have an evil face and an evil heart, and the beauty will be gone. It is this man I fear."

"Why? Why?" asked the flier.

"Someday such a man, in a machine like yours, might fly in the sky and drop huge stones upon the Great Wall of China," said the Emperor. **E**

D READ AND DISCUSS

Comprehension

What is the flying man up to now?

E HERE'S HOW

Reading Focus

I see that the Emperor says the flier created something without knowing what it would do. Then he says he does not fear the flier. Instead, he fears another man who might use the machine to drop stones on the Great Wall. I can **draw the conclusion** that the Emperor ordered the man executed because he feared the flying machine could be used as a weapon against his country.

Comprehension

What do you think the Emperor means when he says, "What is the life of one man against those of a million others?"

B   YOUR TURN

Literary Focus

Think about the **biographical** information you know about Bradbury's views on technology. Why was a long-ago China a good setting for this story? Why do you think Bradbury chose not to set the story in a location he knew better, such as the United States?

_____

_____

_____

_____

_____

_____

_____

C   HERE'S HOW

Reading Focus

The Emperor seems to get a lot of pleasure from his own invention, especially the tiny birds. I know that he had the man who created the flying machine killed. Therefore, I can **draw the conclusion** that the Emperor feels that only birds should fly. I think that he is afraid of change in his peaceful country.

No one moved or said a word.

90   "Off with his head," said the Emperor.

The executioner swung his silver ax.

"Burn the kite and the inventor's body. Bury their ashes together," said the Emperor.

He turned to his servant who had seen the man flying. "Say nothing about this. It was all a dream. If

100   the story ever gets out, you will die."

"You are kind, Emperor," said the servant.

"No, not kind," said the old man. Beyond the garden wall he saw the guards burning the beautiful machine of paper and bamboo. "No, only confused and afraid." He saw the guards digging a pit to bury the ashes. "What is the life of one man against those of a million others? I must take comfort from that thought." **A**

He took the key from his neck and once more wound up the beautiful little garden. He stood looking out at the Great

110   Wall, the peaceful town, the green fields, the rivers and streams. He sighed. The tiny garden began to move. Tiny people walked in forests. Among the tiny trees flew little bits of bright blue and yellow color, flying in that small sky.

"Oh," said the Emperor, closing his eyes, "look at the birds, look at the birds!" **B C**

Comprehension Wrap-Up

1. The Emperor does not kill the servant who saw the flying machine but instead swears him to secrecy. Why does he not do the same thing for the man who created the flying machine?

2. Discuss the two inventions in this story. Why does the Emperor see the beauty only in his own invention?

THE DRAGON

By Ray Bradbury

GRAPHIC STORY

Here is what Ray Bradbury has said about "The Dragon":

Chinese lacquered art with dragon representation.

It is hard to talk about 'The Dragon' without giving away its secret, telling you the surprise. So all I can talk about is the boy I was that became the young man who thought about, and the older man who wrote, this story. I loved dinosaurs from the age of five, when I saw the film *The Lost World,* filled with prehistoric monsters. I became even more enamored with these beasts when at age thirteen, *King Kong* fell off the Empire State and landed on me in the front row of the Elite Theater. I never recovered. Later, I met and became friends with Ray Harryhausen, who built and film-animated dinosaurs in his garage when we were both eighteen. We dedicated our lives to these monsters, to dragons in all their shapes and forms. Simultaneously, we loved airplanes, rocket ships, trolley cars, and trains. From this amalgam of loves came our lives and careers. We wound up doing *The Beast from 20,000 Fathoms* as our first film. Not very good, but a beginning. He went on to *Mighty Joe Young* and I to *Moby Dick* and its great sea-beast. When I was in my thirties I wrote 'The Dragon' and combined two of these loves. You'll have to read the story to find out which ones. Read on. **B**

Ray

Introduction to *The Dragon* (Graphic Version) by Ray Bradbury with art by Vicente Segrelles. Copyright © 1955 and renewed © 1983 by Ray Bradbury. Reproduced by permission of **Don Congdon Associates, Inc.**

438 Unit 1 · Collection 4

A HERE'S HOW

Literary Focus

This introduction quotes Ray Bradbury talking about his story "The Dragon." But instead of talking about the story itself, he talks about himself as a young boy. This tells me that the **biographical** information he is giving is going to show up in the story somehow.

B YOUR TURN

Literary Focus

Underline three pieces of **biographical** information that Bradbury reveals in this introduction.

IN OTHER WORDS When I was a boy, I fell in love with dinosaurs and other monsters. Later, I became friends with an artist who built and filmed dinosaurs in his garage. We also loved airplanes, rocket ships, and trains. Our lives and careers followed these interests.

Vocabulary

You are told that by the time the sun rises, the people the dragon has killed are "strewn hither-thither." *Strewn* means "spread by scattering" and *hither-thither* loosely means "here and there." What does this description tell you about the way the dragon treats his victims?

_____

_____

_____

B READ AND DISCUSS

Comprehension

What has the author set up for us with the knights' conversation?

The Dragon **439**

IN OTHER WORDS Two knights are talking about how the swamp they are in is a very scary place.

IN OTHER WORDS There is a dragon that no one can beat. However, the knights decide they are going to try to beat it!

C | **YOUR TURN**

Reading Focus

One of the knights tells the other to "gird on your armor" if he is afraid. *Gird* means "to secure." If the knight is telling the other man to put on and secure his armor, what **conclusion** can you draw about the meaning of *armor*?

_____

_____

_____

D | **READ AND DISCUSS**

Comprehension

What information has the author given us in these first four panels?

E | **YOUR TURN**

Vocabulary

Review how the phrase *in transit* is used in the description at the bottom of this page. What other words do you know that begin with *trans-*? What do the meanings of these words have in common? Knowing this, guess what *in transit* means. Check your answer in a dictionary.

_____

_____

A   YOUR TURN

Vocabulary

Centuries ago, knights wore *mail*, or a metal covering, to protect themselves in battle. They also used *lances*, or steel-tipped spears. Knowing this, describe in your own words what the knights do in the fourth box on this page.

_____

_____

_____

_____

B   YOUR TURN

Reading Focus

The last box on the page describes how the dragon approaches the knights. What **conclusions** can you draw about what the dragon will do next? Circle the verbs that help you do this.

_____

_____

_____

C   READ AND DISCUSS

Comprehension

How do the illustrations help build suspense?

IN OTHER WORDS The dragon is coming closer and closer to the knights. The two knights race off to attack the great dragon.

142   **The Dragon**

C HERE'S HOW

Vocabulary

I am not sure what *brunt* means in the last box on this page. But I do know that the "brunt" of the dragon's shoulder was strong enough to throw the knight and his horse 100 feet. I know that it would take a lot of force to do this. Maybe *brunt* means something like "force." I will check this definition in a dictionary.

D READ AND DISCUSS

Comprehension

What has happened to the knights?

IN OTHER WORDS The dragon comes toward the knights as they attack. One of the knights is knocked off his horse by the dragon.

Comprehension

How do the train engineers figure into a story about knights and a mighty dragon?

B (HERE'S HOW)

Reading Focus

I was surprised when a train suddenly appeared on the last page of this story. At first I did not understand what the train had to do with the dragon and the knights. But then I realized that the train was actually what the knights thought was the dragon. The conversation between the train engineers gave me the evidence for this **conclusion**. That must be what Ray Bradbury meant when he said in the introduction that he "put together two of these loves." He wanted to write about dragons and he wanted to write about trains.

The Dragon **443**

IN OTHER WORDS What the knights have thought is a dragon turns out to actually be a train! The men on the train see the knights get hit. However, there is nothing they can do about it. The train keeps moving along.

Applying Your Skills

from Ray Bradbury Is on Fire!, The Flying Machine, and The Dragon

COMPREHENSION WRAP-UP

1. Go back to the opening of "The Dragon." How does the knights' description of the dragon connect to the train?

2. How does the author create a convincing, frightening story with such an odd idea in "The Dragon"?

LITERARY FOCUS: LITERARY CRITICISM: BIOGRAPHICAL APPROACH

DIRECTIONS: Explain in two sentences or less how you think Ray Bradbury's feelings about technology affect his writing.

_____

_____

READING FOCUS: DRAWING CONCLUSIONS

DIRECTIONS: Find evidence from "Ray Bradbury Is On Fire!" and "The Flying Machine" that explains how you could reach each conclusion listed below.

Conclusion	Evidence
"Ray Bradbury Is on Fire!": One of the reasons why Ray Bradbury writes is to learn more about his own thoughts.	
"The Flying Machine": Ray Bradbury believes that inventors need to understand all of the different ways science can be used.	

Word Box

bamboo

criticize

gird

VOCABULARY REVIEW

DIRECTIONS: Each sentence below includes an underlined vocabulary word. Circle the sentence in which the underlined word is used correctly.

1. I gird the windows by pushing them open.

2. I never work with her because I know she will criticize my ideas.

Steam Rising: The Revolutionary Power of Paddleboats *and* Summaries of "Steam Rising"

Based on the magazine article by The World Almanac

INFORMATIONAL TEXT FOCUS: EVALUATING A SUMMARY

Summaries of informational texts exist in many places. You might read them in newspapers or magazines, in book reviews, or online. The purpose of these summaries is to give you a quick overview of an article. However, if a summary is not written correctly, you will not really understand what the article is about. When writing a summary, the writer should do the following:

1. Identify the article's title and author.

2. State the topic of the article.

3. State main ideas in the order they appear in the article.

4. Include details that support the main ideas, such as names of people and places and important dates.

5. Include quotation marks around any parts of the article that appear in the summary, whether it is one word or an entire paragraph.

VOCABULARY

Practice saying these words out loud.

twinkling (TWIN KLING) *n.:* an instant; originally, the time required to wink.

upriver (UP RIH VUHR) *adv.:* toward the source of a river.

method (MEH THUD) *n.:* way of doing or getting something.

INTO THE ARTICLE

The article you are about to read discusses the history of paddle steamboats in the United States. Today, very few boats are powered by steam. Ninety-five percent of the ships built now are powered by diesel fuel instead. Yet the history of the American steamboat remains alive. Tourist steamboats run up and down rivers in various part of the country, including Louisiana, Kentucky, and Wisconsin.

SKILLS FOCUS

Informational Text Skills
Compare an original text to a summary; evaluate a summary.

STEAM RISING: THE REVOLUTIONARY POWER OF PADDLEBOATS

Based on the magazine article by The World Almanac

"S-t-e-a-m-boat a-comin'!" and the scene changes! . . . all in a twinkling the dead town is alive and moving."
—from *Life on the Mississippi*, by Mark Twain **A**

In the days when paddle steamboats filled the Mississippi River, the famous writer Mark Twain wrote about his love of steamboats in *Life on the Mississippi*. Today, modern visitors still ride these old boats along U.S. rivers. Tourists enjoy the riverbank towns, the calm sound of the running water, and the feeling of being in a different time. **B**

Business Need

10   The steamboat was not invented for fun, however. The boat was made to help the country's businesses. Before paddle steamboats, going from Louisville, Kentucky, to New Orleans, Louisiana, took four-months. After their invention, business was able to move full steam ahead.

  Paddle steamboats were created for river travel. A giant wheel is built into the back or side of a boat with a flat bottom. This helps it move easily through shallow water. Burning wood or coal turns water into steam, and the steam turns the wheel.

  For many years, boats had been powered by sails that
20 depended on the wind. By the 1700s American leaders wanted boats that could travel upriver, against the wind. John Fitch came up with the idea of a steamboat as early as 1785. **C** In 1790, he

---

A (HERE'S HOW)

Language Coach

I have never heard of a *twinkling* before. But I have heard of *twinkle*. Mark Twain seems to be saying that the town changes really fast once the boat comes. Based on **context clues**, I think that *twinkling* must mean "moment." It makes sense to say "in a moment the dead town is alive."

B (READ AND DISCUSS)

Comprehension

What do we learn about modern-day travelers and the steamboat?

C (READ AND DISCUSS)

Comprehension

What was so special about the paddle steamboats?

A (READ AND DISCUSS)

Comprehension

How does this information connect to what you read on the first page?

B (HERE'S HOW)

Reading Focus

I wrote a **summary** of this article and I used this sentence. I showed that I borrowed the sentence by putting it in quotation marks, like this: "Fulton soon became rich."

C (READ AND DISCUSS)

Comprehension

What is the point of these statistics?

D (HERE'S HOW)

Reading Focus

If I were writing a **summary** of this article, I would have to include all of the main ideas. I know that every main idea in this article has to do with paddle steamboats. But each idea makes a different statement about these boats. To find each main idea and list it in the order it appears, I need to return to the beginning of the article and review each paragraph.

and a partner sent a model between two towns in Pennsylvania. But they could not raise enough money to build a full-size working steamboat.

Robert Fulton

Robert Fulton invented the first successful model. As a boy, Fulton spent time in shops that made machines. There, he trained in art as a teenager. After that he went to England and studied science. In 1802, with money from the U.S. official
30 Robert R. Livingston, Fulton sent a paddle steamboat up a French river.

Along with money, Livingston had steam in politics. He was able to get all rights to trade on New York's rivers by promising a ship that could go four miles per hour. Fulton kept that promise by building the *Clermont*. This boat ran at almost five miles per hour. The ship helped businesses send goods more quickly. Fulton soon became rich. **A** **B**

River Trade

Early steamboats were sometimes dangerous. But builders learned from mistakes and made better boats. In addition,
40 Congress supported major improvements along major rivers. These things, along with business growth, helped lead to the steamboat's rise. In 1814, records show that 21 steamboats visited New Orleans. By 1833, that number had grown to more than 1,200. **C**

By the 1850s, when Mark Twain was on the river, paddleboats had become very fancy. "And the boat IS a rather pretty sight, too," he wrote in *Life on the Mississippi*. These boats helped the Mississippi become the main U.S. river. Until railroads went across the country in the 1870s, nothing replaced the great
50 U.S. steamboat. In many ways, nothing ever has. **D**

Summaries of "Steam Rising"

Summary #1

"Steam Rising" tells about the rise of the U.S. paddle steamboat. It includes its design, its inventors, and the importance of this method of travel in the country's history. As steamboats were built, trade along the country's rivers increased. Fancy steamboats went up and down the Mississippi in the 1850s, taking goods and people to many places far away. "Steam Rising" is about paddle steamboats and how important they are to people who love boats. Fans of this special method of travel still exist today. Mark Twain, the famous U.S. author, said it best:

60 "And the boat is a rather pretty sight, too." **E**

Summary #2

In "Steam Rising: The Revolutionary Power of Paddleboats," author Jessica Cohn talks about the invention, creation and impact of the paddle steamboat. Steamboats played a major role in the rise of America's businesses. Americans in the 1700s knew that, in order to grow, businesses needed to use rivers to travel and to move goods. As early as 1784, inventors were working with ideas for a steamboat that would be able to travel upstream. Building such a boat cost a lot of money, however.

Robert Fulton made the first working steamboat. He
70 paddled it up a French river in 1802. Fulton studied art and science. With both money and other help from U.S. official Robert R. Livingston, Fulton was able to build his steamboat. Fulton's steamboats allowed businesses to send goods more quickly. The boats later made Fulton rich.

Steamboat designs changed, becoming safer as well as prettier. The use of steamboats also increased. By 1833, records show that 1,200 steamboats visited New Orleans. The steamboat played an important role in U.S. businesses for many years. **G**

E ┃ HERE'S HOW ┃

Reading Focus

The Preparing to Read page before the article had a list of things that should be included in a good **summary**. I see that some of those things are missing here, like the full title and the author's name. Also, while the writer tells me some of the main ideas, he or she does not give me a lot of supporting details. For example, I do not know why steamboats were built or why trade increased once they were built.

F ┃ YOUR TURN ┃

Reading Focus

Does this **summary** explain the main ideas of the article? Does it include enough supporting details? Explain how it is different from Summary #1.

_____

_____

_____

_____

_____

G ┃ READ AND DISCUSS ┃

Comprehension

What do these summaries show you?

Skills Practice

Steam Rising: The Revolutionary Power of Paddleboats *and* Summaries of "Steam Rising"

USE A VENN DIAGRAM

Use the Venn diagram below to compare the two article **summaries** you just read. Write what the summaries had in common in the part of the diagram where the circles overlap. Write what was different about Summary #1 in the left circle. Write what was different about Summary #2 in the right circle. As you write, think back to the Preparing to Read page and remember the five things a writer should do when writing a summary.

Summary #1   Summary #2

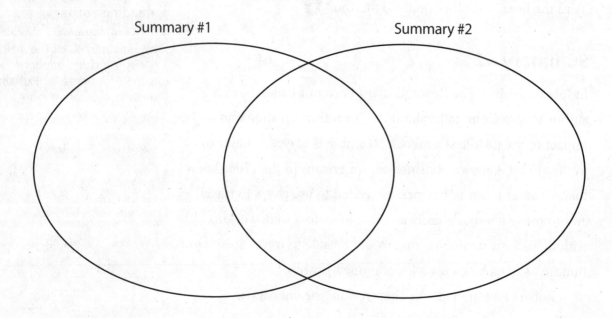

Applying Your Skills

Steam Rising: The Revolutionary Power of Paddleboats *and* Summaries of "Steam Rising"

COMPREHENSION WRAP-UP

1. How does the author back up her comment that "nothing replaced the great U.S. steamboat" even though she discusses the rise of the railroads? What does she really mean?

2. Discuss the importance of steamboats throughout our nation's history.

INFORMATIONAL TEXT FOCUS: EVALUATING A SUMMARY

DIRECTIONS: On the lines below, write a short **summary** of "Steam Rising: The Revolutionary Power of Paddleboats." Use the Venn diagram you completed on the previous page to give you ideas about how to start.

_____

_____

_____

_____

_____

_____

_____

_____

VOCABULARY REVIEW

DIRECTIONS: Fill in the blank with the correct vocabulary word from the Word Box.

Word Box

twinkling

upriver

method

1. The thief took my purse from me in a(n) _____; I didn't even see him do it.

2. Her _____ for cutting tomatoes is better than my way.

3. The town dock is located _____, close to the lake.

Skills Review

Collection 4

VOCABULARY REVIEW

DIRECTIONS: In each exercise, circle the word that does not match the meaning of the other words.

Word Box

impact

impression

distinctive

establish

bamboo

criticize

gird

twinkling

upriver

method

shrieked

corpse

chatted

chicken

break

fly

1. screamed/shrieked/whispered
2. moment/forever/twinkling
3. chatted/talked/ignored
4. brave/daring/chicken
5. idea/impression/confusion
6. secure/gird/untie
7. criticize/judge/shrug
8. bamboo/tree/chair
9. speed/crawl/fly
10. alive/breathing/corpse
11. special/distinctive/ordinary

Skills Review

Collection 4

LANGUAGE COACH: MULTIPLE-MEANING WORDS

DIRECTIONS: The words listed below all have **multiple, or more than one, meanings**. For each word, write two sentences in which you use that word as the part of speech indicated. Use a dictionary to help you.

1. bear

Noun:_____

Verb:_____

2. mind

Noun:_____

Verb:_____

3. light

Noun:_____

Adjective:_____

4. train

Noun:_____

Verb:_____

5. grave

Noun:_____

Adjective:_____

ORAL LANGUAGE ACTIVITY

DIRECTIONS: Working with a partner, draw **conclusions** about the writers who created the two summaries of the "Steam Rising" article. To begin, discuss the following questions:

- What seems to be the goal of the writer of Summary #1? The writer of Summary #2?

- Is one summary more complete than the other? What does this say about the two writers?

Elements of Nonfiction

Literary and Academic Vocabulary for Collection 5

LITERARY VOCABULARY

biography (BY AH GRUH FEE) *n.:* story of a person's life written by another person.

He wanted to share his life stories, so he hired someone to write his biography.

coherence (KOH HIHR UHNS) *n.:* one idea flows from another and important details are easy to follow.

The biography described the events of the bank robbery in order, which gave the story coherence.

main idea (MAYN I DEE AH) *n.:* the writer's most important message in a text.

The main idea of the story was that good things happen to good people.

ACADEMIC VOCABULARY

observation (OHB ZUHR VAY SHUHN) *n.:* the act of taking notice of something; study.

The observation of human nature is important to authors who write personal essays.

emphasize (EHM FUH SYZ) *v.:* give importance to; pay special attention to.

The writer tended to emphasize points she felt would be more interesting to her readers.

reactions (REE AK SHUNZ) *n.:* responses.

The students' reactions to the story let the teacher know that they really liked it.

define (DEE FYN) *v.:* give the meaning of something.

The writer is able to define the emotions of the character.

from Harriet Tubman: Conductor on the Underground Railroad

By Ann Petry

LITERARY FOCUS: BIOGRAPHY AND COHERENCE

A **biography** is the story of someone's life written by another person. For example, there have been biographies written about famous athletes, movie stars, and U.S. presidents. A good biography has **coherence**. That means that all the details come together in a way that makes the biography easy to understand. For example, an athlete's biography may give details about the person's childhood and how he or she affected the sports world as an adult.

READING FOCUS: FINDING THE MAIN IDEA

All of the important details in a biography must support the **main idea**, or the central message of the text. In the biography of an athlete, for example, the main idea might be: "An athlete must train hard to become successful." To find the main idea, look for important details, like examples of a person's hard work. Then think about what *all* of the details add up to.

SKILLS FOCUS

Literary Skills
Understand characteristics of biography; understand coherence.

Reading Skills
Identify the main idea; identify supporting sentences.

VOCABULARY

Make flashcards for the words below. On each card, write the word on the front and its definition on the back.

fugitives (FYOO JUH TIHVZ) *n.:* people who run from danger.

incomprehensible (IHN KAHM PRIH HEHN SUH BUHL) *adj.:* impossible to understand.

incentive (IHN SEHN TIHV) *n.:* reason for doing something.

dispel (DIHS PEHL) *v.:* scatter.

eloquence (EHL UH KWEHNS) *n.:* ability to write or speak well.

from HARRIET TUBMAN: CONDUCTOR ON THE UNDERGROUND RAILROAD

By Ann Petry

INTO THE BIOGRAPHY

In the United States in the 1800s, there were many people trying to help slaves escape to freedom. These people led the slaves along the Underground Railroad. This was not an actual railroad. It was a network of people called "conductors" who helped slaves flee from slavery in the South to freedom in the North. One of these conductors was Harriet Tubman. She was often called "the Moses" of her people. In the Bible, Moses helped the people of Israel escape slavery in Egypt.

The Railroad Runs to Canada

Along the Eastern Shore of Maryland, in Dorchester County, in Caroline County, the masters kept hearing whispers about the man named Moses, who was running off slaves. At first they did not believe in his existence. The stories about him were fantastic, unbelievable. Yet they watched for him. They offered rewards for his capture. **A B**

They never saw him. Now and then they heard whispered rumors to the effect that he was in the neighborhood. The woods were searched. The roads were watched. There was never anything to indicate his whereabouts. But a few days afterward, a goodly number of slaves would be gone from the plantation. Neither the master nor the overseer had heard or seen anything unusual in the quarter.[1] Sometimes one or the other would vaguely remember having heard a whippoorwill call somewhere

10

---

1. **quarter:** area in a plantation where enslaved blacks lived. It consisted of windowless, one-room cabins made of logs and mud.

A ⟨ HERE'S HOW ⟩

Literary Focus

I can tell that this is a **biography** because it tells about a person. The person is called "Moses." I think that "Moses" is really Harriet Tubman, because of the title of the biography and what I read in the Into the Biography paragraph.

B ⟨ HERE'S HOW ⟩

Reading Focus

As I read on, I know to pay close attention in order to find the **main idea**. I can already tell that "Moses's" actions and the reasons for them will likely be the main idea of this biography.

A **READ AND DISCUSS**

Comprehension

What has the author set up for us? **Follow-up**: What does this use of animal signals tell us about Moses?

B **HERE'S HOW**

Vocabulary

I do not know what *fugitives* means. I may be able to find out by using clues in this paragraph, though. The phrase "runaway slaves" is used in the next sentence. I bet that *fugitives* means "people who run from danger." I checked my dictionary, and I was right.

in the woods, close by, late at night. Though it was the wrong season for whippoorwills.

Sometimes the masters thought they had heard the cry of a hoot owl, repeated, and would remember having thought that the intervals between the low moaning cry were wrong, that

20 it had been repeated four times in succession instead of three. There was never anything more than that to suggest that all was not well in the quarter. Yet, when morning came, they invariably discovered that a group of the finest slaves had taken to their heels. **A**

IN OTHER WORDS Slave owners in Maryland heard rumors about a mysterious man named Moses who helped slaves escape to freedom in the North. The owners never saw Moses, but sometimes they heard unusual bird calls. The next morning, several slaves would be missing. The bird calls were signals between Moses and the slaves to put their plan of escape into action.

Unfortunately, the discovery was almost always made on a Sunday. Thus a whole day was lost before the machinery of pursuit could be set in motion. The posters offering rewards for the fugitives could not be printed until Monday. **B** The men who made a living hunting for runaway slaves were out of reach,

30 off in the woods with their dogs and their guns, in pursuit of four-footed game, or they were in camp meetings saying their prayers with their wives and families beside them.

Harriet Tubman could have told them that there was far more involved in this matter of running off slaves than signaling the would-be runaways by imitating the call of a whippoorwill, or a hoot owl, far more involved than a matter of waiting for a clear night when the North Star was visible.

IN OTHER WORDS "Moses" was actually Harriet Tubman, a former slave. She helped slaves escape on Saturday nights. That way, slave owners, who discovered the missing slaves on

Sunday, could not try to find them until Monday. Most people took Sunday off to go hunting or to go to church.

In December 1851, when she started out with the band of fugitives that she planned to take to Canada, she had been in the vicinity of the plantation for days, planning the trip, carefully selecting the slaves that she would take with her.

She had announced her arrival in the quarter by singing the forbidden spiritual[2]—"Go down, Moses, 'way down to Egypt Land"—singing it softly outside the door of a slave cabin, late at night. The husky voice was beautiful even when it was barely more than a murmur borne on the wind. **C**

Once she had made her presence known, word of her coming spread from cabin to cabin. The slaves whispered to each other, ear to mouth, mouth to ear, "Moses is here." "Moses has come." "Get ready. Moses is back again." The ones who had agreed to go North with her put ashcake[3] and salt herring in an old bandanna, hastily tied it into a bundle, and then waited patiently for the signal that meant it was time to start.

IN OTHER WORDS Helping slaves escape was very hard work. On one of her trips, in December 1851, Tubman helped several slaves escape from Maryland to Canada. She went to the area of the plantation (very large farm) and stayed a few days to plan the escape. She let the slaves know she was there by singing a song about Moses outside of their cabins. Those who were going to travel with Tubman packed some food and waited for her signal.

There were eleven in this party, including one of her brothers and his wife. It was the largest group that she had ever conducted, but she was determined that more and more slaves should know what freedom was like. **D**

---

2. **forbidden spiritual:** Spirituals are religious songs, some of which are based on the biblical story of the Israelites' escape from slavery in Egypt. Plantation owners feared that the singing of spirituals might lead to rebellion.
3. **ashcake:** cornmeal bread baked in hot ashes.

C READ AND DISCUSS

Comprehension
What have we learned about Moses now?

D YOUR TURN

Reading Focus
Re-read lines 55–57. What is Tubman's goal? Could this also be the **main idea** of the selection? Explain.

_____
_____
_____
_____
_____
_____
_____
_____
_____
_____

from **Harriet Tubman: Conductor on the Underground Railroad** 159

A **READ AND DISCUSS**

Comprehension

Why does the author name several escaped slaves in talking about the Fugitive Slave Law? **Follow-up:** How did the enforcement of this law impact Harriet?

B **YOUR TURN**

Literary Focus

For a **biography** to have **coherence**, it needs to give details. Details help you understand the person's life. Underline some details you find out about Harriet Tubman's life in lines 64–68.

She had to take them all the way to Canada. The Fugitive

Slave Law [4] was no longer a great many incomprehensible words

60   written down on the country's law books. The new law had

become a reality. It was Thomas Sims, a boy, picked up on the

streets of Boston at night and shipped back to Georgia. It was

Jerry and Shadrach, arrested and jailed with no warning. **A**

She had never been in Canada. The route beyond

Philadelphia was strange to her. But she could not let the

runaways who accompanied her know this. As they walked along,

she told them stories of her own first flight; she kept painting

vivid word pictures of what it would be like to be free. **B**

IN OTHER WORDS There were eleven slaves travelling with Tubman on this trip—her largest group. Because of a new law, slaves who escaped to the northern part of the United States (where slavery was illegal) could still be caught and taken back South. So, this time she had to take the fugitives farther north, to Canada. Canada was new to her, but she did not want the runaways to know she was unsure of herself, so she told them stories along the way.

But there were so many of them this time. She knew

70   moments of doubt, when she was half afraid and kept looking

back over her shoulder, imagining that she heard the sound

of pursuit. They would certainly be pursued. Eleven of them.

Eleven thousand dollars' worth of flesh and bone and muscle that

belonged to Maryland planters. If they were caught, the eleven

runaways would be whipped and sold South, but she—she would

probably be hanged.

They tried to sleep during the day but they never could

wholly relax into sleep. She could tell by the positions they

assumed, by their restless movements. And they walked at night.

80   Their progress was slow. It took them three nights of walking

---

4.   **Fugitive Slave Law:** Harsh federal law passed in 1850 stating that fugitives who escaped from slavery to free states could be forced to return to their owners. As a result, those who escaped were safe only in Canada. The law also made it a crime for a free person to help fugitives or to prevent their return.

to reach the first stop. She had told them about the place where they would stay, promising warmth and good food, holding these things out to them as an incentive to keep going. **C**

IN OTHER WORDS Traveling with such a large group was even more dangerous than usual. The slave owners would definitely try to find the runaways. If they were caught, the slaves would be whipped and Tubman would probably be hanged. Everyone was nervous. But Tubman knew of places to stop on their journey—homes that would give food and shelter for the night.

When she knocked on the door of a farmhouse, a place where she and her parties of runaways had always been welcome, always been given shelter and plenty to eat, there was no answer. She knocked again, softly. A voice from within said, "Who is it?" There was fear in the voice.

She knew instantly from the sound of the voice that there was something wrong. She said, "A friend with friends," the password on the Underground Railroad.

The door opened, slowly. The man who stood in the doorway looked at her coldly, looked with unconcealed astonishment and fear at the eleven disheveled runaways who were standing near her. **D** Then he shouted, "Too many, too many. It's not safe. My place was searched last week. It's not safe!" and slammed the door in her face. **E**

She turned away from the house, frowning. She had promised her passengers food and rest and warmth, and instead of that, there would be hunger and cold and more walking over the frozen ground. Somehow she would have to instill courage into these eleven people, most of them strangers, would have to feed them on hope and bright dreams of freedom instead of the fried pork and corn bread and milk she had promised them.

They stumbled along behind her, half dead for sleep, and she urged them on, though she was as tired and as discouraged as they were. She had never been in Canada, but she kept painting

90

100

C YOUR TURN

Vocabulary

What do you think *incentive* means? Think about what you already know: The group was tired, cold, and hungry. They moved slowly and Tubman wanted them to keep going. She told them about warmth and good food—things they wanted. What does it mean that she held "these things out to them as an *incentive* to keep going"?

_____

_____

_____

D HERE'S HOW

Vocabulary

I do not know what the words *unconcealed* and *astonishment* mean. I checked my dictionary, and *unconcealed* means "not hidden from sight" and *astonishment* means "great surprise." This tells me that the man in the doorway made no effort to hide his surprise that Harriet Tubman and her group had come to his home.

E READ AND DISCUSS

Comprehension

What is happening with Harriet Tubman and her group? **Follow-up:** What does this turn of events show you about the trip they are taking?

Comprehension

How did Harriet manage to keep her group going even when they were tired, afraid or not scared enough? **Follow-up:** What does this show us about Harriet Tubman?

Reading Focus

At first I was not sure why the biography included a description of how Tubman and her group were turned away. Nothing really happened. But now I think that these details help support the **main idea**. They show me how hard Tubman worked to help people be free.

110
wondrous word pictures of what it would be like. She managed to dispel their fear of pursuit so that they would not become hysterical, panic-stricken. Then she had to bring some of the fear back, so that they would stay awake and keep walking though they drooped with sleep. **A**

Yet, during the day, when they lay down deep in a thicket, they never really slept, because if a twig snapped or the wind sighed in the branches of a pine tree, they jumped to their feet, afraid of their own shadows, shivering and shaking. It was very cold, but they dared not make fires because someone would see the smoke and wonder about it. **B**

IN OTHER WORDS Tubman brought the group to a house on the Underground Railroad that she had been to before. But this time she was turned away. The owners, who could get in trouble with the law, were too afraid to hide eleven runaways. The group had to go on without food, warmth, or sleep. Tubman tried to keep the runaways' spirits up with stories about Canada.

120
She kept thinking, eleven of them. Eleven thousand dollars' worth of slaves. And she had to take them all the way to Canada. Sometimes she told them about Thomas Garrett, in Wilmington.[5] She said he was their friend even though he did not know them. He was the friend of all fugitives. He called them God's poor. He was a Quaker[6] and his speech was a little different from that of other people. His clothing was different, too. He wore the wide-brimmed hat that the Quakers wear.

130
She said that he had thick white hair, soft, almost like a baby's, and the kindest eyes she had ever seen. He was a big man and strong, but he had never used his strength to harm anyone, always to help people. He would give all of them a new pair of shoes. Everybody. He always did. Once they reached his house

5. **Wilmington:** city in Delaware.
6. **Quaker:** member of the Society of Friends, a religious group active in the movement to end slavery.

in Wilmington, they would be safe. He would see to it that they were.

She described the house where he lived, told them about the store where he sold shoes. She said he kept a pail of milk and a loaf of bread in the drawer of his desk so that he would have food ready at hand for any of God's poor who should suddenly appear before him, fainting with hunger. There was a hidden room in the store. A whole wall swung open, and behind it was a room where he could hide fugitives. On the wall there were shelves filled with small boxes—boxes of shoes—so that you would never guess that the wall actually opened.

140

While she talked, she kept watching them. They did not believe her. She could tell by their expressions. They were thinking. New shoes, Thomas Garrett, Quaker, Wilmington—what foolishness was this? Who knew if she told the truth? Where was she taking them anyway? **C**

IN OTHER WORDS Tubman told the group about Thomas Garrett, a man from Delaware who helped runaway slaves. He had a secret room in his store where he could hide them. Once they reached his house, Garrett would give them each a pair of shoes and some food. Despite her hopeful stories, Tubman could tell that the runaways did not believe her.

That night they reached the next stop—a farm that belonged to a German. She made the runaways take shelter behind trees at the edge of the fields before she knocked at the door. She hesitated before she approached the door, thinking, suppose that he too should refuse shelter, suppose—Then she thought, *Lord, I'm going to hold steady on to You and You've got to see me through*—and knocked softly. **D**

150

She heard the familiar guttural voice say, "Who's there?"

She answered quickly, "A friend with friends."

He opened the door and greeted her warmly. "How many this time?" he asked.

"Eleven," she said and waited, doubting, wondering.

C **HERE'S HOW**

Reading Focus

I think I know why the runaways did not believe Tubman's story about Thomas Garrett. Before, Tubman had told them about a place on the Underground Railroad where they could sleep and get food. But the owners of that house turned them away. The runaways probably think everything Tubman says is untrue. Tubman's struggle to gain the runways' trust could also be related to the **main idea**.

D **YOUR TURN**

Literary Focus

Here the author tells us that Tubman hesitated, or stopped, and said a prayer before knocking on the door. How do these details add to the **biography** about Harriet Tubman and the goal she is trying to accomplish?

_____

_____

_____

_____

160   He said, "Good. Bring them in."

He and his wife fed them in the lamp-lit kitchen, their faces glowing as they offered food and more food, urging them to eat, saying there was plenty for everybody, have more milk, have more bread, have more meat.

They spent the night in the warm kitchen. They really slept, all that night and until dusk the next day. When they left, it was with reluctance. They had all been warm and safe and well-fed. It was hard to exchange the security offered by that clean, warm kitchen for the darkness and the cold of a December night. **Ⓐ**

IN OTHER WORDS Tubman and the group stopped at the next house on the Underground Railroad. This time the owners took them in and give them lots of food and a place to sleep. The next day, it was hard to leave the warm house and go out into the cold December night.

"Go On or Die"

170   Harriet had found it hard to leave the warmth and friendliness, too. But she urged them on. For a while, as they walked, they seemed to carry in them a measure of contentment; some of the serenity and the cleanliness of that big, warm kitchen lingered on inside them. But as they walked farther and farther away from the warmth and the light, the cold and the darkness entered into them. They fell silent, sullen, suspicious. **Ⓑ** She waited for the moment when some one of them would turn mutinous. It did not happen that night.

Two nights later, she was aware that the feet behind her
180 were moving slower and slower. She heard the irritability in their voices, knew that soon someone would refuse to go on.

She started talking about William Still and the Philadelphia Vigilance Committee.[7] No one commented. No one asked any questions. She told them the story of William and Ellen Craft

---

7. **Philadelphia Vigilance Committee:** group that offered help to people escaping slavery. William Still, a free African American, was chairman of the committee.

Ⓐ READ AND DISCUSS

Comprehension
What is going on now?

Ⓑ HERE'S HOW

Language Coach
My teacher says that the **root** of the word *suspicion* is the Latin word *suspicio*, meaning "mistrust." This seems to make sense. The word *suspicious* here tells me that the group may not have trusted Harriet when they left the house.

and how they escaped from Georgia. Ellen was so fair that she looked as though she were white, and so she dressed up in a man's clothing and she looked like a wealthy young planter. Her husband, William, who was dark, played the role of her slave. Thus they traveled from Macon, Georgia, to Philadelphia, riding

190 on the trains, staying at the finest hotels. Ellen pretended to be very ill—her right arm was in a sling and her right hand was bandaged because she was supposed to have rheumatism.[8] Thus she avoided having to sign the register at the hotels, for she could not read or write. They finally arrived safely in Philadelphia and then went on to Boston. **C**

No one said anything. Not one of them seemed to have heard her.

She told them about Frederick Douglass, the most famous of the escaped

200 slaves, of his eloquence, of his magnificent appearance. **D** Then she told them of her own first, vain effort at running away, evoking the memory of that miserable life she had led as a child, reliving it for a moment in the telling.

© Corbis

IN OTHER WORDS The runaways became bad-tempered. Again, Tubman told them stories to keep their minds off of their troubles. She told them about William Still, a free African American who helped escaping slaves. She told them stories about Ellen Craft and Frederick Douglass, both former slaves who had run away. Tubman even told them her own story, but the group did not say anything.

But they had been tired too long, hungry too long, afraid too long, footsore too long. One of them suddenly cried out in despair, "Let me go back. It is better to be a slave than to suffer like this in order to be free."

---

8. **rheumatism** (ROO MUH TIHZ UHM): painful swelling and stiffness of the joints or muscles.

from **Harriet Tubman: Conductor on the Underground Railroad** **165**

C **YOUR TURN**

Reading Focus

In this paragraph, the author mentions people who escaped slavery or helped others to escape slavery. How is this connected to the **main idea** of the story?

_____

_____

_____

D **YOUR TURN**

Language Coach

The Latin **root** *loqui* means "to speak." Knowing this, what might the word *eloquence* mean? Use a dictionary to check your answer.

_____

_____

_____

A **READ AND DISCUSS**

Comprehension

What is going on between Harriet and her group?
Follow-up: How does Harriet carrying a gun connect to what we know about her?

B **HERE'S HOW**

Literary Focus

I wonder how this **detail** is important to the biography. I know that all of the slaves in the group wanted to be free so badly that they risked their lives to escape. If one of them wants to turn around and go back to a life of slavery, their journey must be very difficult.

210 She carried a gun with her on these trips. She had never used it—except as a threat. Now, as she aimed it, she experienced a feeling of guilt, remembering that time, years ago, when she had prayed for the death of Edward Brodas, the Master, and then, not too long afterward, had heard that great wailing cry that came from the throats of the field hands, and knew from the sound that the Master was dead. **A**

One of the runaways said again, "Let me go back. Let me go back," and stood still, and then turned around and said, over his shoulder, "I am going back." **B**

220 She lifted the gun, aimed it at the despairing slave. She said, "Go on with us or die." The husky, low-pitched voice was grim.

He hesitated for a moment and then he joined the others. They started walking again. She tried to explain to them why none of them could go back to the plantation. If a runaway returned, he would turn traitor; the master and the overseer would force him to turn traitor. The returned slave would disclose the stopping places, the hiding places, the corn stacks they had used with the full knowledge of the owner of the farm, the name of the German farmer who had fed them and sheltered

230 them. These people who had risked their own security to help runaways would be ruined, fined, imprisoned.

She said, "We got to go free or die. And freedom's not bought with dust."

IN OTHER WORDS One of the runaways said he wanted to go back to Maryland. Tubman aimed a gun at him and threatened to kill him if he did not continue with the group. He agreed to continue. Tubman explained that runaways who went back to slavery would be forced to tell their owners everything they knew about the Underground Railroad.

This time she told them about the long agony of the Middle Passage[9] on the old slave ships, about the black horror of the

9. **Middle Passage:** route traveled by ships carrying captured Africans across the Atlantic Ocean to the Americas. The captives endured the horrors of the Middle Passage crammed into holds, airless cargo areas below deck.

holds, about the chains and the whips. They too knew these stories. But she wanted to remind them of the long, hard way they had come, about the long, hard way they had yet to go. She told them about Thomas Sims, the boy picked up on the streets of Boston and sent back to Georgia. She said when they got him back to Savannah, got him in prison there, they whipped him until a doctor who was standing by watching said, "You will kill him if you strike him again!" His master said, "Let him die!"

Thus she forced them to go on. Sometimes she thought she had become nothing but a voice speaking in the darkness, cajoling, urging, threatening. Sometimes she told them things to make them laugh; sometimes she sang to them and heard the eleven voices behind her blending softly with hers, and then she knew that for the moment all was well with them.

She gave the impression of being a short, muscular, indomitable woman who could never be defeated. **C** Yet at any moment she was liable to be seized by one of those curious fits of sleep, which might last for a few minutes or for hours.[10]

Even on this trip, she suddenly fell asleep in the woods. The runaways, ragged, dirty, hungry, cold, did not steal the gun as they might have and set off by themselves or turn back. They sat on the ground near her and waited patiently until she awakened. They had come to trust her implicitly, totally. They, too, had come to believe her repeated statement, "We got to go free or die." She was leading them into freedom, and so they waited until she was ready to go on. **D** **E**

IN OTHER WORDS Tubman told the group more stories. Some of her stories were funny and some were scary. Sometimes they all sang together. Once in a while, because of a head injury, Tubman would suddenly go to sleep. When this happened, the runaways waited by her side until she woke

---

10. Harriet's losses of consciousness were caused by a serious head injury that she had suffered as a teenager. Harriet had tried to protect someone else from punishment, and an enraged overseer threw a two-pound weight at her head.

C **YOUR TURN**

Vocabulary

Look up the word *indomitable* in a dictionary. Write the definition on the lines, below. How does this detail help you picture what Harriet Tubman looked like?

_____

_____

_____

D **READ AND DISCUSS**

Comprehension

How does the gun fit into the story now?

E **YOUR TURN**

Literary Focus

How do all of the details about Tubman on this page give the biography **coherence**? Why is it important to know details about how Tubman was feeling and thinking?

_____

_____

_____

A READ AND DISCUSS

Comprehension

How can we describe William Still's record keeping of the slaves who used the Underground Railroad?

B HERE'S HOW

Literary Focus

I think things are looking up for Tubman and the runaways. They met Thomas Garrett, William Still, and Reverend J. W. Loguen. All of these details are about Tubman getting help from other people who help runaway slaves. This adds **coherence** to the story.

up. They did not steal her gun or go off on their own. They trusted her to lead them to freedom.

Finally, they reached Thomas Garrett's house in Wilmington, Delaware. Just as Harriet had promised, Garrett gave them all new shoes, and provided carriages to take them on to the next stop.

By slow stages they reached Philadelphia, where William Still hastily recorded their names, and the plantations whence they had come, and something of the life they had led in slavery. Then he carefully hid what he had written, for fear it might be discovered. In 1872 he published this record in book form and called it *The Underground Railroad*. In the foreword to his book he said: "While I knew the danger of keeping strict records, and while I did not then dream that in my day slavery would be blotted out, or that the time would come when I could publish these records, it used to afford me great satisfaction to take them down, fresh from the lips of fugitives on the way to freedom, and to preserve them as they had given them." **A**

William Still, who was familiar with all the station stops on the Underground Railroad, supplied Harriet with money and sent her and her eleven fugitives on to Burlington, New Jersey.

Harriet felt safer now, though there were danger spots ahead. But the biggest part of her job was over. As they went farther and farther north, it grew colder; she was aware of the wind on the Jersey ferry and aware of the cold damp in New York. From New York they went on to Syracuse,[11] where the temperature was even lower.

In Syracuse she met the Reverend J. W. Loguen, known as "Jarm" Loguen. This was the beginning of a lifelong friendship. Both Harriet and Jarm Loguen were to become friends and supporters of Old John Brown.[12] **B**

---

11. **Syracuse:** city in central New York State.
12. **John Brown** (1800–1859): abolitionist (opponent of slavery) who was active in the Underground Railroad. In 1859, Brown led a raid on the federal arsenal at Harpers Ferry, then in Virginia, in hopes of inspiring a slave uprising. Federal troops overpowered Brown and his followers, and Brown was convicted of treason and was hanged.

From Syracuse they went north again, into a colder, snowier city—Rochester. Here they almost certainly stayed with Frederick Douglass, for he wrote in his autobiography:

"On one occasion I had eleven fugitives at the same time under my roof, and it was necessary for them to remain with me until I could collect sufficient money to get them to Canada. It was the largest number I ever had at any one time, and I had some difficulty in providing so many with food and shelter, but, as may well be imagined, they were not very fastidious in either direction, and were well content with very plain food, and a strip of carpet on the floor for a bed, or a place on the straw in the barn loft." **C**

Late in December 1851, Harriet arrived in St. Catharines, Canada West (now Ontario), with the eleven fugitives. It had taken almost a month to complete this journey. **D**

IN OTHER WORDS The group reached Thomas Garrett's house. He gave them new shoes and carriages. In Philadelphia, William Still wrote down information about the slaves so he could tell their stories later. In Syracuse, Reverend J. W. Loguen helped them. In Rochester, Frederick Douglass helped them. It grew colder, but the group was getting closer to freedom. Finally, after a month-long journey, the group reached freedom in Canada.

Comprehension Wrap-Up

1. Discuss Harriet Tubman and the kind of person she was.

2. Discuss the ups and downs the group of eleven experienced during their trip from Maryland to Canada.

3. Discuss the idea that the slave masters thought "Moses" was a man. What would lead them to think this?

C **YOUR TURN**

Vocabulary

What do you think *fastidious* means? Look at the clues in this paragraph. Douglass says the runaway slaves were not *fastidious*. They were happy with very plain food and a simple bed. Based on these clues, write a definition for *fastidious*. Check your answer against a dictionary.

_____

_____

_____

_____

D **READ AND DISCUSS**

Comprehension

What has happened by the end of the selection?

from Harriet Tubman: Conductor on the Underground Railroad

USE A TIME LINE

When a **biography** is long and has lots of details, it helps to write down some of the main events in the order they happened. This helps you keep track of the story more easily. In the time line below, write a sentence about three of the main events in "*from* Harriet Tubman: Conductor on the Underground Railroad." Put the events in the correct order. The first one has been done for you.

Harriet Tubman begins a journey with eleven runaway slaves in December 1851.

Applying Your Skills

from Harriet Tubman: Conductor on the Underground Railroad

LITERARY FOCUS: BIOGRAPHY AND COHERENCE

DIRECTIONS: The author of this **biography** creates **coherence** by including lots of details about Tubman and her group's trip. Fill in the chart below with some details that helped describe the most important events that took place on this trip to Canada.

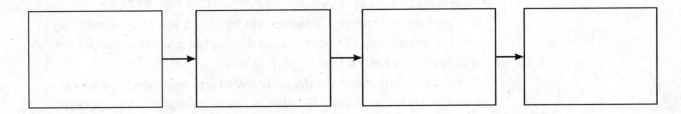

READING FOCUS: FINDING THE MAIN IDEA

DIRECTIONS: Write details from the biography in the chart below. Then fill in the **main idea** that you can draw from *all* of these details. (Hint: The main idea should have to do with the biography's subject, Harriet Tubman.)

Biography Title: *Harriet Tubman: Conductor on the Underground Railroad*
Important Detail:
Important Detail:
Important Detail:
Main Idea of Biography:

VOCABULARY REVIEW

DIRECTIONS: Circle clues in each sentence that make the boldfaced word's meaning clearer.

1. The **fugitives** fled from the dangerous war zone to a safer place.

2. I could not understand the directions at all; they were completely **incomprehensible**.

3. My brother delivered his wonderful speech with confidence and **eloquence**.

Fragment on Slavery, 1854

Based on the note by Abraham Lincoln

from What to the Slave Is the Fourth of July?

Based on the speech by Frederick Douglass

INFORMATIONAL TEXT FOCUS: PROPOSITION AND SUPPORT

In a persuasive argument, a writer will try to get you to do something or think a certain way. For example, an article that gives five reasons why you should not smoke is a kind of persuasive argument.

A persuasive argument usually begins with a **proposition**—the writer's opinion. Then the writer will give the reader reasons that **support** the proposition. It is up to you to decide whether each reason is believable. How do you recognize support for a proposition? Look for the following:

- **facts:** true details (like survey results) or **statistics** (facts in number form).

- **examples:** instances that illustrate reasons or facts.

- **anecdotes:** brief stories, such as personal experiences.

- definitions and opinions from experts.

To support the proposition that people should not smoke, a writer might give statistics about the number of smokers who die from lung cancer each year. The writer might also share anecdotes from people who got sick as a result of smoking.

VOCABULARY

With a partner, practice using these words in complete sentences.

prove (PROOV) *v.:* to test the truth of something.

issue (IH SHOO) *n.:* matter in dispute; concern; problem.

justice (JUHS TIS) *n.:* deserved, fair treatment.

prejudice (PREH JUH DIHS) *n.:* an already formed opinion, often incorrect, about a group or individual.

liberty (LIH BUHR TEE) *n.:* state of being free.

SKILLS FOCUS

Informational Text Skills
Understand proposition and support.

FRAGMENT ON SLAVERY, 1854

Based on the note by Abraham Lincoln

INTO THE NOTE

Abraham Lincoln was president during the American Civil War, in which Northern and Southern states fought over slavery and other issues. In 1863, Lincoln signed the Emancipation Proclamation. This document freed all American slaves in the Southern states. The following selection is Lincoln's notes for an argument against slavery. They date from 1854, years before he became president.

© The Corcoran Gallery of Art/Corbis

Let's say that a person called "A" can prove that he has the right to make another person, called "B," his slave. Why can't B use the same argument, and prove that he can make A his slave? **A**

You say A is white, and B is black. So people with lighter skin have the right to make people with darker skin slaves? Be careful. By this rule you will become a slave to the first man you meet who has lighter skin than you.

You do not mean color exactly? You mean the whites are smarter than blacks and so have the right to make them slaves?
10 Be careful again. By this rule, you will become a slave to the first man you meet who is smarter than you.

But, you say, it is an issue of what is best for you. If it helps your life, then you have the right to make another person your slave. Very well. And if it helps his life, then he has the right to make you his slave. **B** **C**

Comprehension Wrap-up

1. Discuss the way these arguments and Lincoln's reasoning connect to the world we live in today.

A 〔 HERE'S HOW 〕

Reading Focus

I know that this is a persuasive essay. The author is trying to make me think a certain way. I bet the **proposition** is in the first paragraph. If I make the question in lines 2–3 into a statement, that could be the proposition. In my own words, the proposition is: "If A can prove that he can make B a slave, then B can prove that he can make A a slave." Now I need to keep reading to find **support** the writer gives for this statement.

B 〔 YOUR TURN 〕

Reading Focus

Circle any **examples** that support Lincoln's **proposition**.

C 〔 READ AND DISCUSS 〕

Comprehension

What is Lincoln doing with all of these examples?

from WHAT TO THE SLAVE IS THE FOURTH OF JULY?

Based on the speech by Frederick Douglass

A (HERE'S HOW)

Vocabulary

I already read the definition of *justice* on the Preparing to Read page. It means "deserved, fair treatment." So it looks like Douglass is asking why black people should celebrate fair treatment, since they do not have that.

B (YOUR TURN)

Reading Focus

Douglass has already said many things, but not his **proposition**. He does say what his subject is, though. The subject is what Douglass' proposition will target. What is the subject of this speech? Underline it.

C (HERE'S HOW)

Reading Focus

I think that the first sentence of this paragraph is Douglass' **proposition**. In my own words, his proposition is: "Slavery is wrong and should be eliminated."

INTO THE SPEECH

Frederick Douglass was a former slave who spoke out strongly against slavery. A few years after writing his autobiography in 1845, Douglass launched a newspaper dedicated to the anti-slavery cause. He gave this speech on July 5, 1852, in Rochester, New York.

Fellow citizens, please let me ask, why did you want me to speak here today? What does your national independence mean to me or other black people? Are the Declaration of Independence's great ideas of freedom and justice given to us? **A**

Fellow citizens, above your happiness, I hear the sad cry of millions. My subject, fellow citizens, is "American Slavery." I look at this day and its celebrations from the slave's point of view. Standing here, caring about American slaves, I can say that the actions of this nation never looked worse to me than on this Fourth of July. **B**

I will question and criticize everything that supports slavery, with all the power I can. It is the great sin of America! I will not mislead you. I will not forgive you. I will use the strongest language I can. Yet any man whose thinking is not shaped by prejudice, or who does not want to own slaves, will agree with my words. **C**

What part of anti-slavery beliefs do you want me to explain? What part of the subject do the people of this country need help understanding? Must I try to prove that slaves are people? That point is agreed upon already. Nobody doubts it. The slaveholders themselves admit it by making laws that slaves must follow. They admit it when they punish slaves for disobeying them. There are seventy-two crimes in the State of Virginia, which, if committed by a black man, could be punished by death. Only two of these crimes have the same punishment for a white man.

These laws show that whites believe that slaves know the difference between right and wrong. They admit that slaves are human. Many Southern laws forbid teaching slaves to read and
30 write. When you can point to any such laws about animals, then you can ask whether slaves are people.

For now it is enough to agree that black people are human beings. Is it not amazing that, while we are doing the same work and other things as whites, we are asked to prove that we are human? **D**

Do you want me to argue that men should have liberty? **E** That they are the rightful owners of their own bodies? You have already said so. Do I have to explain why slavery is wrong? Is that a question for voters? Should it be treated as a problem that is hard to understand? How would I look in front of you
40 today, arguing whether or not men have a natural right to freedom? To do so would be to make myself look silly. There is not a man anywhere who does not know that it is wrong for him to be a slave.

Do I need to argue that a system marked with blood and filled with evil is wrong? No, I will not. I have better uses for my time and strength than to make such arguments.

At a time like this, harsh words are needed. Oh! If I had the ability, and could get people to listen, I would today use strong words. We need the storm, the whirlwind, and the earthquake.
50 The nation must be forced to feel. The nation must agree to do the right thing. It must understand that these crimes against God and man are wrong. **F**

Comprehension Wrap-Up

1. How does Douglass's speech reflect his beliefs about slavery and what needs to happen?

D YOUR TURN

Reading Focus

Douglass comes up with different arguments to **support** his **proposition** that slavery is wrong. State one of his arguments in your own words. (Hint: Look at lines 19–34.)

_____

_____

_____

_____

E HERE'S HOW

Language Coach

My teacher says the **origin** of the word _liberty_ is the Latin word _liber_, meaning "free." This makes sense because _liberty_ means "the state of being free."

F READ AND DISCUSS

Comprehension

It now becomes clearer why Douglass kept saying that he was not going to argue certain things. What does he say is needed more than just arguments?

Fragment on Slavery, 1854; *from* What to the Slave is the Fourth of July?

USE A CONCEPT MAP

A graphic organizer is an easy way to track all of the **support** a writer gives you for a **proposition**. Complete the exercise below by stating the proposition of one of the last two selections you read. Then, supply three supporting details in the surrounding circles.

Selection title: _____

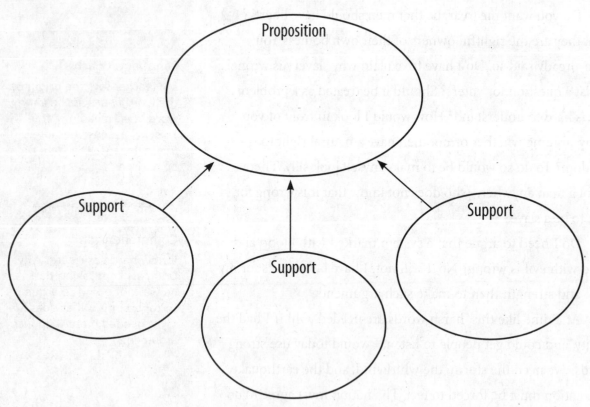

Fragment on Slavery, 1854; *from* What to the Slave Is the Fourth of July?

INFORMATIONAL TEXT FOCUS: PROPOSITION AND SUPPORT

DIRECTIONS: Circle the correct answer to each question.

1. What is Lincoln's **proposition** in "Fragment on Slavery, 1854"?

   a) It is right for one person to enslave another.

   b) There is no such thing as slavery.

   c) Some people have more intellect than others.

   d) If one person is allowed to make another person a slave, then the other person can make the first person a slave.

2. What does Lincoln's **proposition** tell us about his opinion of slavery?

   a) Slavery is acceptable because there are good arguments for it.

   b) Slavery is unacceptable because there are no good arguments for it.

   c) He does not have an opinion on slavery.

   d) He thinks that everyone should have his or her own opinion about slavery.

3. Which of these arguments does Douglass use to **support** his **proposition** that slavery is wrong?

   a) There are laws written just for slaves.

   b) Slaves are punished for crimes they commit.

   c) Both a and b.

   d) Neither a nor b.

VOCABULARY REVIEW

DIRECTIONS: Explain what *liberty* is in your own words. (Hint: Think about what life might be like without liberty. What things would you NOT be able to do?)

_____

_____

_____

_____

Skills Review

Collection 5

VOCABULARY REVIEW

DIRECTIONS: Unscramble each vocabulary word by using the definition underneath. Each word can be found in the Word Box.

Word Box

observation

emphasize

fugitives

dispel

issue

prove

prejudice

liberty

reactions

incentive

define

justice

1. pidels: _____
to scatter

2. efinde: _____
to give characteristics

3. givefutis: _____
people fleeing from danger

4. pvreo: _____
test the truth

5. esius: _____
concern

6. cartiones: _____
responses

7. venticine: _____
motivation

8. tyblrie: _____
state of being free

Imagine the following situation: Marc meets someone who has a *prejudice* against teenagers. Marc then tries to persuade the person that this *prejudice* is incorrect.

What happened with Marc? Use what you know about the meaning of *prejudice* to explain the rest of the story in your own words.

_____

_____

_____

_____

Skills Review

Collection 5

LANGUAGE COACH: WORD ORIGINS

The Latin root *cedere means* "to go." This is a **word origin**. Many words in English are built on this root. By understanding the Latin root, you can better understand the meaning of many words in English. Each of the words in the table come from *cedere*.

DIRECTIONS: Use a dictionary to look up the meaning of each word in the table below. Write the definition in the correct box. Then write an original sentence using the word.

Word	Definition	Original Sentence
Concede		
Precede		
Recede		

ORAL LANGUAGE ACTIVITY

In the second and third selections in this collection, Abraham Lincoln and Frederick Douglass give their **propositions** on slavery. They **support** their propositions with facts and examples.

Prepare a brief speech giving your proposition on an issue that you care about. Use one of the following phrases in your talk: "In my opinion . . ." or "I believe that . . ." Be sure to support your proposition with at least two of the following:

- facts (including statistics)
- examples
- definitions
- opinions of experts on the subject
- anecdotes

Collection

6

Reading for Life

© Stefano Pattera/North American Solar Challenge

Literary and Academic Vocabulary for Collection 6

LITERARY VOCABULARY

preview (PREE VYOO) *v.:* quickly glance over a text before reading it more closely.

When you preview, you may just read the headings and look at the pictures.

skimming (SKIHM IHNG) *n.:* quickly looking over a document.

The student only looked at the headings and photo captions when skimming his new textbook.

scanning (SKAN IHNG) *v.:* looking for the particular information you want in a document.

She began by scanning the directions, looking for the part about batteries.

graphics (GRAF IHKS) *n.:* graphs, tables, maps, cartoons, photos, and illustrations that present visual information in a document.

Graphics like diagrams may help explain the information in the text.

ACADEMIC VOCABULARY

specify (SPEHS UH FY) *v.:* mention or describe in detail.

When signing up with a phone company, be sure to specify which service you are choosing.

sequence (SEE KWUHNS) *n.:* order.

With technical directions, you must follow each step in the correct sequence.

fundamental (FUHN DUH MEHN TUHL) *adj.:* basic; essential.

Manuals give fundamental information, so read them carefully.

critical (KRIHT IH KUHL) *adj.:* very important, vital.

It is critical to read directions closely so you do not make a mistake.

Skateboard Park Documents

INFORMATIONAL TEXT FOCUS: USING INFORMATION TO SOLVE PROBLEMS

Using information can help you solve a problem. For example, imagine that you want to fix a broken net at your community basketball court. To do this, you may need information about who is in charge of the court. Information can come from different kinds of **documents**, like:

- **Workplace documents**, such as memos, e-mails, and reports.
- **Public documents**, such as government publications, schedules, and Web sites.
- **Consumer documents**, such as contracts, advertisements, and manuals.

Once you have found and read the documents you need, it is important to compare and contrast them. By doing this, you can decide which ones have the most dependable information.

READING FOCUS: PREVIEWING

Another way to judge documents is to **preview** them. When you preview, you look over the text you are about to read. Be sure to notice any titles, headings, boldfaced terms, and illustrations. These features often make it easier to see what lies ahead in your reading. For example, think about previewing a newspaper article. If you read the headline and then look at any photos and captions, you will have a much better idea of what the entire article is about.

VOCABULARY

Working with a partner, practice using these words in sentences.

potentially (POH TEHN SHUH LEE) *adv.:* possibly.

proposal (PRUH POHZ UHL) *n.:* suggestion.

hazards (HAZ UHRDZ) *n.:* dangers; things that can cause danger.

INTO THE DOCUMENTS

A town has a problem. Some people in the town want to build a skateboard park. Others do not want the park. The town's Parks and Recreation Department has done some research. The city council has held a public meeting on the issue. The following workplace, public, and consumer documents give some information about the skateboard park problem.

SKILLS FOCUS

Informational Text Skills
Use information from documents to solve a problem.

Reading Skills
Preview a text.

Skateboard Park Documents

Read with a Purpose Read these workplace, public, and consumer documents to solve a skateboarding problem.

From: A. Longboard, Assistant Director of Parks and Recreation
To: J. Cool, Director of Parks and Recreation
Re: Establishment of a Permanent Skateboard Park

CRITICAL ISSUES

A. Need. Ten percent of the families in this city, about seven thousand households, include at least one skateboarder. The city provides no designated space for skateboarding. Police reports show that citations for illegal skating are rising every month. This problem is particularly acute in downtown areas, leading to complaints from businesses. The nearest public skateboard park is twenty miles to the east in Mogul, where illegal skating dropped sharply when its park opened last year.

B. Liability.[1] California AB 1296 states that persons who skateboard on public property are expected to know that it is a potentially dangerous sport. They cannot sue the city, county, or state for their injuries as long as the city has passed an ordinance[2] requiring

- helmet, kneepads, and elbow pads for skaters
- clear and visible signs warning citizens of this requirement
- citations for skaters who violate the ordinance

---

1. **liability** (ly uh BIHL uh tee): legal responsibility.
2. **ordinance** (AWR duh nuhns): law; rule.

Such an ordinance was enacted by our city council on July 15, 2000. Therefore, building a skateboard park would not pose a liability risk.

C. Cost. Local groups have raised half the necessary $140,000. The Parks and Recreation Department's budget can fund the other half. Costs will be minimal—only inspection for damage and yearly maintenance.

D. Location. The city already owns two sites:

- 1.3 acres of the park area between 180th Avenue and 360th Drive, bordered by Drab Street and Grinding Drive, two heavily used thoroughfares. On two sides of the park are neighborhood houses.
- 2.1 acres in the 15-acre sports park at Ramp and Spin avenues. This site is set back from heavily traveled roads but still offers excellent access and visibility from service roads within the park. It is also three-tenths of a mile from the fire station and paramedic aid. There are no residential neighborhoods bordering the complex.

Vocabulary **potentially** (poh TEHN shuh lee) *adv.:* possibly.

IN OTHER WORDS This memorandum (memo) presents four issues concerning a new skateboard park. The first section, under "Need," explains why the city should build a skateboard park. The second section, under "Liability," tells the reader that even if the city builds the park, the city is not responsible if a skater is hurt there. The third section, under "Cost," explains how the city and its residents will pay for the new park. The fourth section, under "Location," introduces two locations that might be good spots for the park.

Sidebar

A · HERE'S HOW

Reading Focus

When I **preview** this document, I see that it is some kind of letter. I think that a memorandum is a document from a **workplace** since job titles are listed. The "From" line shows who wrote the letter. The "To" line shows who read it. The "Re:" line explains that the letter will be about creating a skateboard park.

B · HERE'S HOW

Vocabulary

I am not sure what *budget* means. It must have something to do with money, though. I know that groups have already raised $140,000 for the park. I also know that the rest of the money needed will come from the Parks and Recreation *budget*. I can conclude that a *budget* is an amount of money put aside for a reason.

C · YOUR TURN

Reading Focus

How do the two possible locations for the skateboard park compare? **Use the information** in this document to compare and contrast the locations. Circle the site that you think is best.

D · READ AND DISCUSS

Comprehension

According to this information, why is there a need for a skateboard park?

Skateboard Park Documents **183**

A YOUR TURN

Reading Focus

Preview this new document. Underline the heading. Do you think this is a **workplace**, **public**, or **consumer document**? What about the heading makes you think this?

_____

_____

_____

B YOUR TURN

Vocabulary

Review the definition of _hazards_ on the Preparing to Read page. Then find both times the word _risks_ is used in these two paragraphs. How are _hazards_ and _risks_ the same? How are they different? Use a dictionary if you need to review the definition of _risk_.

_____

_____

_____

C HERE'S HOW

Language Coach

Some **prefixes** change their spelling when added to certain words. The prefix _in-_ means "no" or "not," like in the word _incorrect_. I see the word _illiterate_ in this line. Here, the prefix _il-_ has the same meaning as _in-_. _Illiterate_ means "not able to read and write."

The City Beat

by N. PARKER **A**

A lively debate occurred at last Tuesday's packed city council meeting on the subject of whether to establish a skateboard park. Mayor Gridlock made a few opening remarks and then turned the microphone over to J. Cool, Director of Parks and Recreation. Mr. Cool read from portions of a report prepared by his staff, who had investigated the need for and the liability, risks, cost, and possible location of a park. Several members of the community spoke.

K. Skater said, "Skateboarding is a challenging sport. It's good for us. But right now we have no place to skate, and so kids are getting tickets for illegal skating. Lots of people say it's too dangerous, but that's not true. Kids get hurt in every sport, but you can make it a lot less dangerous for us if you give us a smooth place to practice. Still, we skaters have to be responsible and only take risks we can handle. That teaches us a lot." **B**

D. T. Merchant remarked, "I am a store owner downtown. These skaters use our curbs and handrails as their personal skating ramps. They threaten pedestrians and scare people. If we build them an alternative, I believe most will use it. Then the police can concentrate on the few who break the rules."

G. Homeowner had this to say: "Skaters are illiterate bums. They think safety **C** gear means thick hair gel. They have no respect. They will disturb my neighborhood all night long with their subhuman noise. I would like to remind the city council— I pay taxes and I vote. A skateboard park? Not in my backyard!"

© David Young_Wolff/Photo Edit, Inc.

IN OTHER WORDS This page is part of a two-page newspaper column called "The City Beat." The reporter, N. Parker, shares what happened at a recent city council meeting about the new skateboard park. After the mayor and head of the Parks and Recreations Department spoke, different people from the city also spoke. First, K. Skater explained why skaters need a park. Then D.T. Merchant, a business owner, said that a new park would keep skaters away from curbs and railings. G. Homeowner was the third speaker. This person explained why some voters would not support a skateboard park.

F. Parent: "My son is an outstanding citizen. He is respectful and well behaved. He also lives to skateboard. This city has placed my son at risk by failing to give him a safe place to skate. If we were talking about building a basketball court, nobody would think twice before agreeing. I'm a voter too, and I expect the city council to be responsive to the needs of *all* citizens."

Finally, S. B. Owner said, "I am the owner of the Skate Bowl. Skateboarding is not a fad. It is here to stay. You may not like the way some skaters act or look, but I know them all. They're great kids. Seems like most of the good folks here tonight are worried about safety. So here's what I propose: I will sell all safety gear at my store at 50 percent off. That's less than it costs me, folks. All that you parents have to do is fill out the emergency information card for your skater and return it to me. I'll see that the information is entered in a database that paramedics, hospital workers, and police officers can access. I'll also make sure that everyone who comes to my store knows what the Consumer Product Safety Commission says: "'Kids who want to skate are going to skate. Let's help them skate safely.'"

D

Mr. Owner's proposal was met with a standing ovation. Plans to move ahead with the new skateboard park project will be put to a formal vote at next month's regular session.

Vocabulary **proposal** (pruh POHZ uhl) *n.*: suggestion.

Comprehension

How do all of the different citizen comments add to the debate? **Follow-up:** How does the information Mr. Owner shares add to the argument?

IN OTHER WORDS This is the second page of the newspaper column. N. Parker reports that F. Parent spoke in favor of a park because it would give children a safe place to skate. The final speaker was S.B. Owner, who spoke in full support of skaters. He offered to sell all safety equipment at his skate shop at 50 percent off if parents of skaters agreed to fill out an emergency info card. This information would then be shared with police and health workers, in case a skater has an accident. N. Parker reports that other people at the meeting clapped for Mr. Owner's plan and that a vote on the park will be held next month.

Reading Focus

This is an example of a **consumer document**. What information can you gather from it? How can you use this information to better understand the previous document that describes the debate?

_____

_____

_____

_____

_____

_____

Reading Focus

Previewing a consumer document is sometimes different than previewing other kinds of documents. For example, if you just look at the heading and boldface print in this document, you may not notice the very important small text at the bottom. Why is this small text so important?

_____

_____

_____

_____

_____

_____

COUPON

50% OFF   DISCOUNT COUPON FOR A 50% OFF

S. B. OWNER'S

SKATE BOWL

This coupon entitles bearer,

_____

to **50 PERCENT OFF**
the regular list price on all helmets,
kneepads, and elbow pads.

Discount does not extend to shoes, padded clothing, boards, trucks, stickers, or any other equipment. Discount does not include state or local sales tax. Discount is not good in combination with any other discount or coupon. Bearer must show photo identification, such as a school ID or a yearbook photograph. B

Skateboard Park Documents **615**

IN OTHER WORDS This page shows a coupon from the skate shop S.B. Owner runs, called the Skate Bowl. The coupon is a 50 percent off discount on helmets, kneepads, and elbow pads. The small print at the bottom of the coupon explains what products are not included in the discount. The small print also explains that the discount does not include tax and cannot be used with any other coupon. Finally, the coupon requires that anyone using it must show photo identification.

Excerpts from

Consumer Product Safety Commission: Document 93 C

Approximately 26,000 persons go to hospital emergency rooms each year for skateboarding-related injuries. Several factors—lack of protective equipment, poor board maintenance, and irregular riding surfaces—are involved in these accidents.

Who gets injured. Six of every ten skateboard injuries happen to children under fifteen years of age. Skateboarders who have been skating for less than a week suffer one third of the injuries; riders with a year or more of skating experience have the next highest number of injuries.

Injuries to first-time skateboarders are, for the most part, caused by falls. Experienced riders suffer injuries mostly when they fall after their skateboards strike rocks and other irregularities in the riding surface, or when they attempt difficult stunts.

Environmental hazards. Irregular surfaces account for more than half the skateboarding injuries caused by falls. Before riding, skateboarders should check the surface for holes, bumps, rocks, and debris. Areas set aside for skateboarding generally have smoother riding surfaces. Skateboarding in the street can result in collisions with cars, causing serious injury or even death. **D**

The skateboard. Before using their boards, riders should check them for hazards, such as loose, broken, or cracked parts; sharp edges; slippery top surfaces; and wheels with nicks and cracks. Serious defects should be corrected by a qualified repair person.

Protective gear. Protective gear—such as slip-resistant, closed shoes, helmets, and specially designed padding—may not fully protect skateboarders from fractures, but its use is recommended because such gear can reduce the number and severity of injuries.

The protective gear currently on the market is not subject to federal performance standards, and so careful selection by consumers is necessary. In a helmet, look for proper fit and a chin strap; make sure the helmet does not block the rider's vision and hearing. Body padding should fit comfortably. If it is tight, it can restrict circulation and reduce the skater's ability to move freely. Loose-fitting padding, on the other hand, can slip off or slide out of position.

Source: U.S. Consumer Product Safety Commission, Washington, D.C. 20207 **E**

Vocabulary **hazards** (HAZ uhrdz) *n.:* dangers; things that can cause danger.

> **Read with a Purpose** Now that you've read these documents, how would you solve the skateboarding problem?

C **HERE'S HOW**

Reading Focus

I want to **preview** this new **document**. First, I will read the heading. I do not know what *excerpts* means. I can look it up in a dictionary. *Excerpts* are "passages from a text." This document is part of a larger one.

D **YOUR TURN**

Reading Focus

There are many facts on this page. How does this **information** support the ideas and opinions in the first and second documents? Give at least two examples.

_____

_____

_____

E **HERE'S HOW**

Reading Focus

This document includes "Source" information at the end. This tells me that the information in the document comes from a government agency. I can feel comfortable **using the information** in the document, since I know that it came from a respected group.

IN OTHER WORDS The last document in this selection is an excerpt from, or part of, an information sheet about skateboarding injuries. The sheet was published by the Consumer Product Safety Commission, a government agency that checks the safety of different products. The excerpt explains how many people go to the hospital with skateboarding injuries and who tends to get injured most. The excerpt also includes information on how *where* a person is skating can increase the danger for injury. Finally, the document reminds skaters to carefully check their boards and wear the proper safety equipment.

Skateboard Park Documents

USE A VENN DIAGRAM

DIRECTIONS: Filling in a Venn diagram is a great way to compare and contrast the information in documents. In the diagram below, write useful information from the "Skateboard Park Documents" in the left circle. Then, after you have read "SweetPlayer Documents," write useful information from that selection in the right circle. If the same kind of information is found in both documents, write that information in the section where the circles overlap.

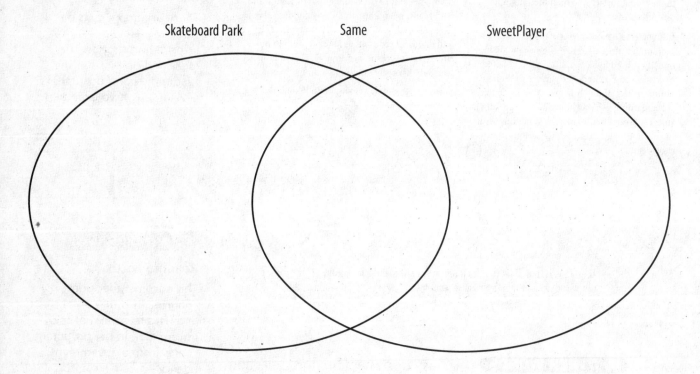

Skateboard Park   Same   SweetPlayer

Applying Your Skills

Skateboard Park Documents

COMPREHENSION WRAP-UP

1. Discuss the three documents presented here. How is the information in each document different? How does this information work for or against the skateboard park?

INFORMATIONAL TEXT FOCUS: USING INFORMATION TO SOLVE PROBLEMS

DIRECTIONS: Use the chart below to compare and contrast the **documents** in this selection. Put a checkmark in the boxes that describe each document.

	Critical issues Memorandum	The City Beat Column	Excerpts from *Consumer Product Safety Commission: Document 93*
It is a public document.			
It is a workplace document.			
It contains facts.			
It contains opinions.			
Its information supports a skateboard park.			
Its information is against a skateboard park.			

READING FOCUS: PREVIEWING

DIRECTIONS: Preview "SweetPlayer Documents" on page 193. Check headings, subheadings, illustrations, and boldface words. What do you predict you will learn?

_____

Word Box

potentially

proposal

hazards

VOCABULARY REVIEW

DIRECTIONS: Imagine that a streetlight near your home is rusty and in danger of falling over. Write a sentence describing this issue that uses two of the words in the Word Box.

_____

Preparing to Read

SweetPlayer Documents

INFORMATIONAL TEXT FOCUS: CONSUMER DOCUMENTS

Consumer documents give you information that you need to make smart buying decisions. You have probably already seen many different kinds of these documents, such as warranties, contracts, and instruction manuals. Every consumer document includes the following:

- The **elements** of a consumer document are the types of information in the document. For example, a contract for cell phone service will tell you what services you get and what you pay in return.

- The **features** of a consumer document are the details unique to that document. For example, the contract for one kind of cell phone service may give you more free minutes than the contract for another type of service.

READING FOCUS: SKIMMING AND SCANNING

You can use **skimming** and **scanning** to get the information you need from consumer documents. Skimming is reading quickly. When you skim, you get a general—but not very detailed—idea of what you are reading. For example, skimming is a good way to get a basic understanding of the elements of a consumer document. Scanning is looking for specific information. You can scan titles, headings, graphics, and key words in italics or boldface to locate what you are looking for. When reading a consumer document, you might scan headings to find specific features.

Informational Text Skills
Analyze consumer documents; analyze and understand elements and features of informational texts.

Reading Skills
Skim and scan texts.

VOCABULARY

Practice saying these words out loud.

abide (UH BYD) (with *by*) *v.:* accept and follow.

liable (LY UH BUHL) *adj.:* legally responsible.

INTO THE DOCUMENTS

Many products come with consumer documents. Some documents tell how a product works, such as directions or manuals. Contracts are also important documents. A user's agreement is a type of contract that tells what the buyer promises. A warranty tells what the company promises. In this selection, a boy named Juan looks at consumer documents before buying new computer software.

SweetPlayer Documents

Choosing an MP3 Player Now Juan is ready to use that high-speed modem. His first stop? MP3s and fast downloads! MP3 is an audio format, a software code that turns sounds into information a computer can understand. MP3 squeezes good sound quality into a small package. The sound-size combination makes MP3 the most popular audio format used today. Juan checks out the rules for downloading MP3s on the Internet.

IS IT LEGAL?

The Internet is full of music. You can get your favorite hit in MP3 format with a single click. It's easy, it's free—and it could be illegal. Many music sites contain music that someone has digitally copied from a CD and then placed where other people can download it. It's a convenient and popular practice, but it is not legal. So what is legal? **B**

1. You may rip tracks from a CD you own to a computer as long as they are for your own use and not for the use of other people.

2. You may download free promotional tracks. This is an increasingly popular way for artists to introduce their work to you. Free and promotional tracks are clearly marked, usually under the heading "Free Music." There are often CDs for sale by the artist, too. Watch

out, though. If a friend wants the same track, he or she will have to download it. It is not legal for you to copy a CD you downloaded from the Internet.

3. You may buy the track for your own use. Many sites, including those of more and more record companies, are now offering songs for sale in this manner.

Rule of thumb: If the way in which music is to be downloaded doesn't fit any of the three situations described above, the process probably isn't legal. When in doubt, check the copyright notice on the site. **C** **D**

Internet

© Jack Hollingsworth/Photodisc/Getty Images

IN OTHER WORDS This page discusses when ripping tracks from a CD and downloading songs is legal—and when it is illegal. Songs, like books, have copyrights. A copyright is a person's or company's legal right to copy, publish, or sell something. Downloading copyrighted songs for free is often illegal. However, many record companies now allow you to buy songs and *then* download them. Once you buy a song, it is yours to play as often as you like. However, it is illegal to then copy that song onto a CD for your friends.

A | HERE'S HOW

Reading Focus

When I **scan** this page, I see from the title that these are "SweetPlayer Documents." I do not know what SweetPlayer is. When I **skim** further, I see that Juan is looking for MP3 software. SweetPlayer must be some kind of MP3 software.

B | HERE'S HOW

Language Coach

I know that the word *illegal* is similar to the word *legal*. *Legal* means "something okay under the law." I already know il- is a **prefix** like *non-*. I see at the end of the paragraph that downloading some music is *not* legal. *Illegal* means "not legal."

C | YOUR TURN

Vocabulary

The In Other Words paragraph gives you the definition of *copyright*. Now imagine you are unsure if downloading from a certain site is legal. Why does it make sense for you to read the site's *copyright*? What would you expect the *copyright* to tell you?

D | READ AND DISCUSS

Comprehension

What does this box say about downloading music?

Juan can't wait to start listening to music on the family's computer. He needs the right software and has narrowed his search to a product called SweetPlayer—but which version should he get? Let's look at the Internet advertisement.

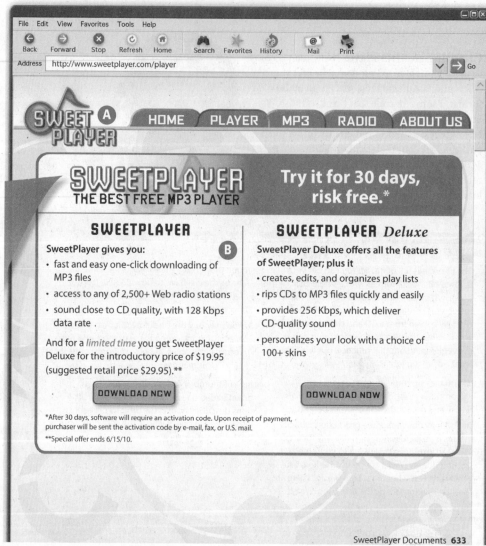

SweetPlayer Documents **633**

A YOUR TURN

Reading Focus

One common **feature** of advertisements is the cost of the product. **Scan** this advertisement to find out how much SweetPlayer costs. How about SweetPlayer Deluxe? Which product would you most like to buy? Explain your answer.

_____

_____

_____

_____

_____

_____

_____

_____

B READ AND DISCUSS

Comprehension

What do we learn in this box about SweetPlayer?

IN OTHER WORDS This page shows you an advertisement for SweetPlayer on the company's Web site. Customers are encouraged to try either SweetPlayer or SweetPlayer Deluxe for free for 30 days. (Small print at the bottom of the advertisement explains that after 30 days, you will need a paid activation code.) The left side of the advertisement explains what you get when you use SweetPlayer. The right side explains additional features you can use when you use SweetPlayer Deluxe. Each version of the player can be downloaded by clicking the "Download Now" button.

Following Download Directions Juan clicks on the button to download SweetPlayer Deluxe. The following downloading directions appear on the screen:

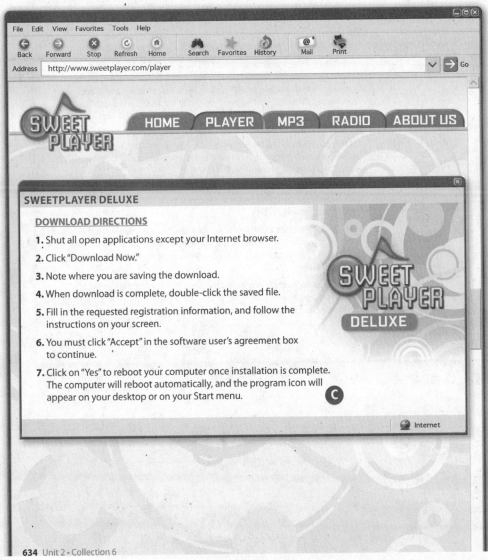

File   Edit   View   Favorites   Tools   Help

Back   Forward   Stop   Refresh   Home   Search   Favorites   History   Mail   Print

Address   http://www.sweetplayer.com/player   Go

HOME   PLAYER   MP3   RADIO   ABOUT US

SWEETPLAYER DELUXE

DOWNLOAD DIRECTIONS

1. Shut all open applications except your Internet browser.
2. Click "Download Now."
3. Note where you are saving the download.
4. When download is complete, double-click the saved file.
5. Fill in the requested registration information, and follow the instructions on your screen.
6. You must click "Accept" in the software user's agreement box to continue.
7. Click on "Yes" to reboot your computer once installation is complete. The computer will reboot automatically, and the program icon will appear on your desktop or on your Start menu.

SWEET PLAYER DELUXE

Internet

634 Unit 2 • Collection 6

IN OTHER WORDS This page shows the seven steps Juan needs to follow to download SweetPlayer Deluxe. Many of these steps will take place after the software is actually downloaded. For example, Juan will need to accept a software user's agreement before he can use the player.

C   **YOUR TURN**

Reading Focus

Which common **elements** of technical directions do you see so far? (Hint: Think of other technical directions you have read.)

_____

_____

_____

_____

_____

_____

Vocabulary

 A **HERE'S HOW**

I am not sure of the exact meaning of *license* here. I do know that if you have a driver's *license*, you are allowed to drive. I think the "*license* to use this software" must be something that allows me to use the player. The definition of *license* must be close to "permission to use or do something."

Reading Focus

B **HERE'S HOW**

When I **scan** the user's agreement, I recognize common **elements** of this kind of agreement. It tells how a person may use the product. If I **skim** to look for details, I can find out more about the **features** of this agreement. I see that the company is sure to tell me that I cannot use the software on two computers at the same time. This might be an important **feature**.

Reading Focus

C **YOUR TURN**

Why would it be a mistake only to **skim** or **scan** a software user's agreement before you accept it?

_____

_____

_____

Reading a Software User's Agreement Even though he plans to click "Accept," Juan reads the software user's agreement carefully. (Remember that a user agreement is a form of contract.) It is long and complicated. Here are the parts that grab Juan's attention.

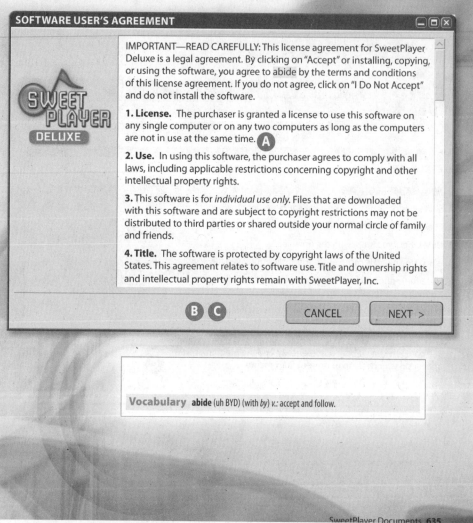

SOFTWARE USER'S AGREEMENT

IMPORTANT—READ CAREFULLY: This license agreement for SweetPlayer Deluxe is a legal agreement. By clicking on "Accept" or installing, copying, or using the software, you agree to abide by the terms and conditions of this license agreement. If you do not agree, click on "I Do Not Accept" and do not install the software.

1. License. The purchaser is granted a license to use this software on any single computer or on any two computers as long as the computers are not in use at the same time. **A**

2. Use. In using this software, the purchaser agrees to comply with all laws, including applicable restrictions concerning copyright and other intellectual property rights.

3. This software is for *individual use only*. Files that are downloaded with this software and are subject to copyright restrictions may not be distributed to third parties or shared outside your normal circle of family and friends.

4. Title. The software is protected by copyright laws of the United States. This agreement relates to software use. Title and ownership rights and intellectual property rights remain with SweetPlayer, Inc.

B **C**   CANCEL   NEXT >

Vocabulary **abide** (uh BYD) (with *by*) *v*.: accept and follow.

SweetPlayer Documents **635**

IN OTHER WORDS This page shows you the first page of the Software User's Agreement that Juan has to accept to use SweetPlayer Deluxe. This legal agreement explains how a customer can use the player. The agreement includes the number of computers on which the program can be used. The agreement also reminds the customer that both the player and any files are protected by copyrights.

WARRANTY

Reading a Limited Warranty Before clicking on "Accept,"
Juan also reads the warranty.

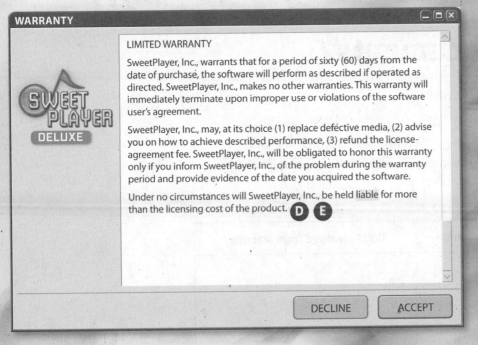

WARRANTY

LIMITED WARRANTY

SweetPlayer, Inc., warrants that for a period of sixty (60) days from the date of purchase, the software will perform as described if operated as directed. SweetPlayer, Inc., makes no other warranties. This warranty will immediately terminate upon improper use or violations of the software user's agreement.

SweetPlayer, Inc., may, at its choice (1) replace defective media, (2) advise you on how to achieve described performance, (3) refund the license-agreement fee. SweetPlayer, Inc., will be obligated to honor this warranty only if you inform SweetPlayer, Inc., of the problem during the warranty period and provide evidence of the date you acquired the software.

Under no circumstances will SweetPlayer, Inc., be held liable for more than the licensing cost of the product. **D** **E**

DECLINE   ACCEPT

Now Juan is ready to go! He knows what he can legally do and
what the company must legally provide. He clicks "Accept."

D **YOUR TURN**

Reading Focus

Circle two **features** in the SweetPlayer warranty.

E **READ AND DISCUSS**

Comprehension

When Juan accepts the user's agreement, what does that mean? **Follow-up:** What other information is important for Juan to understand?

IN OTHER WORDS This page gives you a look at the limited warranty Juan needs to accept. Remember that a warranty tells what a company promises its customers. The first paragraph of this warranty explains that SweetPlayer, Inc. promises its product will perform as described for 60 days. The customer must use the product just as the company says, though. The second paragraph of the warranty lists three ways in which SweetPlayer, Inc. might communicate with the customer. The final paragraph states that the company is only liable, or legally responsible, for the cost of the license. A customer cannot sue the company for an amount of money higher than the license fee.

Skills Practice

SweetPlayer Documents

USE A SKIMMING AND SCANNING CHART

DIRECTIONS: Remember that **skimming** is reading quickly, and **scanning** is looking for specific information. Review "SweetPlayer Documents" and complete the chart below with the information you learned from skimming and scanning each page.

Page	What I learned from skimming	What I learned from scanning
193		
194		
195		
196		
197		

Applying Your Skills

SweetPlayer Documents

COMPREHENSION WRAP-UP

1. How do laws affect the downloading and copying of music?

2. What would happen if someone simply clicked "Accept" without reading the contract?

INFORMATIONAL TEXT FOCUS: CONSUMER DOCUMENTS

DIRECTIONS: The list below includes some of the **elements** and **features** of the **consumer documents** you just read. Circle anything that is an element. Underline anything that is a feature.

one-click downloading

directions for downloading

license agreement

software can be used on any two computers

ad for 30-day trial

60-day guarantee that software will work

READING FOCUS: SKIMMING AND SCANNING

DIRECTIONS: Skim the next selection in this collection, "Guide to Computers," for 30 seconds. Then write two general ideas you gathered from skimming on the lines below.

1. _____

2. _____

Next, **scan** the document for the answers to the following question:

What steps do you follow to set up a desktop computer?

_____

_____

VOCABULARY REVIEW

DIRECTIONS: Look again at the definition of *abide* on the Preparing to Read page. Then find the word *abide* in "SweetPlayer Documents." What does Juan agree to *abide* by in the Software User's Agreement? What do you think this means?

_____

_____

Guide to Computers

INFORMATIONAL TEXT FOCUS: TECHNICAL DIRECTIONS

Many products come with instruction manuals that explain how the product works. Sometimes a product is a scientific, electronic, or mechanical device, like a computer. Then the instruction manuals are called **technical directions**. Technical directions usually contain:

- a list of parts or a glossary of key terms that you will need to know.

- step-by-step instructions you need to follow to put together and use the product.

- graphics, such as illustrations, diagrams, and photos, that show you key steps.

READING FOCUS: UNDERSTANDING GRAPHICS

The **graphics** in technical directions can be a big help in understanding how a product works. Graphics can also guide you as you try to follow step-by-step instructions. Often, these graphics are labeled as "figures." For example, as you read "Guide to Computers," you will come across several figures illustrating what certain computer parts look like. Take the time to notice graphics and the information each provides.

VOCABULARY

Make flashcards for the words below. On each card, write the word on the front and its definition on the back.

functions (FUHNGK SHUHNZ) *n.:* uses or jobs something performs.

corresponding (KAWR UH SPAHN DIHNG) *adj.:* matching; equivalent.

secure (SIH KYUR) *v.:* fix firmly in place.

INTO THE DIRECTIONS

Computers are an example of a type of product that always comes with technical directions. The following selection begins with a description of the parts of a computer. The document continues by describing what each of these parts does. Finally, the document describes how to set up the computer.

SKILLS FOCUS

Informational Text Skills
Understand technical directions; follow technical directions and steps in a process; analyze instruction manuals.

Reading Skills
Understand graphics.

GUIDE TO COMPUTERS

Figure 1 *Believe it or not, this MP3 player contains a computer!*

Read with a Purpose
Read to figure out the purpose of this set of technical directions.

WHAT IS A COMPUTER?

Did a computer help you wake up this morning? You might think of a computer as something you use to send e-mails or surf the Internet, but computers are around you all of the time. Computers are in alarm clocks, cars, phones, and even MP3 players. An MP3 player, like the one in **Figure 1,** allows you to build your own music lists and carry thousands of songs with you wherever you go.

A **computer** is an electronic device that performs tasks by processing and storing information. A computer performs a task when it is given a command and has the instructions necessary to carry out that command. Computers do not operate by themselves, or "think." **A**

Basic Functions

The basic functions a computer performs are shown in **Figure 2.** The information you give to a computer is called *input.* Downloading songs onto your MP3 player or setting your alarm clock is a type of input. To perform a task, a computer processes the input, changing it to a desired form. Processing could mean adding a list of numbers, executing a drawing, or even moving a piece of equipment. Input doesn't have to be processed immediately; it can be stored until it is needed. Computers store information in their *memory.* For example, your MP3 player stores the songs you have chosen to input. It can then process this stored information by playing the songs you request. *Output* is the final result of the task performed by the computer. The output of an MP3 player is the music you hear when you put on your headphones! **B** **C**

Vocabulary **functions** (FUHNGK shuhnz) *n.:* uses; purposes.

A **HERE'S HOW**

Reading Focus

After reading the first paragraph and looking at the **graphic,** I can tell that this is a document about computers. I do not think this is the start of the **technical directions,** though. I will read further to find the technical directions.

B **READ AND DISCUSS**

Comprehension

What point is the author trying to make here?

C **HERE'S HOW**

Vocabulary

Sometimes it is easier to understand a new word by putting a familiar word that means the same thing in its place. If I re-read the In Other Words paragraph, I see that *functions* can mean "jobs." If I replace *functions* with "jobs," the subheading would read "Basic Jobs." That makes a lot of sense when I read the first sentence in this paragraph.

IN OTHER WORDS This page begins by explaining what a computer is and the different ways computers play a role in your everyday life. It then continues to explain the functions, or jobs, that a computer performs. It lists three important terms and their definitions. *Input* is the information you give a computer to process, or work to examine or analyze. *Memory* is where computers store information. *Output* is the result of the processing work the computer performed. In the left column of the page, the illustration Figure 1 shows an MP3 player.

YOUR TURN

Reading Focus

This **graphic's** label tells you that it is a diagram of the functions of a computer. What do the boxes and arrows help you picture?

_____

_____

_____

_____

_____

 YOUR TURN

Vocabulary

You know from the In Other Words paragraph that *processing* means "working to examine data." How do you think *processes* is connected to this definition?

_____

_____

_____

_____

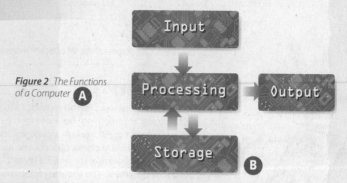

Figure 2 *The Functions of a Computer* A

COMPUTER HARDWARE

For each function of a computer, there is a corresponding part of the computer where that function occurs. *Hardware* refers to the parts, or equipment, that make up a computer. As you read about each piece of hardware, refer to **Figure 3**.

Input Devices

An *input device* is a piece of hardware that feeds information to the computer. You can enter information into a computer by using a keyboard, mouse, scanner, digitizing pad and pen, or digitizing camera—or even your own voice!

Central Processing Unit

A computer performs tasks within an area called the *central processing unit,* or CPU. In a personal computer, the CPU is a microprocessor. Input goes through the CPU for immediate processing or for storage in memory. The CPU is where the computer does calculations, solves problems, and executes the instructions given to it. Some computers now come with two—or more—CPUs to process information more effectively.

Vocabulary **corresponding** (kawr uh SPAHN dihng) *adj.:* matching; equivalent.

IN OTHER WORDS This page is the beginning of a list of the different hardware, or pieces of equipment, that make up a computer. A computer's input devices and central processing unit are described first. Figure 2 is a flowchart that illustrates how to think about the different functions, or jobs, of a computer. These functions are described on the previous page.

Memory

Information can be stored in the computer's memory until it is needed. CD-ROMs, DVDs, and flash drives inserted into a computer and hard disks inside a computer have memory to store information. Two other types of memory are *ROM* (read-only memory) and *RAM* (random-access memory).

ROM is permanent. It handles functions such as computer start-up, maintenance, and hardware management. ROM normally cannot be added to or changed, and it cannot be lost when the computer is turned off. On the other hand, RAM is temporary. It stores information only while that information is being used. RAM is sometimes called working memory. The more RAM a computer has, the more information can be input and the more powerful the computer is. **C** **D**

Figure 3 *Computer Hardware*

Keyboard · Mouse · Modem · CPU · RAM · ROM · CD/DVD drive · Hard disk

IN OTHER WORDS This page and the next page continue to describe the hardware that makes up a computer. On these pages, the two types of memory (ROM and RAM) are defined, as well as output devices and modems.

C YOUR TURN

Reading Focus

This section is about computer hardware. What part of **technical directions** is this—a parts list or instructions? Why is this part of the document important?

_____

_____

_____

_____

_____

D YOUR TURN

Language Coach

Many words have **multiple**, or more than one, **meanings**. These words are spelled the same, yet are meant to mean different things. Look at the way *handles* is used in the first line of the second paragraph. You already know that a *handle* can help you carry a box or other object. But here *handles* means something else. Guess another meaning of *handles*. (Hint: The functions listed in the sentence are all something ROM *does*.) Check your answer with a dictionary.

_____

_____

_____

_____

A **READ AND DISCUSS**

Comprehension

What does this part say about the computer's hardware?

B **HERE'S HOW**

Reading Focus

As I read about the different parts of a computer, I had trouble understanding what the text is describing. Now that I see the **graphic**, I have a clear picture in my mind of what the text is explaining.

Output Devices

Once a computer performs a task, it shows the results of the task on an *output device*. Monitors, printers, and speaker systems are all examples of output devices.

Modems

One piece of computer hardware that serves as an input device as well as an output device is a *modem*. Modems allow computers to communicate. One computer can input information into another computer over a telephone or cable line as long as each computer has its own network connection. In this way, modems permit computers to "talk" with other computers. **A**

B

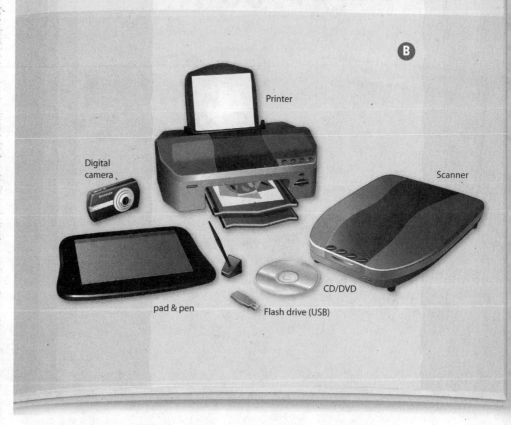

Printer

Digital camera

Scanner

pad & pen

Flash drive (USB)

CD/DVD

IN OTHER WORDS Figure 3 runs across the bottom of both pages. This figure illustrates what all the hardware described in the manual (and more) looks like, from a mouse to a Flash drive.

THE INTERNET—A GLOBAL NETWORK

Thanks to high-speed connections and computer software, it is possible to connect many computers and allow them to communicate with one another. That's what the **Internet** is—a huge computer network consisting of millions of computers that can all share information with one another. **C D**

How the Internet Works

Computers can connect to one another on the Internet by using a modem to dial into an Internet service provider, or ISP. A home computer connects to an ISP over a phone or cable line. A school, business, or other group can connect all of its computers to form a local area network (LAN). Then, a single network connection can be used to connect the LAN to an ISP. As depicted in **Figure 4,** ISPs are connected globally by satellite. And that's how computers go global!

Figure 4 *Through a series of connections like these, every computer on the Internet can store information.*

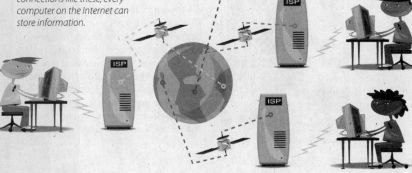

IN OTHER WORDS This page gives a quick explanation of the Internet—a huge, global computer network. It also explains how it is possible for computers to connect to one another at home, in a school or business, or across the world. Figure 4 shows how one person's computer is linked to their friends' computers by his or her Internet service provider's satellites.

Vocabulary

I am not sure of what *consisting* means. I do know that when a computer is a part of a network, there are other computers in the network, too. So *consisting* might mean "made up of" here. I can try replacing *consisting* with my definition: "a huge computer network made up of millions of computers." My definition seems to work.

D (READ AND DISCUSS)

Comprehension

What is the purpose of the Internet?

Reading Focus

How are the **graphics** on this page different from other graphics in this selection? What is the purpose of each graphic?

_____

_____

_____

_____

_____

_____

_____

_____

_____

Vocabulary

The directions have not told me what *connectors* are. I do know they plug into other things. Plus I know that *connect*, part of *connector*, means "bring things together." *Connectors* must be parts that join two pieces of computer equipment together.

HOW TO SET UP A DESKTOP COMPUTER A

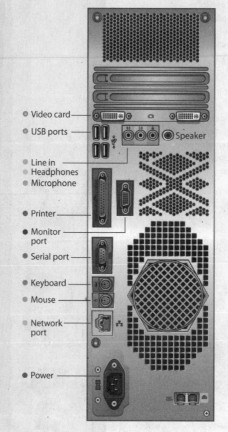

- Video card
- USB ports
- Line in
- Headphones
- Microphone
- Printer
- Monitor port
- Serial port
- Keyboard
- Mouse
- Network port
- Power

Speaker

Monitor

STEP 1 **Connect the monitor to the computer.**

The monitor has two cords. One cord, the **monitor interface cable,** lets the computer communicate with the monitor. The monitor cable connects to the video port (the port designated for monitors) at the back of the computer. The connector on this cord is a plug with pins in it; the pins correspond to holes in the video port on the computer. This cable probably has screws to secure the connection. The other cord is the **monitor's power cord,** which plugs into the wall outlet or **surge protector,** a plug-in device that protects electronic equipment from high-voltage electrical surges (see Step 5). B

Figure 5 *Computer Connections*

Vocabulary **secure** (sih KYUR) *v.:* fix firmly in place.

IN OTHER WORDS This page introduces the five-step process of setting up a desktop computer. Step 1, connecting your monitor to your computer, is described in detail with both words and an illustration above it. Figure 5, which runs down the left side of the page, points out the many connections that can be made from the back of your computer.

USB

STEP 2 Connect the printer to the computer.

The connector on the cable that is attached to your printer is most likely a USB cable. USB ports (USB stands for Universal Serial Bus) can accept any device with a USB connector. Connect one end to the back of your printer. Then connect the other end to an available USB port on the back of your computer where you see a **printer** or **peripherals icon.**

Keyboard/mouse

STEP 3 Connect the keyboard and mouse.

Look at the **connector** on the cord that is attached to the keyboard or mouse. If this connector is round, plug the cord into a matching port on the back of the computer. (See Figure 5 illustration on page 645.) If the connector on the cord is flat, plug it into any available USB port. (See Step 2 illustration.) If you are using a cordless keyboard or mouse, connect it to the computer using the manufacturer's technical directions.

Network

STEP 4 Connect the modem to the computer by using a network cable.

Connect the **network cable** to the network port on the back of your computer. Connect the other end of the network cable to your modem. As long as you have an active Internet connection, the software should automatically detect that you are connected to the Internet when your computer starts.

Power cord

STEP 5 Connect the power cords.

The **power cord** is a three-pronged, grounded cord that you attach to your computer. First, attach one end of the power cord to the computer; then, plug the other end of the cord into a **surge protector**. Plug the surge protector into a grounded wall outlet. Turn on the monitor and then the computer, and you are ready to go! **C D**

C READ AND DISCUSS

Comprehension

Why would a diagram and text both be included in the directions?

D HERE'S HOW

Reading Focus

I can see how important it is to follow the steps in **technical directions** in the order they are given. A person needs to first connect all of the hardware using the right cables. Otherwise, when the power is connected, the computer will not work.

IN OTHER WORDS This page contains the other four steps in the five-step process. As with Step 1, each step is described with a full paragraph and an illustration. Important terms are shown in boldfaced type.

Skills Practice

Guide to Computers

USE A GRAPHICS TABLE

DIRECTIONS: Remember that **graphics** can be a big help when trying to read technical directions. Take a look at the steps in the table below. These steps detail how to get started with a new portable CD player and headphones. In the "graphics" column, draw your own illustrations to make each step clear.

Technical Directions	Graphics
1. Take the CD Player and head phones out of the box and remove all of the parts.	
2. Turn the CD player over and insert batteries.	
3. Plug the headphone wire into the CD player.	
4. Press the "play" button, and enjoy!	

Applying Your Skills

Guide to Computers

COMPREHENSION WRAP-UP

1. Discuss how a clock can be thought of as a kind of computer. Describe what a clock does by using its different parts. Why might technical directions be needed for something as simple as a clock?

2. Using the illustrations in the selection, discuss the computer's parts and what they do. Why is it important to know the parts and actions of an electronic device?

INFORMATIONAL TEXT FOCUS: TECHNICAL DIRECTIONS

DIRECTIONS: Review the **technical directions** you just read to answer the following questions.

1. You need to connect the modem to your new computer, but you do not know what it looks like. Where can you look for help?

   _____

2. You are trying to explain the difference between ROM and RAM, but you keep mixing up the two. Where can you find this information?

   _____

3. You have connected the printer, keyboard, and mouse, but something seems to be missing. Where can you double-check the steps?

   _____

READING FOCUS: UNDERSTANDING GRAPHICS

DIRECTIONS: Imagine that the writers who created the technical directions have asked for your feedback on the **graphics**. On a separate piece of paper, draw **A)** a new graphic you would like to see or **B)** how you would change one of the existing graphics.

VOCABULARY REVIEW

DIRECTIONS: On the blank line next to each word, write the word from the Word Box that means exactly or nearly the same thing.

Word Box

functions

corresponding

secure

1. matching _____

2. jobs _____

Collection 6

DIRECTIONS: Complete the vocabulary flashcards below. Include each word's part of speech, pronunciation, and definition. Then write a short sample sentence using each word.

potentially	**abide**
part of speech:_____	part of speech:_____
pronunciation:_____	pronunciation:_____
definition:_____	definition:_____
sample sentence:_____	sample sentence:_____
_____	_____
_____	_____

sequence	**functions**
part of speech:_____	part of speech:_____
pronunciation:_____	pronunciation:_____
definition:_____	definition:_____
sample sentence:_____	sample sentence:_____
_____	_____
_____	_____

proposal	**fundamental**
part of speech:_____	part of speech:_____
pronunciation:_____	pronunciation:_____
definition:_____	definition:_____
sample sentence:_____	sample sentence:_____
_____	_____
_____	_____

Skills Review

Collection 6

LANGUAGE COACH: PREFIXES

Prefixes are syllables attached to the beginnings of words. Prefixes change the meaning of words. For example, the word *view* means "look at." The prefix *pre-* means "before or in front of." When you add this prefix to *view*, it becomes *preview*. *Preview* means "look at beforehand." Some prefixes are spelled differently but mean the same thing.

DIRECTIONS: Circle the word with a prefix in each sentence below.

1. It is illegal to park on that street.

2. In the movie, the detectives uncover who stole the jewelry.

3. My teacher told me that I had to rewrite my paper.

4. It is unfashionable to wear that style of pants.

5. Mario thinks football is an impossible sport.

6. We joined hands and stood in a semicircle.

7. The musician has extraordinary skill.

8. We were disconnected when I hung up the phone by accident.

Which two of the above prefixes mean the same thing but are spelled differently? Explain your answer.

_____

_____

WRITING ACTIVITY

DIRECTIONS: There are many different kinds of **informational texts**: workplace documents, public and consumer documents, technical directions, advertisements, warranties, and user agreements. It is important to read informational texts to learn about new products. Write a short paragraph in which you describe the documents you would read before buying a new MP3 player. Explain why you would read these documents carefully.

_____

_____

_____

_____

_____

Collection

7

Poetry

Smithsonian Institution, Washington DC/
Bridgeman Art Library International

Literary and Academic Vocabulary for Collection 7

LITERARY VOCABULARY

narrative poem (NAR AH TIHV PO UHM) *n.:* a poem that tells a story.
"Paul Revere's Ride" is an example of a narrative poem.

lyric poem (LIR IK PO UHM) *n.:* a poem that includes words and phrases that express the thoughts and emotions of the poet or speaker.
Most lyric poems are short and suggest a feeling.

sonnet (SAHN IT) *n.:* a poem with fourteen lines that follows a rhythmic pattern called iambic pentameter.
He read the sonnet aloud to really hear its beat and rhymes.

iambic pentameter (I AM BIK PEN TAM UT UR) *n.:* a line of poetry with five unstressed beats, each followed by five stressed beats.
Each line in a sonnet follows the pattern called iambic pentameter.

ACADEMIC VOCABULARY

intent (IHN TEHNT) *n.:* a purpose, or a plan.
The intent of a narrative poem is to tell a story.

evoke (IH VOHK) *v.:* draw out, or bring forth.
A good poem or story may evoke strong feelings in a reader.

associations (UH SOH SEE AY SHUHNZ) *n.:* connections in the mind between different things.
To understand a narrative poem, you may have to think about the associations between the characters and your own life.

interpretation (IHN TUR PRUH TAY SHUHN) *n.:* explanation of the meaning.
You may have a different interpretation of a poem than your friend.

Valentine for Ernest Mann

By Naomi Shihab Nye

LITERARY FOCUS: LYRIC POEMS

Some poems tell stories. Others express the thoughts and feelings of the speaker. These kinds of poems are called **lyric poems**. Lyric poems are usually short. The feelings they express are not always easy to understand at first. The poems may simply hint at a strong emotion, like music often does.

READING FOCUS: READING A POEM

When you first **read a poem**, do not spend time worrying about finding certain literary elements. Just enjoy reading! When you have finished, read the poem again. This time, pay closer attention to its individual parts. Notice the title, the poet's word choice, and punctuation.

As you read the following lyric poem, remember the following tips:

- **Read to enjoy.** Even the most serious poem can be fun to read. Poets play with words, sounds, rhythms, and rhymes.

- **Read aloud.** Read the poem in a normal voice, as if you were speaking to a friend. The poem's music will come naturally. If possible, also have someone read the poem to you while you concentrate on listening.

- **Pay attention to each word.** Each word in a well-written poem is important to its meaning. Do not be afraid to stop and check a word's definition if it is unclear to you.

VOCABULARY

Practice saying each word out loud.

spirit (SPIHR IHT) *n.:* courage; liveliness.

drifting (DRIHF TING) *v.:* moving without a purpose.

re-invented (REE IN VENT) *v.:* made again or made new.

INTO THE POEM

In "Valentine for Ernest Mann," the poet is the speaker. She is responding to someone who has asked her to write a poem. Instead of sending the person a poem, the poet gives the reader a lesson in finding poetry in unexpected places. She asks the reader to look at the world differently.

SKILLS FOCUS

Literary Skills
Understand the characteristics of lyric poetry.

Reading Skills
Use strategies to read and analyze a poem.

VALENTINE FOR ERNEST MANN

By Naomi Shihab Nye

© Boden/Ledingham/Masterfile

You can't order a poem like you order a taco.
Walk up to the counter, say, "I'll take two"
and expect it to be handed back to you
on a shiny plate.

5   Still, I like your spirit.
Anyone who says, "Here's my address,
write me a poem," deserves something in reply.
So I'll tell a secret instead:
poems hide. In the bottoms of our shoes, **(A)**
10   they are sleeping. They are the shadows
drifting across our ceilings the moment
before we wake up. What we have to do
is live in a way that lets us find them. **(B) (C)**

IN OTHER WORDS The poet is replying to a letter she received in which the person wrote only "Here's my address, write me a poem." She explains that you cannot order a poem like you would order a taco. But she is impressed that the person was brave enough to just say "Write me a poem." So

(A) READ AND DISCUSS

Comprehension

What does the poet set up for us? **Follow-up:** What does the way the poet replied to the letter show us about her view of writing poetry?

(B) YOUR TURN

Reading Focus

Re-read lines 1–13 silently. Then **read** them out loud. How does reading out loud change how you think about the way the poem is written? For example, how does the sentence beginning "In the bottom of our shoes" seem different when read out loud?

_____

_____

_____

(C) HERE'S HOW

Language Coach

The **denotation,** or dictionary definition of *drifting* is "moving without a purpose." The **connotation,** or feeling and association, of *drifting* here is "moving to stay out of sight."

A   HERE'S HOW

Vocabulary

I do not know what
re-invented means, and I need
to know to better understand
the poem. When I look back
at the Preparing to Read
page, I see that its definition
is "made new." I think the
man made the skunks into
something new—valentines.

B   YOUR TURN

Reading Focus

As you **read**, are you paying
attention to each word the
poet chooses to use? The
poet has chosen every word
carefully to express exactly
the right emotion. Look up
any words you are unsure
of to better understand the
poem. Write their definitions
below.

C   READ AND DISCUSS

Comprehension

How does the skunk story
connect to the way the poet
views the starting point and
growth of poetry?

D   HERE'S HOW

Literary Focus

I can tell that this is a **lyric
poem**. It is short and expresses
the poet's thoughts about
writing poetry and where
poems come from. I think the
feeling she expresses in the
poem is happiness that so
many things in life can give
us poetry.

she shares this secret with the person (and with the reader):
"poems hide." She says that poems are everywhere; you
simply have to find them.

Once I knew a man who gave his wife

15 two skunks for a valentine.

He couldn't understand why she was crying.

"I thought they had such beautiful eyes."

And he was serious. He was a serious man

who lived in a serious way. Nothing was ugly

20 just because the world said so. He really

liked those skunks. So, he re-invented them

as valentines and they became beautiful. **A**

At least, to him. And the poems that had been hiding

in the eyes of skunks for centuries

25 crawled out and curled up at his feet. **B** **C**

Maybe if we re-invent whatever our lives give us

we find poems. Check your garage, the odd sock

in your drawer, the person you almost like, but not quite.

And let me know. **D**

IN OTHER WORDS   The poet is now giving an example of
how people can find poems in everyday life. She tells the story
of a man who found two skunks that he thought had very
beautiful eyes. He found them so beautiful that he thought
they would make a good valentine for his wife. To him, the
skunks' eyes were a poem. The poet suggests that people
should try looking at things differently, to see if there is a
poem in them after all.

Comprehension Wrap-Up

1. Discuss the idea of re-inventing objects as valentines. What
   do you view as poetic or beautiful that others might not?

2. How would it be possible to find poetry in the person you
   "almost like"?

Applying Your Skills

Valentine for Ernest Mann

LITERARY FOCUS: LYRIC POEMS

DIRECTIONS: How does "Valentine for Ernest Mann" fit the definition of a **lyric poem**? (Review the description of lyric poems on the Preparing to Read page.) Write your answer on the lines below. Then list three details from the poem to support your answer.

_____

_____

Details from the poem:

1. _____

2. _____

3. _____

READING FOCUS: READING A POEM

DIRECTIONS: Complete the chart below. In the right column, write what you learned while **reading the poem** and following the tips listed in the left column.

Read to enjoy.	
Read aloud.	
Pay attention to each word.	

VOCABULARY REVIEW

DIRECTIONS: Follow the instructions below to write a sentence for two of the vocabulary words in the selection.

1. Use *drifting* in a sentence about a balloon.

_____

2. Use *spirit* in a sentence about a little boy.

_____

Preparing to Read

Paul Revere's Ride

By Henry Wadsworth Longfellow

LITERARY FOCUS: NARRATIVE POETRY: RHYTHM AND METER

A **narrative poem** is a poem that tells a story. Like stories, narrative poems have characters, setting, and plot. Additionally, narrative poems have **rhythm**. Rhythm is the rise and fall of the voice, which is caused by the sounds being pronounced. Rhythm gives a poem a musical quality, and when its sounds are in a regular pattern, we call it **meter**. Read "Paul Revere's Ride" out loud and listen to the way it sounds. The meter may remind you of a running horse: da da DUM da da DUM da da DUM.

READING FOCUS: PARAPHRASING

Paraphrasing means restating a writer's text in your own words. A paraphrase is different than a summary, which retells only the most important points in a text. The first three lines of "Paul Revere's Ride" are paraphrased below.

Original Text	Paraphrase
Lines 1–3: "Listen, my children, and you shall hear / Of the midnight ride of Paul Revere, / On the eighteenth of April in Seventy-five."	Listen to the story of Paul Revere's midnight ride on April 18, 1775.

VOCABULARY

Work with a friend to practice saying these words out loud in complete sentences.

impetuous (IHM PEHCH u UHS) *adj.*: eager.

aghast (UH GAST) *adj.*: shocked; horrified.

INTO THE STORY

This poem is loosely based on real events. On the night of April 18, 1775, Paul Revere and two other men set out to warn American colonists of a British attack. The next day, groups of armed colonists stood up to the British soldiers. They fought at Concord and another town called Lexington. These were the first battles of the American Revolution.

SKILLS FOCUS

Literary Skills
Understand the characteristics narrative poetry; understand rhythm and meter.

Reading Skills
Paraphrase a poem.

PAUL REVERE'S RIDE

By Henry Wadsworth Longfellow

Listen, my children, and you shall hear
Of the midnight ride of Paul Revere,
On the eighteenth of April, in Seventy-five;
Hardly a man is now alive
5 Who remembers that famous day and year. **A**

IN OTHER WORDS Listen to the story of Paul Revere's ride. It took place at midnight, on April 18, 1775. Hardly anyone is still alive who remembers that night.

He said to his friend, "If the British march
By land or sea from the town tonight,
Hang a lantern aloft in the belfry[1] arch
Of the North Church tower as a signal light—
10 One, if by land, and two, if by sea;
And I on the opposite shore will be,
Ready to ride and spread the alarm
Through every Middlesex village and farm,
For the country folk to be up and to arm."[2] **B** **C**

IN OTHER WORDS Paul Revere told his friend to watch for the British. The signal that the British were coming would be a light in the bell tower of the church. One light meant the British were coming by land. Two lights meant they were coming by sea. Revere would wait with his horse on the other side of the river. If the British attacked, he would be ready to ride off and warn the local villagers and farmers to arm themselves.

15 Then he said, "Good night!" and with muffled[3] oar
Silently rowed to the Charlestown shore,

1. **belfry** (BEHL FREE): tower for a bell or bells.
2. **to arm**: to get guns.
3. **muffled** (MUHF UHLD): sound covered up or deadened.

Reading Focus

I will pause now and **paraphrase** lines 18–23: A huge British ship is anchored in the bay and its image is reflected in the water.

B **YOUR TURN**

Literary Focus

When you read lines 24–30 aloud, do you begin with a slow **rhythm** or a fast rhythm? Why?

_____

_____

_____

C **READ AND DISCUSS**

Comprehension

What is the speaker letting us know?

Just as the moon rose over the bay,

Where swinging wide at her moorings[4] lay

The Somerset, British man-of-war;

20   A phantom ship, with each mast and spar[5]

Across the moon like a prison bar,

And a huge black hulk, that was magnified

By its own reflection in the tide. **A**

IN OTHER WORDS   Revere said good night to his friend. Then, he very quietly rowed across the bay from Boston to Charlestown. He passed a British warship anchored in the harbor. In the moonlight, its masts looked to him like prison bars. The ship's reflection in the water made it look big and frightening.

Meanwhile, his friend, through alley and street,

25   Wanders and watches with eager ears,

Till in the silence around him he hears

The muster[6] of men at the barrack[7] door,

The sound of arms, and the tramp of feet,

And the measured tread of the grenadiers,[8]

30   Marching down to their boats on the shore. **B** **C**

IN OTHER WORDS   Meanwhile, Revere's friend wandered through the streets of Boston. He looked out for the British soldiers. Finally, he heard them gather their weapons and march down to their boats on the shore.

Then he climbed the tower of the Old North Church,

By the wooden stairs, with stealthy tread,

To the belfry chamber overhead,

And startled the pigeons from their perch

4. **moorings:** cables holding a ship in place so that it doesn't float away.
5. **mast and spar:** poles supporting a ship's sails.
6. **muster:** assembly; gathering.
7. **barrack** (BAR UHK): building for soldiers.
8. **grenadiers** (GREHN UH DIHRZ): foot soldiers who carry and throw grenades.

35　On the somber[9] rafters, that round him made

　　Masses and moving shapes of shade—

　　By the trembling ladder, steep and tall,

　　To the highest window in the wall,

　　Where he paused to listen and look down

40　A moment on the roofs of the town,

　　And the moonlight flowing over all.

IN OTHER WORDS Revere's friend climbed quietly up the wooden stairs to the church tower. He woke up the pigeons roosting there, and they flew around him. Then he climbed the ladder to the highest window. There, he paused and looked down on the roofs of the town.

　　Beneath, in the churchyard, lay the dead,

　　In their night encampment[10] on the hill,

　　Wrapped in silence so deep and still

45　That he could hear, like a sentinel's[11] tread,

　　The watchful night wind, as it went

　　Creeping along from tent to tent,

　　And seeming to whisper, "All is well!" **E**

　　A moment only he feels the spell

50　Of the place and the hour, and the secret dread

　　Of the lonely belfry and the dead;

　　For suddenly all his thoughts are bent

　　On a shadowy something far away,

　　Where the river widens to meet the bay—

55　A line of black that bends and floats **F**

　　On the rising tide, like a bridge of boats.

IN OTHER WORDS He looked down at the graveyard. It reminded him of a military camp, with each stone like a soldier's tent. The night wind was like a lookout, moving from tent to tent to say that all is well. It was a spooky moment.

---

9. **somber**: dark and gloomy.
10. **encampment**: camping place; here, a graveyard.
11. **sentinel's** (SEHN TIHN UHLZ): guard's.

D **YOUR TURN**

Reading Focus
To better understand the text, **paraphrase** lines 31–41.

_____

_____

_____

_____

_____

_____

E **YOUR TURN**

Literary Focus
Remember that a **narrative poem** tells a story. What larger story does this poem fit into?

_____

_____

_____

_____

F **HERE'S HOW**

Language Coach
I know the word *floats* has **multiple**, or more than one, **meanings**. It can also be a verb meaning "moves across the surface of a liquid." It can also be a noun meaning "vehicles in a parade." I think the first definition makes more sense here.

Literary Focus

Re-read lines 68–72. Is the **rhythm** of these lines quick or is it slow? Explain your answer.

_____

_____

_____

_____

B **YOUR TURN**

Vocabulary

The word *lingers* means "stays back." Draw a circle around what Revere stays back and waits to see in line 72.

C **READ AND DISCUSS**

Comprehension

What has happened?

But, suddenly, in the distance, he spotted something moving on the river. It was the British warships.

Meanwhile, impatient to mount and ride,

Booted and spurred, with a heavy stride

On the opposite shore walked Paul Revere.

60 Now he patted his horse's side,

Now gazed at the landscape far and near,

Then, impetuous,[12] stamped the earth,

And turned and tightened his saddle girth;[13]

But mostly he watched with eager search

65 The belfry tower of the Old North Church,

As it rose above the graves on the hill,

Lonely and spectral[14] and somber and still.

And lo! as he looks, on the belfry's height

A glimmer, and then a gleam of light!

70 He springs to the saddle, the bridle he turns,

But lingers and gazes, till full on his sight

A second lamp in the belfry burns!

IN OTHER WORDS Meanwhile, Paul Revere waited impatiently on the other side of the bay. He had on his boots and spurs. He was ready to ride. He patted his horse and he looked around. He stamped his foot. He tightened the strap of his saddle. But, mostly, he watched the bell tower of the church. It looked lonely and ghostly above the graveyard. At last, he saw a light! He jumped on his horse and turned to go. But then, he waited, and he saw the second light in the bell tower.

A hurry of hoofs in a village street,

A shape in the moonlight, a bulk[15] in the dark,

75 And beneath, from the pebbles, in passing, a spark

---

12. **impetuous** (IHM PEHCH oo uhs): impulsive; eager.
13. **girth**: strap that holds the saddle on the horse.
14. **spectral** (SPEHK truhl): ghostly.
15. **bulk**: shape.

© Kevin Fleming/Corbis

D (YOUR TURN)

Language Coach

The word *light* has **multiple meanings**. On the lines below, write two possible meanings for the word *light*. Use a dictionary to help you. Which definition of *light* makes the most sense here?

_____

_____

_____

_____

_____

E (YOUR TURN)

Reading Focus

Stop and re-read lines 73–80. Then **paraphrase** what these lines describe.

_____

_____

_____

_____

_____

_____

_____

_____

_____

Struck out by a steed[16] flying fearless and fleet:

That was all! And yet, through the gloom and the light, **D**

The fate of a nation was riding that night;

And the spark struck out by that steed, in his flight,

80   Kindled the land into flame with its heat. **E**

IN OTHER WORDS   The sound of hoofs hurrying through a village street. A dark shape in the moonlight. A spark made by a horseshoe striking a stone as the horse galloped by. That was all. Yet, the fate of the nation was riding with Paul Revere. The spark of freedom struck that night set the whole land on fire.

He has left the village and mounted the steep,

And beneath him, tranquil[17] and broad and deep,

_____

16. **steed**: horse.
17. **tranquil** (TRANG KWUHL): peaceful.

Is the Mystic,[18] meeting the ocean tides;

And under the alders[19] that skirt its edge,

85   Now soft on the sand, now loud on the ledge,

Is heard the tramp of his steed as he rides. **A**

IN OTHER WORDS He left the village behind and rode up a hill. Below him was the water. He rode along the shore of the Mystic River, under the alder trees. Sometimes the hoofbeats were soft in the sand. Sometimes they were loud on rock.

It was twelve by the village clock,

When he crossed the bridge into Medford town.

He heard the crowing of the cock,

90   And the barking of the farmer's dog,

And felt the damp of the river fog,

That rises after the sun goes down. **B**

IN OTHER WORDS At midnight, he crossed the bridge into Medford. He heard a rooster crow. He heard a farmer's dog bark. He felt the dampness of the night fog from the river.

It was one by the village clock,

When he galloped into Lexington.

95   He saw the gilded[20] weathercock[21]

Swim in the moonlight as he passed,

And the meetinghouse windows, blank and bare,

Gaze at him with a spectral glare,

As if they already stood aghast[22]

100   At the bloody work they would look upon. **C**

IN OTHER WORDS At one o'clock, he rode into Lexington. He saw a weather vane turn. The windows of the meeting-

---

18. **Mystic:** Mystic River.
19. **alders:** a type of tree.
20. **gilded:** coated with gold.
21. **weathercock:** weather vane shaped like a bird.
22. **aghast** (UH GAST): struck with horror.

A **HERE'S HOW**

Literary Focus

I think that I would read lines 81–86 with a firm, steady **rhythm**. This is similar to the way a horse would slow down going up a hill. The view of the river and the ocean tides would need a smooth, flowing rhythm. I like trying out different rhythms as I read this poem.

B **READ AND DISCUSS**

Comprehension

What is going on now?

C **YOUR TURN**

Literary Focus

What conflict is this **narrative poem** highlighting?

_____

_____

_____

_____

_____

_____

house seemed to stare at him like ghosts. It was as if they were already horrified by the bloodshed they would see.

It was two by the village clock,
When he came to the bridge in Concord town.
He heard the bleating of the flock,
And the twitter of birds among the trees,
105 And felt the breath of the morning breeze
Blowing over the meadows brown.
And one was safe and asleep in his bed
Who at the bridge would be first to fall,
Who that day would be lying dead,
110 Pierced by a British musket ball.[23]

IN OTHER WORDS At two o'clock, he came to Concord. He heard sheep bleating. He heard birds chirping in the trees. He felt the morning breeze blowing over the grass. One man, safe asleep in his bed, would be the first to die in battle that same day.

You know the rest. In the books you have read,
How the British Regulars[24] fired and fled—
How the farmers gave them ball for ball,
From behind each fence and farmyard wall,
115 Chasing the redcoats down the lane,
Then crossing the fields to emerge again
Under the trees at the turn of the road,
And only pausing to fire and load. **D E**

IN OTHER WORDS You know the rest. You've read about it in books. The British soldiers fired, then ran away. The farmers chased them off, shooting at them, pausing only to reload their guns.

---

23. **musket ball:** ammunition that was fired from the muskets, or long-barreled guns.
24. **British Regulars:** British soldiers.

D HERE'S HOW

Literaray Focus

In lines 111–118, the **rhythm** of these lines helps me imagine the fighting between the colonists and the British soldiers.

E READ AND DISCUSS

Comprehension

What is the poet describing here?

Vocabulary

In line 122, *defiance* means "refusal to obey." Underline any words in that line that could help you figure out this meaning.

So through the night rode Paul Revere;

120 And so through the night went his cry of alarm

To every Middlesex village and farm—

A cry of defiance and not of fear,

A voice in the darkness, a knock at the door,

And a word that shall echo forevermore! **A**

125 For, borne[25] on the night wind of the Past,

Through all our history, to the last,

In the hour of darkness and peril and need,

The people will waken and listen to hear

The hurrying hoofbeats of that steed,

130 And the midnight message of Paul Revere. **B**

IN OTHER WORDS So Paul Revere rode through the night. He spread the alarm all across Middlesex. It was a cry of defiance, not fear. A voice in the darkness, a knock at the door, and a word that will echo forever. For, all through our history, at times of danger, the people will wake up to the sound of that horse's hoofbeats, and the midnight message of Paul Revere.

Comprehension Wrap up

1. Talk about Longfellow's purpose for writing this poem.
2. This poem opens with the line "Listen, my children." Do you think this is a children's poem?

---

25. **borne**: carried.

Applying Your Skills

Paul Revere's Ride

LITERARY FOCUS: NARRATIVE POETRY: RHYTHM AND METER

DIRECTIONS: Complete the chart below by listing the different elements of the **narrative poem** "Paul Revere's Ride."

Characters	Setting	Conflict
1.	2.	3.

READING FOCUS: PARAPHRASING

DIRECTIONS: Practice **paraphrasing** by restating the lines below from "Paul Revere's Ride." Refer back to the poem if you need to check the context. Try to do this exercise without using the "In Other Words" sections.

Original Text	My Paraphrase
Lines 57–59: "Meanwhile, impatient to mount and ride, / Booted and spurred with a heavy stride / On the opposite shore walked Paul Revere."	1.

VOCABULARY REVIEW

DIRECTIONS: Fill in the blanks with the correct words from the Word Box.

Word Box

impetuous

aghast

1. The men stood _____ as they prepared for the bloody fight ahead.

2. The young, _____ soldier could not sleep through the night.

On the Grasshopper and the Cricket

By John Keats

LITERARY FOCUS: SONNET

A **sonnet** is a fourteen line poem usually written with a specific meter called **iambic pentameter**. In iambic pentameter, every line of a poem contains five unstressed syllables, each followed by a stressed syllable. A stressed syllable is pronounced more forcefully than an unstressed syllable. For example, in the word *party*, the first syllable, "par," is stressed, and the second syllable, "ty," is unstressed. The markings below indicate the unstressed syllables (˘) and the stressed syllables (/) in the first line of Keats's poem.

˘ / ˘ / ˘ ˘ / ˘ / ˘ /

The poetry of earth is never dead.

READING FOCUS: USING FORM TO FIND MEANING

The sonnet you are about to read is in the Italian **form**. In this form, the poet makes his or her point in the first eight lines. Then he or she responds to the point in the last six lines. For example, in the poem you are about to read, John Keats makes a point about nature in the first eight lines. He then develops this point in the next six lines.

You can use the form of a sonnet to help you understand it. First, identify the point the poet is making. Then read the rest of the poem to see what else he or she says about that point.

VOCABULARY

Working with a partner, use the following words in complete sentences.

wrought (RAWT) *v.:* formed or made.

drowsiness (DRAU ZEE NEHS) *n.:* the condition of being sleepy.

INTO THE POEM

The speaker of the poem you are about to read celebrates the "poetry" of nature. Two very small insects that chirp very loudly, the grasshopper and the cricket, are spotlighted in this poem. The speaker uses them as proof that the earth is always alive and full of poetry.

SKILLS FOCUS

Literary Skills
Understand the characteristics of a sonnet.

Reading Skills
Use a poem's form to find its meaning.

ON THE GRASSHOPPER AND THE CRICKET

By John Keats

Huts at Walberswick, Suffolk (collage and w/c on paper), Mc Kechnie,
Christine/Private Collection/The Bridgeman Art Library International

The poetry of earth is never dead:
    When all the birds are faint with the hot sun,
    And hide in cooling trees, a voice will run
From hedge to hedge about the new-mown mead;[1]
5 That is the Grasshopper's—he takes the lead
In summer luxury—he has never done **A**
With his delights; for when tired out with fun
He rests at ease beneath some pleasant weed. **B**

IN OTHER WORDS Keats is telling the reader you can find
poetry in nature even on the hottest summer days. When the
birds are too hot to sing "poetry" and are hiding in the shade,

---

1. **mead** (MEED) *n.:* meadow.

A **HERE'S HOW**

Literary Focus

I am pretty sure that this
poem is written in **iambic
pentameter**. I can first
check this by testing a line
to see if it has five stressed
syllables. In line 4, I see that
the following five syllables
are stressed: "hedge,"
"hedge," "bout," "new,"
and "mead." The syllables
before and after these five
are unstressed. Now I am
sure that this poem is written
in iambic pentameter.

B **YOUR TURN**

Reading Focus

This sonnet is in Italian **form**.
The poet's point must be
included in the first eight
lines. What point do you
think Keats makes in
lines 1–8?

_____

_____

_____

I would usually expect to hear the phrase "ever increasing," not "increasing ever," which Keats writes in this line. I think Keats uses this **inverted word order** to keep the poem's rhythm the same throughout.

 READ AND DISCUSS

Comprehension

How does the poem explain the line "The poetry of earth is never dead"?

the grasshopper will begin singing. He enjoys singing in the heat very much. When he is tired, he rests comfortably under a weed.

The poetry of earth is ceasing never:

10   On a lone winter evening, when the frost

Has wrought a silence, from the stove there shrills

The Cricket's song, in warmth increasing ever, **A**

And seems to one in drowsiness half lost,

The Grasshopper's among some grassy hills. **B**

IN OTHER WORDS Keats now explains that you can also find poetry in nature on the coldest winter day. When it is too cold outside for any animal to make noise, a cricket living inside a warm stove will sing. The cricket's song may remind sleepy listeners of the happy summer song of the grasshopper.

Comprehension Wrap-Up

1. Discuss Keats's view of nature and the way it plays out in the poem. How might you describe Keats's view of the world?

Applying Your Skills

On the Grasshopper and the Cricket

LITERARY FOCUS: SONNET

DIRECTIONS: Use your new knowledge of **sonnets** to complete each sentence below. Write your answers on the lines provided.

1. Each line in a sonnet has _____ stressed syllables, or beats.

2. In iambic pentameter, each stressed syllable is followed by a(n) _____ syllable.

Copy a line from the poem into the box below. Circle each stressed syllable. Underline every unstressed syllable.

```
```

READING FOCUS: USING FORM TO FIND MEANING

DIRECTIONS: In the table below, answer the questions about the point Keats makes in his sonnet.

What point does Keats make in lines 1–8?	
Which line best describes this point?	
What do lines 9–14 have to do with this point?	

VOCABULARY REVIEW

DIRECTIONS: Circle the word that means the same thing as the boldfaced vocabulary word.

1. **wrought**   a) broke   b) made   c) found

2. **drowsiness**   a) sleepiness   b) happiness   c) sadness

Skills Review

Collection 7

VOCABULARY REVIEW

DIRECTIONS: For each word in Column A, choose the correct meaning in Column B.
Write the letter on the line next to the word.

Column A		Column B
1. wrought	_____	a) high
2. lingers	_____	b) plan or purpose
3. drifting	_____	c) to draw out
4. aloft	_____	d) stays back
5. intent	_____	e) explanation of meaning
6. spirit	_____	f) formed or made
7. drowsiness	_____	g) the condition of being sleepy
8. evoke	_____	h) to make again
9. re-invent	_____	i) courage or liveliness
10. interpretation	_____	j) being carried along as if by a current of air or water.

Collection 7

LANGUAGE COACH: CONNOTATIONS

All words have **denotations**, or dictionary definitions. All words also have **connotations**, or the feelings and associations a word brings forth. For example, the denotation of the word *sobbing* is the same as the denotation for the word *crying*. However, *sobbing* has a much stronger connotation. Someone who is sobbing is doing more than just crying—they are breathing in and out in short breaths and weeping.

DIRECTIONS: For the vocabulary words listed below, the denotations are given. Complete the exercise by giving their connotations.

1. wrought

   a. Denotation: formed or made.

   b. Connotation:_____

2. re-invent

   a. Denotation: make new again.

   b. Connotation:_____

3. evoke

   a. Denotation: draw out.

   b. Connotation:_____

ORAL LANGUAGE ACTIVITY

Poets intend for readers to read their poems aloud. By reading a poem aloud, you can appreciate the music of the lines. You may also have a better understanding of the meaning of the language.

Practice reading aloud one of the two poems from this collection. Then read the poem aloud to a partner. Discuss with your partner what happened when you read the poem aloud. In your discussion, complete the following statements:

1. As the reader, I learned . . .
2. As the listener, I learned . . .

Elements of Drama

© David Sutherland/Corbis

Literary and Academic Vocabulary for Collection 8

LITERARY VOCABULARY

drama (DRAH MUH) *n.:* a story written to be acted out in front of people.

I went to see the drama of Romeo and Juliet *at the local playhouse.*

acts (AKTS) *n.:* smaller parts of a long play.

I read the first act of The Diary of Anne Frank.

stage directions *n.:* text that tells what is happening on stage.

When I read a play, I know what the actors should be doing by reading the stage directions.

dialogue (DI UH LOHG) *n.:* conversations between characters in any type of story or play.

The dialogue between characters is very important. By listening closely to what the characters are saying to each other, you can find out more about a story.

ACADEMIC VOCABULARY

contribute to (KUHN TRIHB YOUT TOO) *v.:* play a part in; bring about.

A comical character can contribute humor to a play.

insight (IHN SYT) *n.:* understanding how things work or how people think or act.

Good stage directions provide insight to the characters' thoughts and feelings.

evident (EHV UH DUHNT) *adj.:* plain; clear; obvious.

Her actions made it evident that she was happy.

express (EHK SPREHS) *v.:* show; put into words.

He found it difficult to express what he was feeling.

The Diary of Anne Frank
Act One, Scenes 1 and 2

By Frances Goodrich and Albert Hackett

LITERARY FOCUS: ELEMENTS OF DRAMA

A **drama**, or play, is a work of literature that can be performed by actors for an audience, or simply read by one person. A drama must include **dialogue**, the lines the characters speak, and **stage directions**, which describe what is happening on stage. Like most literature, drama focuses on a set of **characters** that have problems, or **conflicts**. Over the course of the play, the characters try to solve those problems. The main parts of a drama are **exposition** (when characters and setting are established), **complications** (conflicts that arise), **climax** (when the conflict reaches its most suspenseful moment), and **resolution** (when the conflict is resolved).

READING FOCUS: MAKING INFERENCES

When you read drama, **make inferences**, or educated guesses, about the characters' personalities and why they act as they do. Making inferences from clues in the text will allow you to better understand the characters.

VOCABULARY

Work with a partner to practice using these words in complete sentences.

conspicuous (KUHN SPIHK YU UHS) *adj.*: noticeable.

interval (IN TER VUHL) *n.*: time between.

unabashed (UN A BASHT) *adj.*: not embarrassed.

INTO THE PLAY

This is a true story, and Anne Frank was a real person. The Frank family and four other Jews hid for more than two years in a few small rooms above Mr. Frank's office and warehouse in the Dutch city of Amsterdam. In August of 1944, the Nazi police raided their hiding place and sent them to concentration camps. Of the eight people hiding together, only Mr. Frank survived. Before you read the play, note the list of characters and the setting. Most of the play is told in the form of a flashback—a break in the present action that shows events that happened in the past.

SKILLS FOCUS

Literary Skills
Understand elements of drama.

Reading Skills
Make inferences.

THE DIARY OF ANNE FRANK

By Frances Goodrich and Albert Hackett

Characters

Occupants of the Secret Annex:

Anne Frank

Margot Frank, her older sister

Mr. Frank, their father

Mrs. Frank, their mother

Peter Van Daan

Mr. Van Daan, his father

Mrs. Van Daan, his mother

Mr. Dussel, a dentist

Workers in Mr. Frank's Business:

Miep Gies,[1] a young Dutchwoman

Mr. Kraler,[2] a Dutchman

Setting: Amsterdam, the Netherlands, July 1942 to August 1944; November 1945. Netherlands and Holland are the same country. The people and language of the Netherlands are called Dutch. **A B**

© Anne Frank House, Amsterdam/ Hulton Archive/Getty Images

A **HERE'S HOW**

Literary Focus

I can see that this box lists all of the **characters** in the play.

B **HERE'S HOW**

Literary Focus

I see that this **drama** is set in Amsterdam in the 1940s.

Act One

• SCENE 1

The scene remains the same throughout the play. It is the top floor of a warehouse and office building in Amsterdam, Holland. The sharply peaked roof of the building is outlined against a sea of other rooftops stretching away into the distance. Nearby is the belfry[3] *of a church tower, the Westertoren, whose*

---

1. **Miep Gies** (MEEP KHEES).
2. **Kraler** (KRAH LUHR).
3. **belfry** (BEHL FREE): bell tower.

Act 1, Scenes 1 & 2 of *The Diary of Anne Frank* by Albert Hackett and Frances Goodrich Hackett. Copyright © 1956 by Albert Hackett, Frances Goodrich Hackett, and Otto Frank. Reproduced by permission of **Random House, Inc.** Electronic format by permission of **Abrams Artists Agency.**

carillon[4] rings out the hours. Occasionally faint sounds float up from below: the voices of children playing in the street, the tramp of marching feet, a boat whistle from the canal.[5]

10   *The three rooms of the top floor and a small attic space above are exposed to our view. The largest of the rooms is in the center, with two small rooms, slightly raised, on either side. On the right is a bathroom, out of sight. A narrow, steep flight of stairs at the back leads up to the attic. The rooms are sparsely furnished, with a few chairs, cots, a table or two. The windows are painted over or covered with makeshift blackout curtains.[6] In the main room there is a sink, a gas ring for cooking, and a wood-burning stove for warmth.*

    The room on the left is hardly more than a closet. There
20 *is a skylight[7] in the sloping ceiling. Directly under this room is a small, steep stairwell, with steps leading down to a door. This is the only entrance from the building below. When the door is opened, we see that it has been concealed on the outer side by a bookcase attached to it.*

    The curtain rises on an empty stage. It is late afternoon, November 1945.

    The rooms are dusty, the curtains in rags. Chairs and tables are overturned.

    The door at the foot of the small stairwell swings open.
30 MR. FRANK *comes up the steps into view. He is a gentle, cultured[8] European in his middle years. There is still a trace of a German accent in his speech.*

    He stands looking slowly around, making a supreme effort at self-control. He is weak, ill. His clothes are threadbare.

    After a second he drops his rucksack on the couch and moves slowly about. He opens the door to one of the smaller rooms and

HERE'S HOW

Literary Focus
I know that these opening paragraphs are all part of the **exposition**—establishing the setting and characters.

4. **carillon** (KAR UH LAHN): set of bells, each of which produces a single tone.
5. **canal**: artificial waterway. Amsterdam, which was built on soggy ground, has more than one hundred canals, built to help drain the land. The canals are used like streets.
6. **blackout curtains**: curtains that cover the window at night so that no light shows outside.
7. **skylight**: window.
8. **cultured** (KUHL CHUHRD): civilized; well mannered; learned.

then abruptly closes it again, turning away. He goes to the window at the back, looking off at the Westertoren as its carillon strikes the hour of six; then he moves restlessly on.

40   *From the street below we hear the sound of a barrel organ[9] and children's voices at play. There is a many-colored scarf hanging from a nail.* MR. FRANK *takes it, putting it around his neck. As he starts back for his rucksack, his eye is caught by something lying on the floor. It is a woman's white glove. He holds it in his hand and suddenly all of his self-control is gone. He breaks down crying.* **B**

     We hear footsteps on the stairs. MIEP GIES *comes up, looking for* MR. FRANK. MIEP *is a Dutchwoman of about twenty-two. She wears a coat and hat, ready to go home. She is pregnant.*

50 *Her attitude toward* MR. FRANK *is protective, compassionate.[10]*

© Joan Marcus

Miep. Are you all right, Mr. Frank?

Mr. Frank (*quickly controlling himself*). Yes, Miep, yes. **C**

Miep. Everyone in the office has gone home. . . . It's after six. (*Then, pleading*)[11] Don't stay up here, Mr. Frank. What's the use of torturing yourself like this?

60 **Mr. Frank.** I've come to say goodbye . . . I'm leaving here, Miep.

Miep. What do you mean? Where are you going? Where?

Mr. Frank. I don't know yet. I haven't decided.

Miep. Mr. Frank, you can't leave here! This is your home! Amsterdam is your home. Your business is here, waiting for you. . . . You're needed here. . . . Now that the war is over, there are things that . . .

Mr. Frank. I can't stay in Amsterdam, Miep. It has too many memories for me. Everywhere, there's something . . . the

---

9. **barrel organ:** musical street instrument shaped like a barrel and played by winding a handle.
10. **compassionate** (KUHM PASH uhn iht): kind.
11. **pleading** (PLEE dihng): begging.

Literary Focus

I know that a **drama** contains the same literary elements as most short stories or novels. I suspect that Mr. Frank's crying is related to the play's **conflict**.

Reading Focus

By **making inferences**, I think that Mr. Frank is upset due to unpleasant memories. I will keep reading to discover more.

house we lived in . . . the school . . . that street organ playing

70 out there . . . I'm not the person you used to know, Miep. I'm a
bitter[12] old man. (*Breaking off*) Forgive me. I shouldn't speak to
you like this . . . after all that you did for us . . . the suffering. . . .
Miep. No. No. It wasn't suffering. You can't say we suffered. (*As
she speaks, she straightens a chair which is overturned.*)
Mr. Frank. I know what you went through, you and Mr. Kraler.
I'll remember it as long as I live. (*He gives one last look around.*)
Come, Miep. (*He starts for the steps, then remembers his rucksack,
going back to get it.*) A
Miep (*hurrying up to a cupboard*). Mr. Frank, did you see? There

80 are some of your papers here. (*She brings a bundle of papers to
him.*) We found them in a heap of rubbish on the floor after . . .
after you left.
Mr. Frank. Burn them. (*He opens his rucksack to put the glove
in it.*)
Miep. But, Mr. Frank, there are letters, notes . . .
Mr. Frank. Burn them. All of them.
Miep. Burn *this*? (*She hands him a paperbound notebook.*)

IN OTHER WORDS Mr. Frank tells Miep that he is leaving
Amsterdam. He thanks her for what she and Mr. Kraler did
for them while they were in hiding. Miep brings him a pile of
his papers, and he says to burn them. He does not want to
remember the past.

Mr. Frank (*quietly*). Anne's diary. (*He opens the diary and
begins to read.*) "Monday, the sixth of July, nineteen forty-two."

90 (*To* MIEP) Nineteen forty-two. Is it possible, Miep? . . . Only
three years ago. (*As he continues his reading, he sits down on
the couch.*) "Dear Diary, since you and I are going to be great
friends, I will start by telling you about myself. My name is
Anne Frank. I am thirteen years old. I was born in Germany the
twelfth of June, nineteen twenty-nine. As my family is Jewish,
we emigrated to Holland when Hitler came to power." B

---

12. **bitter:** unaccepting.

[*As* MR. FRANK *reads on, another voice joins his, as if coming from the air. It is* ANNE'S *voice.*]

Mr. Frank and Anne's Voice. "My father started a business, importing[13] spice and herbs. Things went well for us until nineteen forty. Then the war came, and the Dutch capitulation, followed by the arrival of the Germans. Then things got very bad for the Jews."

[MR. FRANK'S *voice dies out.* ANNE'S *voice continues alone. The lights dim slowly to darkness.* **C** *The curtain falls on the scene.*]

Anne's Voice. You could not do this and you could not do that. They forced Father out of his business. We had to wear yellow stars.[14] I had to turn in my bike. I couldn't go to a Dutch school anymore. I couldn't go to the movies or ride in an automobile or even on a streetcar, and a million other things. But somehow we children still managed to have fun. Yesterday Father told me we were going into hiding. Where, he wouldn't say. At five o'clock this morning Mother woke me and told me to hurry and get dressed. I was to put on as many clothes as I could. It would look too suspicious if we walked along carrying suitcases. It wasn't until we were on our way that I learned where we were going. Our hiding place was to be upstairs in the building where Father used to have his business. Three other people were coming in with us . . . the Van Daans and their son Peter . . . Father knew the Van Daans but we had never met them. . . .

[*During the last lines the curtain rises on the scene. The lights dim on.* ANNE'S *voice fades out.*]

IN OTHER WORDS Among the papers is Anne's diary. Mr. Frank begins to read from the diary. Anne is writing in 1942, and she is thirteen. She describes life under Nazi rule. All Jews have to wear a large yellow star sewn on their outer clothing. This is so they will be easily recognized as Jews. Jews are not allowed to live a normal life. They cannot go to school, ride bicycles, see

---

13. **importing:** bringing into the country.
14. **yellow stars:** The Nazis ordered all Jews to sew a large Star of David (a six-pointed star) on their outer clothing so that they could be easily recognized as Jews.

Language Coach
I know that adding the **suffix** -*ly* to the adjective *slow* makes it an adverb. *Slowly* describes the speed at which the lights are dimming.

A HERE'S HOW

Literary Focus

I see that the **drama's** setting is similar in Scene 2. However, it is about three years earlier now than it was in Scene 1. I think that when Mr. Frank started reading Anne's diary, it started a flashback—a reflection on past events.

B HERE'S HOW

Vocabulary

I think the word *conspicuous* means "easily seen" or "obvious." The yellow star probably stands out on their clothing.

movies, or do many other things. Now, Anne's family is going into hiding with another family, the Van Daans.

• SCENE 2

It is early morning, July 1942. The rooms are bare, as before, but they are now clean and orderly. **A**

MR. VAN DAAN, *a tall, portly man in his late forties, is in the main room, pacing up and down, nervously smoking a cigarette. His clothes and overcoat are expensive and well cut.*[15]

MRS. VAN DAAN *sits on the couch, clutching her possessions: a hatbox, bags, etc. She is a pretty woman in her early forties. She*
130 *wears a fur coat over her other clothes.*

PETER VAN DAAN *is standing at the window of the room on the right, looking down at the street below. He is a shy, awkward boy of sixteen. He wears a cap, a raincoat, and long Dutch trousers, like plus fours.*[16] *At his feet is a black case, a carrier for his cat.*

The yellow Star of David is conspicuous on all of their clothes. **B**

Mrs. Van Daan (*rising, nervous, excited*). Something's happened to them! I know it!

Mr. Van Daan. Now, Kerli!

140 **Mrs. Van Daan.** Mr. Frank said they'd be here at seven o'clock. He said . . .

Mr. Van Daan. They have two miles to walk. You can't expect . . .

Mrs. Van Daan. They've been picked up. That's what's happened. They've been taken . . .

[MR. VAN DAN *indicates*[17] *that he hears someone coming.*]

Mr. Van Daan. You see?

[PETER *takes up his carrier and his school bag, etc., and goes into the main room as* MR. FRANK *comes up the stairwell from below.* MR. FRANK *looks much younger now. His movements are*
150 *brisk, his manner confident. He wears an overcoat and carries his hat and a small cardboard box. He crosses to the* VAN DAANS, *shaking hands with each of them.*]

---

15. **well cut:** well made.
16. **plus fours:** baggy trousers that end in cuffs just below the knee.
17. **indicates** (IHN DUH KAYTS): shows.

Mr. Frank. Mrs. Van Daan, Mr. Van Daan, Peter. (*Then, in explanation of their lateness*) There were too many of the Green Police[18] on the streets . . . we had to take the long way around.

> **IN OTHER WORDS** It is July 1942. Mr. and Mrs. Van Daan wait in the hiding place with their teenage son, Peter. Mrs. Van Daan is very nervous. She is afraid the Franks have been caught by the Nazis. Then, Mr. Frank enters. He looks younger and healthier than in Scene 1.

[*Up the steps come* MARGOT FRANK, MRS. FRANK, MIEP (*not pregnant now*), *and* MR. KRALER. *All of them carry bags, packages, and so forth. The Star of David is conspicuous on all of the* FRANKS' *clothing.* MARGOT *is eighteen, beautiful, quiet,*
160 *shy.* MRS. FRANK *is a young mother, gently bred,[19] reserved. She, like* MR. FRANK, *has a slight German accent.* MR. KRALER *is a Dutchman, dependable, kindly.*

As MR. KRALER *and* MIEP *go upstage to put down their parcels,* MRS. FRANK *turns back to call* ANNE.]

Mrs. Frank. Anne?

[ANNE *comes running up the stairs. She is thirteen, quick in her movements, interested in everything, mercurial in her emotions.* **C** *She wears a cape and long wool socks and carries a school bag.*]

Mr. Frank (*introducing them*). My wife, Edith. Mr. and Mrs. Van
170 Daan (MRS. FRANK *hurries over, shaking hands with them.*) . . . their son, Peter . . . my daughters, Margot and Anne.

[ANNE *gives a polite little curtsy as she shakes* MR. VAN DAAN'S *hand. Then she immediately starts off on a tour of investigation of her new home, going upstairs to the attic room.*

> **IN OTHER WORDS** The others arrive: Mrs. Frank, Margot (Anne's older sister), Miep, and Mr. Kraler. Anne comes last. Mr. Frank introduces his family to the Van Daans. Anne goes off to explore the hiding place that Miep and Mr. Kraler have set up for them.

---

18. **Green Police:** Nazi police, who wore green uniforms.
19. **gently bred:** well brought up; refined.

C YOUR TURN

Vocabulary

In lines 166–167, Anne's emotions are described as *mercurial.* This word comes from *mercury,* a metal that is extremely changeable. Depending on the temperature, mercury can be a liquid or a solid. Based on this information, how would you describe Anne and her emotions?

_____

_____

_____

_____

Literary Focus

Mrs. Frank sees a **conflict**, or problem, with the ration books because Miep will be obtaining them illegally. How does Mr. Frank address his wife's concern?

_____

_____

_____

_____

MIEP _and_ MR. KRALER _are putting the various things they have brought on the shelves._]

Mr. Kraler. I'm sorry there is still so much confusion.

Mr. Frank. Please. Don't think of it. After all, we'll have plenty of leisure to arrange everything ourselves.

180 **Miep** (_to_ MRS. FRANK). We put the stores of food you sent in here. Your drugs are here . . . soap, linen[20] here.

Mrs. Frank. Thank you, Miep.

Miep. I made up the beds . . . the way Mr. Frank and Mr. Kraler said. (_She starts out._) Forgive me. I have to hurry. I've got to go to the other side of town to get some ration books[21] for you.

Mrs. Van Daan. Ration books? If they see our names on ration books, they'll know we're here.

Mr. Kraler. There isn't anything . . .

Miep. Don't worry. Your names won't be on them. (_As she_
190 _hurries out_) I'll be up later.

Mr. Frank. Thank you, Miep.

Mrs. Frank (_to_ MR. KRALER). It's illegal, then, the ration books? We've never done anything illegal.

Mr. Frank. We won't be living here exactly according to regulations. **A**

[_As_ MR. KRALER _reassures_ MRS. FRANK, _he takes various small things, such as matches and soap, from his pockets, handing them to her._]

Mr. Kraler. This isn't the black market,[22] Mrs. Frank. This
200 is what we call the white market . . . helping all of the hundreds and hundreds who are hiding out in Amsterdam.

[_The carillon is heard playing the quarter-hour before eight._ MR. KRALER _looks at his watch._ ANNE _stops at the window as she comes down the stairs._]

Anne. It's the Westertoren!

---

20. **linen:** sheets, towels, pillowcases, and so forth.
21. **ration books:** books of stamps or coupons issued by the government during wartime. People could purchase scarce items such as food, clothing, and gasoline only with these coupons.
22. **black market:** place or system for buying and selling goods illegally, without ration stamps.

Mr. Kraler. I must go. I must be out of here and downstairs in the office before the workmen get here. (*He starts for the stairs leading out.*) Miep or I, or both of us, will be up each day to bring you food and news and find out what your needs are. **B**

210 Tomorrow I'll get you a better bolt for the door at the foot of the stairs. It needs a bolt that you can throw yourself and open only at our signal. (*To* MR. FRANK) Oh . . . You'll tell them about the noise?

Mr. Frank. I'll tell them.

Mr. Kraler. Goodbye, then, for the moment. I'll come up again, after the workmen leave.

Mr. Frank. Goodbye, Mr. Kraler.

Mrs. Frank (*shaking his hand*). How can we thank you?

[*The others murmur their goodbyes.*]

220 **Mr. Kraler.** I never thought I'd live to see the day when a man like Mr. Frank would have to go into hiding. **C** When you think—

IN OTHER WORDS Miep goes off to get the ration books that will allow her to buy food for the people in the Secret Annex. Mr. Kraler reveals that many Jews are in hiding in Amsterdam. Miep and Mr. Kraler are breaking the law by helping them. Mrs. Frank does not like doing anything illegal. But, under the Nazis, the law is no longer just.

[*He breaks off, going out.* MR. FRANK *follows him down the steps, bolting the door after him. In the interval before he returns,* PETER *goes over to* MARGOT, *shaking hands with her. As* MR. FRANK *comes back up the steps,* MRS. FRANK *questions him anxiously.*] **D**

Mrs. Frank. What did he mean, about the noise?

Mr. Frank. First let us take off some of these clothes.

[*They all start to take off garment after garment. On each of their coats, sweaters, blouses, suits, dresses is another yellow Star*
230 *of David.* MR. *and* MRS. FRANK *are underdressed quite simply. The others wear several things: sweaters, extra dresses, bathrobes, aprons, nightgowns, etc.*]

B READ AND DISCUSS

Comprehension

What are we learning in this scene? **Follow-up:** What part does Miep play in their lives?

C YOUR TURN

Reading Focus

What **inferences** can you make about Mr. Kraler and Miep?

_____

_____

_____

_____

_____

D YOUR TURN

Vocabulary

The word *interval* can mean "the space between" or "time between." Which meaning makes more sense in line 223?

_____

Literary Focus

What must Anne and the others do to avoid any outside **conflicts** while hiding?

_____

_____

_____

_____

Vocabulary

I was not sure about the meaning of *paralyzed*. But when I looked at the word that comes right before it—*motionless*—I knew that *paralyzed* means "not moving." The people were too afraid to move.

Mr. Van Daan. It's a wonder we weren't arrested, walking along the streets . . . Petronella with a fur coat in July . . . and that cat of Peter's crying all the way.

Anne (*as she is removing a pair of panties*). A cat?

Mrs. Frank (*shocked*). Anne, please!

Anne. It's all right. I've got on three more.

[*She pulls off two more. Finally, as they have all removed their surplus[23] clothes, they look to* MR. FRANK, *waiting for him to speak.*]

Mr. Frank. Now. About the noise. While the men are in the building below, we must have complete quiet. Every sound can be heard down there, not only in the workrooms but in the offices too. The men come at about eight-thirty and leave at about five-thirty. So, to be perfectly safe, from eight in the morning until six in the evening we must move only when it is necessary, and then in stockinged feet. We must not speak above a whisper. We must not run any water. We cannot use the sink or even, forgive me, the w.c.[24] The pipes go down through the workrooms. It would be heard. No trash . . . A

(MR. FRANK *stops abruptly as he hears the sound of marching feet from the street below. Everyone is motionless, paralyzed with fear.* B MR. FRANK *goes quietly into the room on the right to look down out of the window.* ANNE *runs after him, peering out with him. The tramping feet pass without stopping. The tension[25] is relieved.* MR. FRANK, *followed by* ANNE, *returns to the main room and resumes his instructions to the group.*) . . . No trash must ever be thrown out which might reveal that someone is living up here . . . not even a potato paring. We must burn everything in the stove at night. This is the way we must live until it is over, if we are to survive.

[*There is silence for a second.*]

Mrs. Frank. Until it is over.

---

23. **surplus:** extra.
24. **w.c.:** short for "water closet," or toilet.
25. **tension** (TEHN SHUHN): strain.

Mr. Frank (*reassuringly*)[26]. **C** After six we can move about
. . . we can talk and laugh and have our supper and read and
play games . . . just as we would at home. (*He looks at his watch.*)
And now I think it would be wise if we all went to our rooms, and
were settled before eight o'clock. Mrs. Van Daan, you and your
husband will be upstairs. I regret that there's no place up there for
Peter. But he will be here, near us. This will be our common room,
where we'll meet to talk and eat and read, like one family. **D**

IN OTHER WORDS Mr. Kraler leaves. The others begin to
undress. Because they could not be seen with suitcases, they
are wearing as many clothes as they could put on. It is July, so
they are very hot. Mr. Frank tells them that they must be silent
all day when there are workers in the building.

Mr. Van Daan. And where do you and Mrs. Frank sleep?

Mr. Frank. This room is also our bedroom.

Mrs. Van Daan. That isn't right. We'll sleep here and you take
the room upstairs.

Mr. Van Daan. It's your place.

Mr. Frank. Please. I've thought this out for weeks. It's the best
arrangement. The only arrangement.

Mrs. Van Daan (*to* MR. FRANK). Never, never can we thank you.
(*Then, to* MRS. FRANK) I don't know what would have happened
to us, if it hadn't been for Mr. Frank.

Mr. Frank. You don't know how your husband helped me when
I came to this country . . . knowing no one . . . not able to speak
the language. I can never repay him for that. (*Going to* MR. VAN
DAAN) May I help you with your things?

Mr. Van Daan. No. No. (*To* MRS. VAN DAAN) Come along,
liefje.[27]

Mrs. Van Daan. You'll be all right, Peter? You're not afraid?

Peter (*embarrassed*). Please, Mother.

270

280

290

---

26. **reassuringly** (REE UH SHOOR IHNG LEE): in a way that restores
confidence.
27. **liefje** (LEEF YAH): Dutch for "little dear one."

C YOUR TURN

Language Coach
Circle the **suffix** that
indicates that *reassuringly* is
an adverb.

D YOUR TURN

Reading Focus
What **inferences** can you
make about Mr. Frank based
on his speech about their
lives in hiding?

_____

_____

_____

_____

_____

_____

A HERE'S HOW

Language Coach

I know that adding the **suffix** *–ly* to the end of a word usually turns that word into an adverb. Here, Anne turns the adjective *sound* into the adverb *soundly.* This means that Anne slept deeply.

[*They start up the stairs to the attic room above.* MR. FRANK *turns to* MRS. FRANK.]

Mr. Frank. You too must have some rest, Edith. You didn't close your eyes last night. Nor you, Margot.

Anne. I slept, Father. Wasn't that funny? I knew it was the last night in my own bed, and yet I slept soundly. A

Mr. Frank. I'm glad, Anne. Now you'll be able to help me straighten things in here. (*To* MRS. FRANK *and* MARGOT) Come with me. . . . You and Margot rest in this room for the time

300　being. (*He picks up their clothes, starting for the room on the right.*)

Mrs. Frank. You're sure . . . ? I could help . . . And Anne hasn't had her milk . . .

Mr. Frank. I'll give it to her. (*To* ANNE *and* PETER) Anne, Peter . . . it's best that you take off your shoes now, before you forget. (*He leads the way to the room, followed by* MARGOT.)

Mrs. Frank. You're sure you're not tired, Anne?

Anne. I feel fine. I'm going to help Father.

Mrs. Frank. Peter, I'm glad you are to be with us.

© Joan Marcus

310 **Peter.** Yes, Mrs. Frank.

[MRS. FRANK *goes to join* MR. FRANK *and* MARGOT. *During the following scene* MR. FRANK *helps* MARGOT *and* MRS. FRANK *to hang up their clothes. Then he persuades them both to lie down and rest. The* VAN DAANS, *in their room above, settle themselves. In the main room* ANNE *and* PETER *remove their shoes.* PETER *takes his cat out of the carrier.*]

IN OTHER WORDS Mr. and Mrs. Van Daan go upstairs to unpack. Mr. Frank tells his wife and Margot that they should rest. He and Anne will arrange things. Unlike her mother and sister, Anne is cheerful and does not seem worried. Peter takes his cat out of its carrier.

Anne. What's your cat's name?

Peter. Mouschi.[28]

Anne. Mouschi! Mouschi! Mouschi! (*She picks up the cat,*
320 *walking away with it. To* PETER) I love cats. I have one . . . a darling little cat. But they made me leave her behind. I left some food and a note for the neighbors to take care of her. . . . I'm going to miss her terribly. What is yours? A him or a her?

Peter. He's a tom.[29] He doesn't like strangers. (*He takes the cat from her, putting it back in its carrier.*)

Anne (*unabashed*). **B** Then I'll have to stop being a stranger, won't I? Is he fixed?

Peter (*startled*). Huh?

Anne. Did you have him fixed?
330 **Peter.** No.

Anne. Oh, you ought to have him fixed—to keep him from— you know, fighting. Where did you go to school?

Peter. Jewish Secondary.

Anne. But that's where Margot and I go! I never saw you around.

Peter. I used to see you . . . sometimes . . .

Anne. You did?

---

28. **Mouschi:** (MOO SHEE).
29. **tom:** male cat.

B (HERE'S HOW)

Vocabulary
I think the word *unabashed* means "not embarrassed." I think this because Anne does not stop trying to get Peter to talk to her. Because the word is in parentheses, it tells the actor how to say that line.

Literary Focus

Why can Peter now remove the Star of David from his clothing without causing **conflict**?

_____

_____

_____

_____

Literary Focus

Anne mentions her friend Jopie, but I doubt that we will actually meet Jopie. Because of this, I do not think that Jopie is one of the play's **characters**.

Peter. . . . in the schoolyard. You were always in the middle of a bunch of kids. (*He takes a penknife from his pocket.*)

Anne. Why didn't you ever come over?

340 **Peter.** I'm sort of a lone wolf. (*He starts to rip off his Star of David.*)

Anne. What are you doing?

Peter. Taking it off.

Anne. But you can't do that. They'll arrest you if you go out without your star.

[*He tosses his knife on the table.*]

Peter. Who's going out? **A**

© Anne Frank Fonds-Basel/Anne Frank House–Amsterdam/Getty Images

IN OTHER WORDS Anne is eager to make friends with Peter and his cat, Mouschi. But Peter does not seem very friendly. They find that they went to the same school, although they never met each other. To Anne's shock, Peter begins ripping the star off his shirt. She says he will be arrested. He points out that they will not be going outside anymore.

Anne. Why, of course! You're right! Of course we don't need them

350 anymore. (*She picks up his knife and starts to take her star off.*) I wonder what our friends will think when we don't show up today?

Peter. I didn't have any dates with anyone.

Anne. Oh, I did. I had a date with Jopie to go and play ping-pong at her house. Do you know Jopie de Waal?[30]

Peter. No.

Anne. Jopie's my best friend. **B** I wonder what she'll think when she telephones and there's no answer? . . . Probably she'll go over to the house. . . . I wonder what she'll think . . . we left everything as if we'd suddenly been called away . . . breakfast

360 dishes in the sink . . . beds not made . . . (*As she pulls off her star, the cloth underneath shows clearly the color and form of the star.*) Look! It's still there! (PETER *goes over to the stove with his star.*) What're you going to do with yours?

---

30. Jopie de Waal: (YOH PEE DUH VAHL).

Peter. Burn it.

Anne. (*She starts to throw hers in, and cannot.*) It's funny, I can't throw mine away. I don't know why.

Peter. You can't throw . . . ? Something they branded you with . . . ? That they made you wear so they could spit on you?

Anne. I know. I know. But after all, it is the Star of David,
370   isn't it?

[*In the bedroom, right,* MARGOT *and* MRS. FRANK *are lying down.* MR. FRANK *starts quietly out.*]

Peter. Maybe it's different for a girl.

[MR. FRANK *comes into the main room.*]

Mr. Frank. Forgive me, Peter. Now let me see. We must find a bed for your cat. (*He goes to a cupboard.*) I'm glad you brought your cat. Anne was feeling so badly about hers. (*Getting a used small washtub*) Here we are. Will it be comfortable in that? **C**

Peter (*gathering up his things*). Thanks.

380   **Mr. Frank** (*opening the door of the room on the left*). And here is your room. But I warn you, Peter, you can't grow anymore. Not an inch, or you'll have to sleep with your feet out of the skylight. Are you hungry?

Peter. No.

Mr. Frank. We have some bread and butter.

Peter. No, thank you.

Mr. Frank. You can have it for luncheon then. And tonight we will have a real supper . . . our first supper together.

Peter. Thanks. Thanks. (*He goes into his room. During the*
390   *following scene he arranges his possessions in his new room.*)

IN OTHER WORDS Anne wonders what their friends will think when they find out the families have disappeared. She takes her star off, too. Peter is burning his, but Anne cannot. To her, the Star of David is still a Jewish symbol, not just a Nazi punishment. Mr. Frank welcomes the cat and shows Peter to his room.

Mr. Frank. That's a nice boy, Peter.

C YOUR TURN

Language Coach

Underline the adverb in this paragraph. Then, circle the **suffix** that tells you it is an adverb.

YOUR TURN

Reading Focus

Based on what you have read about Peter so far, what **inferences** can you make about him as a character?

_____

_____

_____

_____

B **HERE'S HOW**

Literary Focus

At first I thought Annele was a new **character**. Then I realized that would not make any sense considering the setting. Annele is just a nickname for Anne.

Anne. He's awfully shy, isn't he? **A**

Mr. Frank. You'll like him, I know.

Anne. I certainly hope so, since he's the only boy I'm likely to see for months and months.

[MR. FRANK *sits down, taking off his shoes.*]

Mr. Frank. Annele,[31] there's a box there. **B** Will you open it? [*He indicates a carton on the couch.* ANNE *brings it to the center table. In the street below, there is the sound of children playing.*]

400 **Anne** (*as she opens the carton*). You know the way I'm going to think of it here? I'm going to think of it as a boardinghouse.[32] A very peculiar summer boardinghouse, like the one that we— (*She breaks off as she pulls out some photographs.*) Father! My movie stars! I was wondering where they were! I was looking for them this morning . . . and Queen Wilhelmina![33] How wonderful!

Mr. Frank. There's something more. Go on. Look further. (*He goes over to the sink, pouring a glass of milk from a thermos bottle.*)

---

31. **Annele** (AHN UH LUH): Yiddish for "little Anne" (like "Annie").
32. **boardinghouse:** a place that takes paying guests.
33. **Queen Wilhelmina** (WIHL HEHL MEE NAH) (**1880–1962**): queen of the Netherlands from 1890 to 1948.

250 The Diary of Anne Frank

410   **Anne** (*pulling out a pasteboard-bound book*). A diary! (*She throws her arms around her father.*) I've never had a diary. And I've always longed for one. (*She looks around the room.*) Pencil, pencil, pencil, pencil. (*She starts down the stairs.*) I'm going down to the office to get a pencil.

IN OTHER WORDS Anne and her father talk about Peter and his shyness. Mr. Frank has a box for Anne. It has her treasured photos of movie stars and the queen. It also has a new diary. Anne is thrilled. She wants to run down to the office for a pencil.

Mr. Frank. Anne! No! (*He goes after her, catching her by the arm and pulling her back.*)

Anne (*startled*). But there's no one in the building now.

Mr. Frank. It doesn't matter. I don't want you ever to go beyond that door.

420   **Anne** (*sobered*).[34] Never . . . ? Not even at nighttime, when everyone is gone? Or on Sundays? Can't I go down to listen to the radio? **C**

Mr. Frank. Never. I am sorry, Anneke.[35] It isn't safe. No, you must never go beyond that door.

[*For the first time* ANNE *realizes what "going into hiding" means.*]

Anne. I see.

Mr. Frank. It'll be hard, I know. But always remember this, Anneke. There are no walls, there are no bolts, no locks that anyone can put on your mind. Miep will bring us books. We

430   will read history, poetry, mythology. (*He gives her the glass of milk.*) Here's your milk. (*With his arm about her, they go over to the couch, sitting down side by side.*) As a matter of fact, between us, Anne, being here has certain advantages for you. For instance, you remember the battle you had with your mother the other day on the subject of overshoes?[36] You said you'd rather die than wear overshoes? But in the end you had to

---

34. **sobered:** made serious.
35. **Anneke** (AHN uh kuh): another affectionate nickname for Anne.
36. **overshoes:** waterproof shoe covers.

C   YOUR TURN

Literary Focus

What makes Anne realize the seriousness of the **conflict** she is caught in?

_____

_____

_____

Literary Focus

I think Mr. Frank is trying to distract Anne from thinking about the **conflict** of having to hide to be safe. I have underlined what he says in lines 434–438 to ease her mind.

wear them? Well now, you see, for as long as we are here, you will never have to wear overshoes! Isn't that good? **A** And the

440 coat that you inherited from Margot, you won't have to wear that anymore. And the piano! You won't have to practice on the piano. I tell you, this is going to be a fine life for you!

IN OTHER WORDS Mr. Frank stops her. He explains that she must never leave their hiding place, even when there is no one in the building. Anne is shocked. She begins to realize what being in hiding really means. Mr. Frank tries to cheer her up. She can read; she won't have to wear overshoes; she won't have to practice the piano.

[ANNE'S *panic is gone.* PETER *appears in the doorway of his room, with a saucer in his hand. He is carrying his cat.*]
Peter. I . . . I . . . I thought I'd better get some water for Mouschi before . . .
Mr. Frank. Of course.
[*As he starts toward the sink, the carillon begins to chime*[37] *the hour of eight. He tiptoes to the window at the back and looks down at the street below. He turns to* PETER, *indicating in*

450 *pantomime*[38] *that it is too late.* PETER *starts back for his room. He steps on a creaking board. The three of them are frozen for a minute in fear. As* PETER *starts away again,* ANNE *tiptoes over to him and pours some of the milk from her glass into the saucer for the cat.* PETER *squats on the floor, putting the milk before the cat.* MR. FRANK *gives* ANNE *his fountain pen and then goes into the room at the right. For a second* ANNE *watches the cat; then she goes over to the center table and opens her diary.*

In the room at the right, MRS. FRANK *has sat up quickly at the sound of the carillon.* MR. FRANK *comes in and sits down beside her*

460 *on the settee,*[39] *his arm comfortingly around her. Upstairs, in the attic room,* MR. *and* MRS. VAN DAAN *have hung their clothes in the*

---

37. **chime:** ring.
38. **indicating in pantomime** (PAN TUH MYM): acting out rather than speaking.
39. **settee:** small couch.

closet and are now seated on the iron bed. MRS. VAN DAAN *leans back, exhausted.* MR. VAN DAAN *fans her with a newspaper.* **B**

ANNE *starts to write in her diary. The lights dim out; the curtain falls.*

[*In the darkness* ANNE'S *voice comes to us again, faintly at first and then with growing strength.*]

Anne's Voice. I expect I should be describing what it feels like to go into hiding. But I really don't know yet myself. I only know

470   it's funny never to be able to go outdoors . . . never to breathe fresh air . . . never to run and shout and jump. It's the silence in the nights that frightens me most. Every time I hear a creak in the house or a step on the street outside, I'm sure they're coming for us. The days aren't so bad. At least we know that Miep and Mr. Kraler are down there below us in the office. Our protectors, we call them. I asked Father what would happen to them if the Nazis found out they were hiding us. Pim[40] said that they would suffer the same fate that we would. . . . Imagine! They know this, and yet when they come up here, they're always cheerful and

480   gay, as if there were nothing in the world to bother them. . . . Friday, the twenty-first of August, nineteen forty-two. Today I'm going to tell you our general news. Mother is unbearable. She insists on treating me like a baby, which I loathe.[41] Otherwise things are going better. The weather is . . .

[*As* ANNE'S *voice is fading out, the curtain rises on the scene.*] **C** **D**

IN OTHER WORDS Peter wants to turn on the sink to give his cat water. But it's too late; the clock outside chimes eight. The workers would hear him. Anne gives the cat some of her milk. Mr. Frank gives Anne a pen and she begins to write in her diary. As the scene closes, she reads aloud from her diary. She describes what it is like to be in hiding: the boredom, the lack of fresh air, the fear of being caught.

---

40. **Pim:** family nickname for Mr. Frank.
41. **loathe** (LOHTH): hate.

B   **YOUR TURN**

Language Coach

Underline the adverb in this paragraph. Then circle the **suffix** that tells you it is an adverb. What is the definition of this new word?

_____

_____

_____

_____

C   **HERE'S HOW**

Literary Focus

Unlike most **dramas**, this one did not really have a **climax** or a **resolution**. I think this is because this reading is only an excerpt, or a small selection, of the entire play.

D   **READ AND DISCUSS**

Comprehension

What have we learned in this scene?

Skills Practice

The Diary of Anne Frank

USE A CONCEPT MAP

This play has a small number of **characters** because the main characters are in hiding for most of the play. Of the characters you met in the first two scenes, decide which four you feel are most important. Write your four characters in the diagram below. Be sure to include a short explanation of each character's importance.

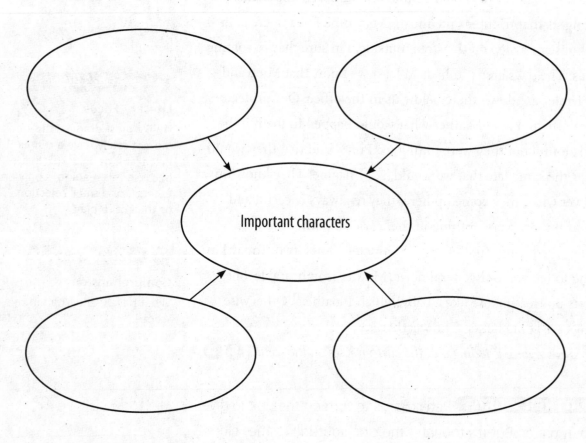

Important characters

Applying Your Skills

The Diary of Anne Frank

LITERARY FOCUS: ELEMENTS OF DRAMA

DIRECTIONS: Answer the following questions about *The Diary of Anne Frank* and the nature of a **drama**.

1. Mrs. Frank is one of the play's:

   a) conflicts.

   b) characters.

   c) expositions.

2. A play's exposition is when:

   a) the conflict is resolved.

   b) the characters exit the stage.

   c) the characters and setting are established.

READING FOCUS: MAKING INFERENCES

DIRECTIONS: Think about the **inferences** you made while reading this selection. With that information in mind, write a paragraph describing one of the play's characters in depth.

_____

_____

_____

_____

_____

_____

VOCABULARY REVIEW

DIRECTIONS: Write "Yes" after each sentence if the vocabulary word is being used correctly. Write "No" if it is not being used correctly.

1. The Frank family tried to be as **conspicuous** as possible on the morning they walked from their home to their hiding spot; they didn't want anyone to notice their extra layers of clothing. _____

2. After an **interval** of a few hours, Miep returned with more supplies. _____

3. Peter was **unabashed** in admitting that he had few friends at school; he wasn't bothered by others' opinions of him. _____

A Tragedy Revealed: A Heroine's Last Days

Based on the article by Ernst Schnabel

INFORMATIONAL TEXT FOCUS: TEXT STRUCTURE AND ORGANIZATION

For a text to be clear, it needs **structure**. Structure is the way a text is **organized**, or how the author presents information. There are three common patterns for structure that authors use:

- **Chronological order:** The author describes events in the order in which they happened, often with **cause-and-effect relationships**. For example, an article about World War II might explain the causes of the war and its effects on the countries involved.

- **Order of importance:** The author makes an argument and then gives supporting details. The details may be in order from most important to least important, or least to most important. Suppose you write an article that argues for a longer lunch period. You could give the most important reasons first.

- **Logical order:** The author arranges supporting details into related groups. This way the connections are clear. For example, a review of a movie may discuss the movie's plot, then the characters, and then the soundtrack.

VOCABULARY

Working with a partner, use the following words in sentences.

legend (LEJ UHND) *n.:* a well-known story.

barrack (BAR UHK) *n.:* a large, plain building where many people are housed.

misery (MIZ UH REE) *n.:* suffering; sadness.

pitiful (PIT I FUHL) *adj.:* lacking; deserving pity.

INTO THE ARTICLE

The following article, written in 1958, tells of the author's journey to find the truth about Anne Frank's last months. Anne was a Jewish girl who hid from the Nazis with her family during World War II. She kept a diary that became a famous book. The author interviewed people who knew Anne. What he learned supported his main argument: Anne suffered but never lost her spirit.

SKILLS FOCUS

Informational Text Skills
Recognize a variety of text patterns that organize information in nonfiction.

A TRAGEDY REVEALED: A HEROINE'S LAST DAYS

Based on the article by Ernst Schnabel

Last year in Amsterdam, Holland, I found an old reel of movie film on which Anne Frank appears. She is seen for only ten seconds. The film was taken for a wedding in 1941, the year before Anne Frank and seven others went into hiding. For just a moment, the camera swings to the left, to a window. There a girl stands alone, looking out into space. It is Anne Frank.

Anne Frank is dead now, but her spirit has shaped the world. Her diary has been read in almost every language. The play based on the diary has been a great success.

10   Last year I set out to find out what happened to this girl who has become a legend. I traveled to the places where she had lived. I talked with forty-two people who knew Anne or who survived the events that killed her. They said the same thing the diary shows. Anne Frank, even in the worst times, had a strong spirit. **A** **B**

The story written in the diary is a story of relationships between people. It is the story of a smart girl who is thirteen when her diary begins and only fifteen when it ends. It is a story without violence, yet it is caused by the worst act of violence in

20   the history of man, Adolf Hitler's murder of six million European Jews. **C**

In the summer of 1942, Anne Frank, her father, her mother, her older sister Margot, and four others were forced into hiding during the Nazi takeover of Holland. Their hiding place was a tiny apartment they called the Secret Annex. It was located in the back of an Amsterdam office building. For twenty-five months they all lived in the Secret Annex. They were protected only by a swinging bookcase and by a few Christians who helped them. Anne Frank's diary talks about their difficult lives in the small space.

A READ AND DISCUSS

Comprehension

What have we learned about Anne Frank so far?

B HERE'S HOW

Vocabulary

I read on the Preparing to Read page that *legend* means "a well-known story." In this case, I do not think Anne herself is a *legend*. I think the story of her life must be the *legend*.

C HERE'S HOW

Reading Focus

I know that a text is usually **organized** in one of three ways: **chronological order**, **order of importance**, or **logical order**. The author has already said he wanted to know what happened to Anne Frank. I think lines 17–18 give me a hint that the author will sometimes use chronological order to do this.

30 The actual diary ends with an entry for August 1, 1944. The play goes further. It tries to recreate the events of August 4, 1944. That was the day the Secret Annex was found and the people inside were arrested.

What really happened on that August day fourteen years ago was far less dramatic than what is shown on the stage. That morning everyone had finished a poor breakfast of fake coffee and bread. Mrs. Frank was about to clear the table. Anne Frank was very likely at work on one of the short stories she often wrote. In a tiny attic room Otto Frank was correcting the English

40 lesson of Peter Van Daan, an eighteen-year-old boy who lived in the Secret Annex. **A**

In the main part of the building, two men and two young women were working at their regular jobs. For more than two years these four had risked their lives to protect their friends. The workers gave them food and brought them news of the outside world. The women were Miep and Elli. The men were Kraler and Koophuis, spice merchants who had worked with Otto Frank before the Nazi takeover.

I spoke to Miep, Elli, and Mr. Koophuis in Amsterdam. The

50 two women had not been arrested after the raid on the Secret Annex. Koophuis had been released in poor health after a few weeks in prison. Kraler, who now lives in Canada, had later escaped from a forced labor camp. **B**

Elli remembered, "A car drove up in front of the house. But cars often stopped. Then the front door opened, and someone came up the stairs. I could hear that there were several men."

Miep said, "The footsteps moved along. Then a door creaked, and a moment later the door to Mr. Kraler's office opened. A fat man said in Dutch, 'Quiet. Stay in your seats.' I did not know what was happening. But then, suddenly, I knew."

Mr. Koophuis is now in very poor health. **C** He added, "I suppose I did not hear them because of the spice mills in the warehouse. The fat man's head was the first thing I knew. He came in. 'You three stay here, understand?' he barked. So we stayed in the office and listened as someone else went upstairs. Doors rattled. Then there were footsteps everywhere. They searched the whole building."

Mr. Kraler wrote and told me, "A police sergeant and three men entered my office. They wanted to see the storerooms in the front part of the building. At the end of the corridor they drew their revolvers and the sergeant ordered me to push aside the bookcase and open the door behind it. He knew everything. The policemen followed me. I could feel their pistols in my back. I was the first to enter the Franks' room. Mrs. Frank was standing at the table. I managed to say 'The Gestapo is here.'"

Otto Frank is now sixty-eight. He has remarried and lives in Switzerland. Of the eight who lived in the Secret Annex, he is the only one who survived. Mr. Frank told me about the events of that morning: "I was showing Peter Van Daan his spelling mistakes when suddenly someone came running up the stairs. Then the door flew open and a man stood before us holding his pistol aimed at my chest.

"In the main room stood a uniformed policeman. He stared into our faces.

"'Where are your valuables?' he asked. I pointed to the cupboard where my cash box was kept. The policeman took it out. Then he looked around. His eye fell on the leather briefcase where Anne kept her diary and all her papers. He opened it and shook everything out. Anne's papers and notebooks and

60

70

80

Reading Focus
The author often skips back and forth between past and present events. What kind of **structural pattern** is he following instead of chronological order? Explain your answer.

_____

_____

_____

_____

90   loose sheets lay scattered at our feet. **A** The policeman put our
valuables into the briefcase and closed it. He asked us whether we
had any weapons. But we had none, of course. Then he said, 'Get
ready.'"

Otto Frank remembered, "No one wept. Anne was very
quiet. Perhaps that was why she did not think to take along her
notebooks. All was lost now. She walked back and forth and did
not even glance at her diary." **B**

As the people left the building, Miep listened. "I heard them
going," she said, "first in the corridor and then down the stairs. I
100 could hear the heavy boots and the footsteps, and then the very
light footsteps of Anne. Through the years she had taught herself
to walk so softly that you could hear her only if you knew what
to listen for. I did not see her. The office door was closed as they
all passed by."

At police headquarters the prisoners were questioned only
briefly. Otto Frank pointed out that after two years in the Secret
Annex, they knew little about other Jews who might be in hiding.

The Franks and their friends were kept at police
headquarters for several days. The men were in one cell, the
110 women in the other. They were fairly comfortable there. The
food was better than the food they had had in the Secret Annex.
The guards left them alone.

Suddenly, all eight were taken to the railroad station and
put on a train. The guards said they were going to Westerbork,
a work camp for Jews in Holland, about eighty miles from
Amsterdam. Mr. Frank said, "We rode in a regular passenger
train. We were together and had been given a little food for
the journey. We were actually cheerful. We knew what was
happening to Jews in Auschwitz. But we hoped our luck would
120 hold. **C**

"As we rode, Anne would not move from the window. It was
summer outside. After two years it was like freedom for her. Can
you understand that?" **D**

One of the people who had known the Franks at Westerbork
was Mrs. de Wiek, who lives in Holland. I visited her home. She

told me that her family, like the Franks, had been in hiding before they were captured. She said: "We had been at Westerbork three or four weeks when the word went around that there were new arrivals. News of that kind ran like wildfire through the camp. My daughter Judy came running to me, calling, 'New people are coming, Mama!'

"The newcomers were standing in a long row. We looked at them. Judy pressed close against me. Most of the people in the camp were adults. I had often wished for a young friend for Judy, who was only fifteen.

"In the long line stood this girl. And I said to Judy, 'Look, there is a friend for you.'

"I saw Anne Frank and Peter Van Daan every day in Westerbork. They were always together, and I often said to my husband, 'Look at those two beautiful young people.'

"Anne was happy there, incredible as it seems. Things were hard for us in the camp. We "convict Jews" who had been arrested in hiding places had to wear blue overalls with a red bib and wooden shoes. Three hundred people lived in each barrack. **E** **F** We were sent to work at five in the morning. The guards all screamed 'Faster, faster!' But Anne was happy. Now she could see new people and talk to them and could laugh. She could laugh while the rest of us thought: Will they send us to the camps in Poland? Will we live through it?

"Otto Frank was quiet. He lived in the men's barracks, but once when Anne was sick, he came over to visit her every evening. He would stand beside her bed for hours, telling her stories. Anne was so like him. When another child, a twelve-year-old boy named David, fell ill, Anne stood by his bed and talked to him. David and Anne always talked about God." **G** **H**

Anne Frank stayed at Westerbork for only three weeks. Early in September a thousand of the "convict Jews" were put on a freight train, with seventy-five people in each car. The Nazis were losing the war. But it was too late. The Franks and their friends were already on the way to Auschwitz, the camp in Poland where four million Jews died.

130

140

150

160

E HERE'S HOW

Vocabulary

I have already read that a *barrack* is a "large, plain building where many people are housed." This seems to make sense. In this case, 300 people are living in the barrack. I know that the Nazis treated the prisoners very badly. So I am sure the *barrack* was plain and uncomfortable.

F YOUR TURN

Language Coach

You can improve your **oral fluency** by trying to pronounce new and unfamiliar words. How many syllables are in the word *barrack*? Are you surprised by how you are supposed to pronounce the second syllable? Why?

_____

_____

G READ AND DISCUSS

Comprehension

What information has Mrs. de Wiek given us about the Frank's?

H YOUR TURN

Reading Focus

The author includes many of Mrs. de Wiek's memories of Anne in one place. What kind of **structural pattern** do you think he is using here?

_____

Mrs. de Wiek was in the same freight car as the Franks. "Now and then the train stopped," she told me. "The guards came to the door and held out their caps and we had to toss our money and valuables into the caps. Anne and Judy sometimes pulled themselves up to the window of the car and described the villages we were passing through. We made the children repeat the addresses where we could meet after the war if we became separated. The Franks chose a meeting place in Switzerland.

170　　On the third night, the train stopped and the doors of the car opened. The tired passengers saw bright lights shining on the train. On the platform, guards were running back and forth shouting orders. Behind them stood officers with huge dogs. As the people poured out of the train, a loudspeaker roared, "Women to the left! Men to the right!" **A**

Mrs. de Wiek, her daughter, Mrs. Frank, Margot, and Anne had a long, hard march to the women's camp at Auschwitz. The next day their heads were shaved. Then the women were put to work digging up grass. As they worked each day, thousands of 180　others were killed in the gas chambers. Black smoke rose from the stacks of the huge buildings where the bodies were burned. **B**

Mrs. de Wiek saw Anne Frank every day. "Anne seemed even more beautiful there," Mrs. de Wiek said. "Of course her long hair was gone. Now you could see that her beauty was in her eyes, which seemed to grow bigger. She was still alert and sweet.

"Though she was the youngest, Anne was the leader in her group of five people. Many people were dying, some of starvation, others of weakness and despair. It was almost impossible not to give up hope. When a person gave up, his face became empty and 190　dead. The Polish woman doctor who had been caring for the sick said to me, 'You will pull through. You still have your face.' **C**

"Anne Frank, too, still had her face, up to the very last. To the last also she was moved by the dreadful things. Who was troubled that every day new people were being selected and gassed? Most of us were beyond feeling. But not Anne. Anne cried when we marched past the children who had been waiting half a day in the rain in front of the gas chambers."

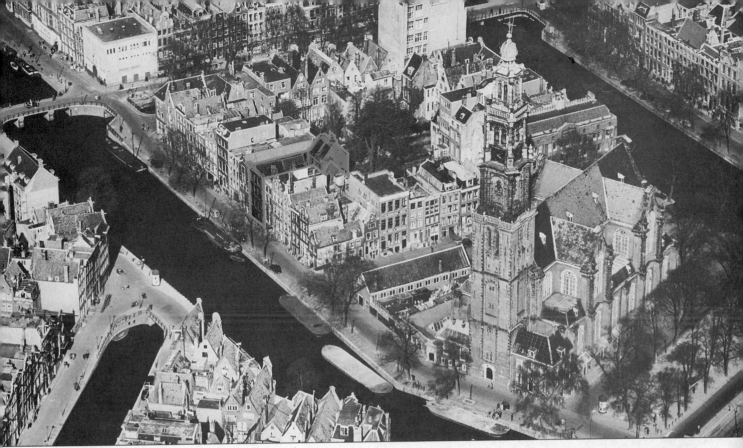

Late in October there was a selection to send prisoners away
from Auschwitz. Only those able to do hard work were being

200 chosen. The women waited naked for hours outside. Then, one
by one, they went back inside for a doctor to check them. Many
of the women lied about their age and health in the hope that
they would escape the almost certain death of Auschwitz. Mrs. de
Wiek was rejected. So was Mrs. Frank. **D**

"Next it was the turn of the two girls, Anne and Margot,"
Mrs. de Wiek recalled. "Anne still had her face. She encouraged
Margot. There they stood for a moment, naked. Anne looked
straight and stood straight. Then they were approved and passed
along. We could not see what was on the other side. Mrs. Frank

210 screamed, 'The children! Oh, God!'"

The record of most of the other people from the Secret
Annex ends at Auschwitz. Mrs. Frank starved to death there
two months later. When the Nazis fled Auschwitz just before
the Russians arrived in January 1945, they took Peter Van Daan
with them. It was bitter cold and the roads were covered with
ice. Peter Van Daan was never heard of again. Only Otto Frank

D **YOUR TURN**

Reading Focus

Since Anne is the focus of
this article, whether she gets
moved from Auschwitz is
the most important detail.
But the author tells us about
what happens to other
people first, in lines 198–204.
What kind of **structural
pattern** is the author using
here?

_____

_____

remained there alive until the prisoners were freed. Anne and Margot had been selected for shipment to Bergen-Belsen, a camp in Germany. A

220   Last year I drove the 225 miles from Amsterdam to Belsen and spent a day there walking over the grounds. My guide first showed me the cemetery where 50,000 Russian prisoners of war, captured in an early battle, were buried in 1941. Next to them is a cemetery for Italians. No one knows exactly how many bodies are in that mass grave. B

About a mile farther we came to the main site of the Bergen-Belsen camp. Anne Frank is buried there somewhere.

The Allies were getting closer, but that did not help the prisoners much. At Bergen-Belsen there were no roll calls, no

230   organization, and almost no sign of the Nazis. Prisoners lived without hope. They died of hunger, thirst, and sickness.

© epa/Corbis

The Auschwitz group had at first been assigned to live in tents. One night a great windstorm brought the tents crashing down. The people living in them were then put in wooden barracks. Mrs. B. of Amsterdam remembered about Anne: "We lived in the same block and saw each other often. In fact, we had a party together. We had saved up some stale bread, and we cut this up and put onions and boiled cabbage on the pieces. Over our feast we nearly forgot our misery for a few hours. We were

240 almost happy in spite of everything." **C**

One of Anne Frank's best friends in Amsterdam was a girl named Lies Goosens. Lies is often mentioned in the diary. She was captured before the Franks were found in the Secret Annex. Anne wrote of her great fears for the safety of her friend. Lies now lives in Jerusalem. But she was in Bergen-Belsen in February 1945 and heard that a group of Dutch Jews had been moved into the next building. **D**

Lies said, "I waited until night. Then I went over to the barbed wire which separated us from the newcomers. I called

250 softly into the darkness, 'Is anyone there?'

"A voice answered, 'I am here. I am Mrs. Van Daan.'

"We had known the Van Daans in Amsterdam. I told her who I was and asked whether Margot or Anne could come to the fence. Mrs. Van Daan answered that Margot was sick but that Anne could probably come.

"I waited, in the darkness. It took a long time. But suddenly I heard a voice: 'Lies? Lies? Where are you?'

"Then I saw Anne beyond the barbed wire. She was in rags. I saw her sunken face in the darkness. Her eyes were very large.

260 We cried and cried as we told each other our sad news.

"My block still had food and clothing. Anne had nothing. She was freezing and starving. I called to her in a whisper, 'Come back tomorrow. I'll bring you something.'

"And Anne called across, 'Yes, tomorrow. I'll come.'

"I saw Anne again when she came to the fence on the following night," Lies continued. "I had packed up a jacket and

Vocabulary

Use clues from lines 232–240 to figure out the meaning of the word *misery*. Write a definition for *misery*. Then check your answer against a dictionary definition.

_____

_____

Reading Focus

What **structural pattern** does the author use in this paragraph? (Hint: It is possible to use more than one kind of pattern in a paragraph.)

_____

_____

_____

READ AND DISCUSS

Comprehension
Now what has happened?
Follow-up: How does this
story fit in with what
we know about these
concentration camps?

B **YOUR TURN**

Vocabulary
Recall the "feast" that the
women had while in the
concentration camp in lines
236–240. Considering this,
what do you think *pitiful*
means?

_____

_____

_____

_____

C **READ AND DISCUSS**

Comprehension
How did Anne's story end?

sugar and a tin of sardines for her. I called out, 'Anne, watch
now!' Then I threw the bundle across the barbed wire.

"But I heard only screams and Anne crying. I shouted,
270 'What's happened?' And she called back, weeping, 'A woman
caught it and won't give it to me.' **A** Then I heard rapid footsteps
as the woman ran away. Next night I had only a pair of stockings,
but this time Anne caught it."

In the last weeks at Bergen-Belsen, Germany was attacked
from both sides by the Russians and the Western Allies. There
was almost no food at all in the camp. The roads were blocked.
The railroads had been bombed. Still, bodies were burning night
and day. Then came an outbreak of typhus, a deadly fever.

Both Anne and Margot Frank caught the disease in late
280 February or early March of 1945. Margot lay unconscious for
several days. Then, she somehow rolled from her bed and died.

The death of Anne Frank passed almost without notice.
I met no one who remembers being with her in that moment.
So many were dying. One woman said, "I feel certain she died
because of her sister's death. Dying is easy for anyone left alone
in a camp." Mrs. B., who had shared the pitiful feast with Anne,
knows a little more: "Anne, who was very sick at the time, was
not informed of her sister's death. But a few days later she sensed
it. Soon afterward she died, peacefully." **B**

290 Three weeks later British troops freed the prisoners at
Bergen-Belsen. **C**

Miep and Elli, the heroic young women who had protected
the Franks for two years, found Anne's papers the week after the
police came to the Secret Annex. "It was terrible when I went up
there," Miep recalled. "Everything had been turned upside down.
On the floor lay clothes, papers, letters, and school notebooks.
And among the clutter lay a notebook with a red-checked
cover. I picked it up, looked at the pages, and recognized Anne's
handwriting."

300 Elli cried as she spoke to me: "The table was still set. There
were plates, cups, and spoons, but the plates were empty. I was so

© Anne Frank Fonds-Basel/Anne Frank House-Amsterdam/Getty Images

frightened. We sat down on the floor and leafed through all the papers. They were all Anne's. We gathered all of them and locked them up in the main office.

"A few days later M. came into the office. M. now had the keys to the building. He said to me, 'I found some more stuff upstairs.' He handed me Anne's papers. How strange, I thought, that *he* should be the one to give these to me. But I took them and locked them up with the others."

310   Miep and Elli did not read the papers they had saved. All of them were kept in the safe until Otto Frank returned to Amsterdam. Thus Anne Frank's voice was saved out of the millions that were silenced. It speaks for those millions and has outlasted the loud shouts of the murderers. **D**

D YOUR TURN

Reading Focus

This story uses many different types of **structural patterns**. Which did you find easiest to read?

_____

_____

_____

_____

Comprehension Wrap-Up

1. As the author mentioned in the beginning of the text, Anne Frank's story has touched people from all over the world. After reading these accounts of her life, what is it about her story that makes her life so memorable?

2. From the author's description of these concentration camps, we understand just how badly the Jewish people were treated. What does this behavior say about people whose prejudices control their actions? How can this type of behavior be kept in check?

3. There are some people who question whether these concentration camps and gas chambers ever really existed. What about this story strongly supports the argument that the camps and the chambers did exist?

Applying Your Skills

A Tragedy Revealed: A Heroine's Last Days

INFORMATIONAL TEXT FOCUS: TEXT STRUCTURE AND ORGANIZATION

DIRECTIONS: The author uses all three of the **structural patterns** described on the Preparing to Read page. Some are used more than others. Fill in the table below with examples of when each pattern was used. One example has been filled in for you.

Pattern	Examples from Article
Chronological order	I learned that the family went to a work camp after leaving the Secret Annex.
Order of importance	
Logical order	

VOCABULARY REVIEW

DIRECTIONS: Circle the word that is an antonym for the boldfaced vocabulary word. Remember that the antonym will be the word that means the opposite of the vocabulary word.

1. **misery:**   a) suffering   b) happiness   c) sadness

2. **pitiful:**   a) lacking   b) disgraceful   c) excellent

Skills Review

Collection 8

VOCABULARY REVIEW

DIRECTIONS: Fill in the blanks with the correct words from the Word Box.

Word Box

contribute

insight

evident

express

inexplicable

conspicuous

emaciated

interval

raucous

unabashed

1. While some may have been embarrassed, I was _____ when I fell down on the dance floor.

2. The judge said it was _____ that the defendant was guilty and he sentenced him to life in prison.

3. The two crying children on the plane were a _____ annoyance to the other passengers.

4. The big, red hat made the man _____, or easily noticed.

5. Because he could not explain how he felt, he wrote a poem to _____ his feelings.

6. After a week of fasting, she looked _____.

7. There was a half hour _____ between the second and third quarters of the football game.

8. By researching Anne Frank, Ernest Schnabel gained an _____ that improved his understanding of her personality.

9. The _____ child kept screaming and knocking chairs over.

10. Steve did not feel confident while taking the test, so he found it _____ that he somehow earned an "A."

Language and Writing

LANGUAGE COACH: ORAL FLUENCY

Many vocabulary words have several syllables, so they may seem hard to pronounce when you first look at them. Using the pronunciation guide will make the task easier and improve your **oral fluency**. The pronunciation guide is found in parentheses after the word and before its definition in a dictionary or glossary. You may find the words easier to say with some practice.

DIRECTIONS: Sound out each word below using the pronunciation guide. Then, put all of the words on flash cards. Write the word on one side and the pronunciation guide on the other. Practice using the flash cards with a partner.

1. legend (LEJ UHND)

2. barrack (BAR UHK)

3. misery (MIZ UH REE)

4. pitiful (PIT I FUHL)

WRITING ACTIVITY

In the article you have just finished reading, the author describes Anne Frank as having a "strong spirit" even at the end of her life. Do you agree with the author's opinion of Anne Frank? Write a brief paragraph in which you agree or disagree that Anne Frank had a strong spirit. Use details from the article to support your opinion.

_____

_____

_____

_____

Index of Authors and Titles